Dog
Anxiety

by Sarah Hodgson

A Wiley Brand

Dog Anxiety For Dummies®

Contents at a Glance

Table of Contents

Introduction

Anxiety isn't an experience unique to humans. Dogs all over the world are suffering, too. This book walks you through the factors contributing to dog stress, from being left alone to fear of new sights, sounds, and stimulations. Many triggers can put your dog on edge, and dogs who are prone to one type of anxiety tend to be more nervous throughout the day. Like anxious people, dogs with anxiety have trouble living in a calm, relaxed state, which can affect their health and well-being.

The challenge with dogs is that we cannot ask them to stretch out on the couch and tell us how they feel. Dogs communicate through postures and actions. In the pages ahead, you learn to decipher their physical communication as you teach them to understand the meaning of a few essential directions, like "come," "stay," and "down." The goal is to be able to predict and respond quickly to prevent your dog from feeling stressed and acting out.

About This Book

Anxiety is a sobering topic; whether it hits when your dog meets a reactive dog, there is a storm surge, or any number of other triggering situations, I cover it all in this book. People often describe these reactions as a sudden switch — their dog is fine one minute, then they're suddenly pacing, drooling, and whining. Dogs can also suffer generalized anxiety when they anticipate something unbearable happening.

Throughout this book, I draw from human experience and use metaphors to help you consider your dog's perspective. For example, how might you feel if someone you depend on doesn't respond to a text promptly? You might text repetitively, call, or have anxious thoughts. It's not hard to imagine a dog's distress when being left alone. The first step is to imagine yourself in your dog's place.

Soon, you'll learn how to read your dog's postures and translate their fears by looking at them. Chapter by chapter, you'll learn to engage in brain games and energy busters and inspire their cooperation with fun lessons and daily structure. Practicing the exercises in this book will build your dog's resilience as they develop a confident, survivalist mentality. The ultimate reward for this time well spent? A loving bond that lasts a lifetime.

Foolish Assumptions

There are a few things I take for granted in this book. I assume that you know the following:

>> You know that your dog is more than paws and a tail, or at least a stump of a tail!

>> You have a dog you're worried about, and you would give anything to make them happy.

>> You don't want to obtain a PhD in animal behavior. You want a practical guide on how to rehabilitate your anxious dog.

If you fit into these categories, this book is for you.

Icons Used in the Book

The book includes the following core icons to ensure you are aware of the most critical things.

TIP

Indicates practical information that can help you make the most of your time.

FUN FACT

Describes interesting facts that add enjoyment and depth to your understanding.

REMEMBER

When you see this icon, you know that the information that follows is important enough to read twice!

WARNING

Highlights information that could be detrimental to your success if you ignore it.

Highlights interesting information that's specific to the professional dog trainers and behaviorists.

Indicates information from another chapter that relates to the
topic at hand. You might want to earmark these sections for
related information.

Beyond the Book

You can find helpful extras — including a glossary and a references
section citing works from various academic journals, scien-
tific research, and books authored by my colleagues — at www.
dummies.com/go/doganxietyfd.

In addition to these extras, I created an easy-to-access Cheat
Sheet that offers quick reminders on how to ease your dog's anxiety and fun ways to build their confidence. You can download this
from www.dummies.com by typing *Dog Anxiety For Dummies* into the
search bar.

Follow me on Instagram or TikTok (@SarahSaysPets) and tune
into my podcast, *Life Unleashed with Sarah Hodgson*, for more quick
tips and visuals on working, playing, and understanding your dog.
Visit www.SarahHodgson.com for free downloads, e-books, and
even virtual training.

Where to Go from Here

The beauty of this book is its flexibility; you can skip to the parts
most relevant to your situation. However, it is a good idea to start
with all the chapters in Part 1, as they lay the groundwork and
explain the underlying issues surrounding anxiety in dogs. You'll
be encouraged to bookmark certain sections, as the information is
referenced often throughout the book.

Does your dog have an emotional episode every time you walk into
another room? Or is your dog fine with short departures but loses
it when you're gone longer than 20 minutes? Part 2 addresses

separation anxiety. For some dogs, being alone triggers the equivalent of a panic attack.

Part 3 looks at containment anxiety. While some dogs find solace in their crate, others may attempt to claw, paw, and free themselves. The reason for this panic can vary from a bad experience, a delayed return, or simply a faulty fire alarm. In the extreme, containment anxiety can extend to any sense of entrapment, be it in a room, a house, a yard, or even a leash. Some dogs even react to being hugged.

Part 4 covers social anxiety. While most dogs are cautious of strangers, when introductions cause extreme anxiety, such as running away, hiding, shrieking in terror, or fear-eliminating, it's important to address these reactions head on. Routine games and interaction can help your dog unpack their extreme fears as you work to create positive associations with their triggers, whether they are to other dogs or puppies, animals, people, or children.

Part 5 focuses on sensory sensitivity. Your dog relies heavily on all their senses: smell, hearing, touch, and sight, although sight is used only to indicate motion. This part focuses on all sensory sensitivities, from sights and sounds to tastes and touch. Dogs experiencing anxiety in these circumstances require a thoughtful and organized approach to overcome their stress and panicked responses.

Whether you read this book chapter by chapter or reference it one section at a time, the information in these pages will teach you how to successfully calm your dog. By providing them with guidance, you can lead your dog to their happy place, teach them healthy self-soothing activities, and enrich both of your lives.

1

Getting Started with Dog Anxiety

Chapter **1**

Understanding Anxiety in Dogs

More than anything, dogs want to feel safe. However, many dogs with anxiety experience life as a series of unpredictable events and startling interruptions, leaving them feeling stressed and unsure. The good news is that you can help unpack your dog's fears and help them learn to enjoy life.

It can be difficult to witness your dog struggling with anxiety, and you can't reason with them or validate their emotions as you can a person. Being routinely anxious takes an emotional toll, whether your dog dreads abandonment, is sensitive to noise, weather, or other sensory stimulation, or views other people and dogs as threatening.

Understanding the similarities between human and dog anxiety will help you appreciate your dog's struggles. Recognizing how your dog comprehends their circumstances and communicates stress will help you guide their rehabilitation with empathy and kindness.

Working through your dog's anxiety is more than training them to make better choices and self-soothe once their anxiety is triggered. The initial goal is to build their general confidence and joy for living. By inspiring fun and happiness through shared interactions, games, and lessons, you can help your dog prioritize your relationship and look to you before they react.

WARNING

Punishment and violence have no part in this process and will only intensify your dog's anxiety. Although you may feel frustrated at times, it's important not to take it out on your dog.

Recognizing Anxiety in Your Dog

All of us can relate to anxiety. Whether you or someone you love receives bad news, experiences financial insecurity, or endures the butterflies before starting a new job, we have all felt it. Coping with anxiety is something we recognize and identify, even at an early age. Many people have a distinct formula for dealing with our anxiety, things like talking to a friend or therapist, going for a walk, or deep breathing. Some people even download an app!

Dogs aren't so lucky. In fact, with limited freedom or ability to express themselves, dogs vent their stress in ways we sometimes deem unacceptable, such as barking, chewing, eliminating, or nipping. Left on their own or unattended, they can suffer greatly.

Unlike people, dogs can't explain unpredictable events, so their tension builds up. Unless you step in and help your dog desensitize triggering events, they will be left with a lot of unresolved triggers and phobias.

REMEMBER

Your dog doesn't identify stress as a separate emotion. When they feel anxiety, it affects their whole being. While there are things they can do to calm themselves, such as run away, dig, or hide, modern dogs often have little agency over their actions and the freedom to choose their own path.

The great disconnect

Your dog doesn't categorize behavior as good or bad. Even for us, right or wrong is often inconsistent; it can be different from house to house, culture to culture, and even person to person. Many couples differ in opinions regarding greeting manners and play. From your dog's perspective, their behavior is a moment-to-moment decision that is more dependent on what alleviates their anxiety or pain. Here are a few examples:

>> When left alone, a dog might tear the house apart or howl for hours — not to punish you for leaving, but because they physically implode when finding themselves alone. This is known as *separation anxiety*.

>> If you can't find your dog before leaving for work or they dig their heels in as you try to get them in the crate, they are not trying to derail your schedule. Many dogs have *containment anxiety* and become visibly upset when forced into small, contained spaces.

>> Dogs don't growl at strangers or other dogs because they're mean; they do so because they're afraid and unable to distance themselves. Dogs with *social anxiety* are often unsure of a strange person, another dog, or of children.

>> When some dogs sense a storm or hear a loud noise, they become terrified. They hide and run away to soothe their distress, not to derail your schedule or plans. This is an example of a *sensory-sensitive* dog.

>> When dogs react to other dogs on leash or from the safety of an enclosure, they are generally afraid and use their behavior to urge the oncoming dog away.

Understand anxiety

Many words describe the range of intensely fearful emotions dogs experience. While these terms might seem interchangeable, it's important to explore the differences before you can get handle on your dog's issues:

>> **Anxiety:** Dogs experience anxiety when they anticipate a future threat or feel uneasy about something that isn't immediately present. This can manifest as restlessness, excessive barking, or destructive behavior. Unlike fear, which is a response to an immediate threat, anxiety is more about the anticipation of possible dangers.

>> **Fear:** Dogs feel fear when they perceive a real or imagined threat in their environment. This might be triggered by routine events or specific stimuli, such as fireworks, a balloon, or a person wearing a hat. While fear is a normal survival instinct, it can become problematic due to a lack of socialization or a learned response. Fortunately, dogs of every age can develop more positive associations through gradual exposure, a process known as *counterconditioning*.

>> **Panic:** When a stressful event is pronounced and inescapable, a dog may develop a panicked response. For example, Jasper, a terrier mix, was fine being left alone in his crate until a smoke alarm went off and fire trucks arrived. Now Jasper panics whenever he hears sirens and is confined.

>> **Phobia:** When dogs have a chronic fear of an unavoidable noise, situation, or traumatic experience that leads to a PTSD-like response, phobic reactions can evolve. Examples include being left alone, experiencing trauma, hearing thunderstorms, and being confined on a leash. Dogs with phobias often become sensitized to related events, such as the sound of rain paired with thunderstorms, or be crated before isolation. For some dogs, similar-sounding events on the radio or TV can also trigger panic.

>> **Aggression:** Dog aggression is a response to perceived threats or stressors. It can result from fear, anxiety, or frustration. Aggressive behaviors can include growling, barking, lunging, and biting. Dog aggression is often a way of trying to protect themselves or their territory.

TIP

Other words I use to represent different levels of anxiety include distress, dread, alarm, caution, and stress.

Your dog's anxiety falls into one of two camps:

>> **Generalized:** Dogs with generalized anxiety are constantly stressed by any number of sensory stimulations, which interferes with their everyday lives and, by association, your life.

>> **Episodic (situational):** These dogs live a relatively stress-free existence until a specific event occurs, such as a thunderstorm, a vacuum, and so on.

KNOWING WHAT ANXIETY IS AND ISN'T

Not all dogs who act up have anxiety. Sometimes, what might seem like anxiety is actually a response to excitement, frustration, age, pain, or illness.

While dogs can't explain their feelings in English, they express them constantly through body postures and subtle interactions. A dog experiencing anxiety shows their stress in various ways, including pacing, whining, lip licking, panting, and soliciting attention. Chapter 2 takes a closer look at dog communication and covers how they express their emotional states.

Recognize your role in their anxiety

Nobody intends to reinforce their dog's anxiety or maladaptive habits. Too often, however, we do just that. The message often gets lost in translation when trying to reassure a dog. Consider these examples:

>> When out for a walk, do you retreat from other dogs, people, and situations that frighten your dog, or do you tighten your hold on the leash, drag your dog toward what they're trying to avoid, or stand still?

>> When you come home to a frenzied dog or a destroyed household, do you stay calm, or do you get frustrated or angry with your dog?

>> When your dog barks or whines incessantly or paws you repeatedly for your attention, do you politely redirect them, or do you give in to their demands?

REMEMBER

Often, our reassurances reinforce our dog's stress. How you'd naturally reassure a friend having a meltdown or panic attack differs from how you should reassure a dog or puppy.

The good news is anxiety isn't a life sentence. Your dog can make more positive associations and learn better coping skills with your guidance and the information in this book. As they become more emotionally stable, your dog will be more confident and relaxed, even in formerly unnerving situations. One of your first goals is to identify what's causing your dog's anxiety and why.

Understanding Why Some Dogs "Misbehave"

Your dog doesn't love their anxiety any more than you do. When fear transforms a moment, their body floods with adrenaline, giving them a jolt of energy to escape or fend off a threat. Even though *you know* they're safe, your dog might not see it the same way. If your dog feels trapped, they'll become frantic and can't be persuaded with reassurances or food. If they are scared, they'll want to flee. Anxious energy is like steam in a pressure cooker, which eventually needs to be released. Although you may not see steam coming from your dog's ears, your dog may run away, bark, or even fight to defend themselves. When left alone, your dog may chew your couch, eliminate inappropriately, or claw at the door frame.

REMEMBER

It's easy to get angry when your dog acts uncontrollably. But remember your dog's not being spiteful; they have no control over their stress reactions. When they get startled, they disconnect from reality. Your frustration can further their emotional dysregulation.

FUN FACT

Dogs learn to recognize our emotions based on our body language and tone of voice. I know it's frustrating to witness your dog's destruction or endure their frantic attempts to pull away or climb on you for attention, but the only way to help your dog is to stay calm and control yourself. You must model the behavior you want them to mirror in order to change your dog's behavior.

WARNING

If you feel overwhelmed, find supportive help beyond these pages. Whether you hire a personal trainer or behavior specialist, ensure they're qualified to treat anxiety. If you're considering supplements or prescription medications to help your dog, you'll find more information in Chapter 5.

Exploring the Roots of Anxiety

To understand the nature of your dog's anxiety, consider our long history with their species. Back when we were cave dwellers, dogs hung around the perimeters and ate our scraps. It was a symbiotic relationship that worked well. Dogs got free food, and in turn, they protected the campsite from other predators.

As we diversified and expanded around the globe, dogs joyfully adapted to our demands and the changing lifestyle. Over the years, dogs endured our selective breeding practices to hone skills like herding and hunting, often resulting in intense physical modification.

When natural behaviors become undesirable

Everything went along hunky dory, at least for a while. For thousands of years, dogs continued to enjoy their free-range lifestyle, hunting prey and maintaining their own schedules. However, as our population ballooned, we built cities, suburbs, and transportation routes. Our beloved dogs were suddenly at risk. Leash laws were enacted to restrict dogs from roaming, and most of their former skills were rendered obsolete. They were brought inside to live among us, and dogs entered a new phase of expectations and reality as intimate members of our immediate family.

Nowadays, many dogs live a fishbowl-like existence, looking out at the world rather than participating in it. Dogs are experiencing an identity crisis! Lacking outlets for their energy and curiosity, we reprimanded them for behaviors they were bred to do. Watchdogs are admonished for barking at passersby, retrievers for carrying the wrong thing, terriers are scolded for digging, and herding dogs for chasing other pets and children. Without enrichment, these highly social, intelligent, and energetic species suffer in ways we cannot imagine.

The "fur baby" paradox

It's common these days for people to think of their dog like one of their children. It's not hard to understand why: We love them like babies, and they demand a similar level of care and attention. Throughout this book, I draw on similarities between dogs and children, as it can be helpful to apply some parenting techniques to dogs. Consider these similarities:

>> Both thrive best with structure, routine, boundaries, and unconditional love.

>> They have similar needs: to eat, drink, sleep, play, and potty.

>> Both act out when overtired or have unmet needs. Puppies get nippy, however, whereas kids cry.

>> Both lack impulse control and emotional regulation. They both need a good model to develop these skills and express emotions properly.

However, it's important to remember that our dogs are *not* people. They are beautifully unique. A primary difference is their brain size, which is about 1/20th of ours. Their head space mostly comprises sensory neurons, enabling them to interpret sound, sights, and smells in unfathomable ways, despite their limited cognitive ability. Whereas our lives are devoted to deep thoughts and postulations, our dogs' lives are committed to sensory interpretation.

FUN FACT

Did you know that dogs can perceive the squeak of a mouse under your floorboard, identify your car's arrival before it turns in the driveway, and sense weather events due to slight changes in barometric pressure? Their sense of smell is so powerful they can identify illnesses like cancer and COVID-19, find people buried beneath the rubble, and even sense our mood fluctuations by whiffing a shift in our hormones. If genius were measured in sensory awareness, our dogs would be at the top of the class.

The bottom line is that it's important not to anthropomorphize your dog too much. Dogs have a magical way of navigating the world that we should stand in awe of rather than disregard. In her book, *Animals Make Us Human*, Temple Grandin identifies anthropomorphism as the phenomenon of treating animals like humans, where reality is exclusively viewed through the lens of human values and experiences.

Pause to consider our somewhat egocentric tendency to overlook the unique qualities of our beloved dogs. Many people unwittingly attribute human motivations and characteristics to their dogs rather than honoring their distinct needs, desires, and natural reactions. It's here, in the light of this denial, that their anxiety often takes root.

Identifying Your Dog's Triggers

Triggers are noises, objects, or sightings that are either unfamiliar and frightening or familiar and scary to your dog. Every dog is unique.

Before diving into the rest of this book, make a list of the things you know or think might be triggering your dog's anxiety. Regardless of what's causing or prompting your dog's anxiety, there is nothing wrong with them that can't be improved, managed, or cured entirely.

Unfortunately, your dog's anxiety cannot be soothed with a quick hug, pat on the head, or favorite treat. When their anxiety is triggered, your dog enters an alternative reality where danger lurks, and bad things could happen. Anxiety feels natural to your dog, and in the moment, nothing you do or say can influence their reaction. The only way to calm your dog down is to get them to a safe place and wait it out.

Trigger stacking occurs when a dog faces multiple triggers without a chance to disengage or soothe their nerves. The accumulation of stresses can intensify the dog's distress, amplifying their emotional reactions and potentially leading to aggression. For example, if a dog is sensitive to thunder, unfamiliar dogs, *and* construction vehicles, experiencing them all at once, such as while out on a walk — can be extremely overwhelming, causing the equivalent of a panic attack.

WARNING

When anxious, your dog will have unique symptoms that range from mild to explosive. If left untreated, your dog's anxiety can result in medical issues, too, such as respiratory and intestinal issues.

ABC: ANTECEDENT-BEHAVIOR-CONSEQUENCE

The pros like to reference their own version of the ABCs when researching and rehabilitating canine anxiety. Here, the letters stand for Antecedent-Behavior-Consequence. This framework analyzes behavior by examining what happens before, during, and after an action. The *antecedent* is what occurs before the behavior, the *behavior* is the action itself, and the *consequence* is what follows the behavior. This framework helps clarify the context and triggers of behavior and its outcomes.

(continued)

(continued)

> Not all dogs respond to interruptive stimuli in the same way. A confident dog might be so conditioned to a noise as to ignore it. Another dog might be excited by the noise if it has been associated with positive events. Other dogs experience an alert response when an unrecognizable event or a stimulus reminds them of a scary experience or immediate danger, causing them to grow anxious. Behaviors can vary from mild reactions like lip licking or turning away to intense reactions like running away or showing aggression.

Soothing Anxiety

We're taught all our lives how to deal with anxiety — we're told to talk it out, to practice mindfulness, or to exercise. Your dog needs similar outlets. Although you might know road construction won't harm you, the barking dog can't get to you, and babies are not zombies, a dog with anxiety isn't so sure. Respect your dog's anxiety and remember, in most instances, there are only two things that will soothe them:

>> **Distance:** Once you identify something causing your dog anxiety, move away from it. When possible, bring your dog into a comforting place, whether that's behind your legs, a room in your home, or a place away from the triggering event. If you're walking outside and your dog gets unnerved by a dog, person, or thing, divert your route and wait to praise or treat your dog until they regain a sense of calm.

>> **Time:** Anxiety fills your dog with stress hormones that may take some time to dissipate. Notice the length of time your dog needs to regain their sense of joy and adventure. Each dog has their own anxiety blueprint. The more you work with them, the faster they'll learn to recover.

While anxiety and fear are warranted reactions from your dog's perspective, they can make different and more positive associations. Chapter 3 explores how freedom, food, and fun inspire joy and confidence.

You Are Not Alone

We all want to be safe. No matter what type of anxiety your dog suffers, simply picking up this book promises results. Remember, anxiety is just one part of their personality — and it's manageable, even curable, in many cases.

With your help, your dog can learn directions, engage in fun activities, and develop a life framed by consistency and reassurances that have been lacking until now.

Each part of this book is dedicated to a specific type of anxiety. You may find that your dog struggles with more than one, and since each part is standalone, you can start anywhere you like! The chapters in this part help build your understanding of dog anxiety and how to identify your dog's triggers. Let's get started!

Chapter **2**

Unpacking the Nature of Anxiety

This chapter is one of the most important in the book. In it, you learn how to identify your dog's mood simply by tuning into their breathing and body language. This will enable you to recognize signs of anxiety before it takes hold of your dog.

Your dog constantly communicates with you and the world around them, something I explain in the pages ahead. Many people don't know how to interpret their dog's interactions, leading to frequent misunderstandings and heightened anxiety. This chapter sheds light on your dog's anxiety and their interactions with the world around them.

Recognizing the Roots of Anxiety

Dog anxiety is a relatively modern phenomenon. Until recently, dogs had more agency to run away, hide, or avoid triggering situations. Modern dog parenting has turned instinctive dog behavior on its head, curtailing their freedom and forcing them to measure up to our standards of how they should conduct their lives.

Dogs don't behave vindictively, nor do they think things like, "Let me bark now to ruin this moment," or "Mom left me alone, so I'm going to chew up the couch," or "I don't want anyone showing affection, so I'm going to ambush all hugs." Instead, their behavior reflects the stress they feel in different situations. Try not to take your dog's actions personally.

For example, people often greet their human family and friends enthusiastically, with smiles, hugs, and face-to-face communication. However, some dogs might see these gestures as threatening. Humans are the only animals who view sustained eye contact and gleaming teeth as friendly; other animals interpret these signals as confrontational or an invitation to play rough. By studying how dogs naturally engage, you can better understand how they perceive your interactions.

TIP

Observe how friendly dogs approach each other, often curving their bodies and lowering their heads. Excited dogs may exhibit more energetic behavior, such as bouncing from side to side or performing a play bow with their front half lowered and their rump and tail raised. Confrontational dogs tend to stiffen their bodies and approach head-on, sometimes circling each other tensely.

Learning to Understand Your Dog's Emotions

All behavior is rooted in emotion. In 1998, neuroscientist Jaak Panksepp outlined emotions in all mammals, not just dogs and humans. This section summarizes the five key emotions motivating your dog's behavior — seeking, curiosity, play, fear, and frustration.

Seeking

Seeking involves fulfilling everyday needs, such as finding food and water. Dogs focused on fulfilling these everyday needs are streamlined in their focus.

Curiosity

Curious dogs love to explore and won't hesitate when socializing or adventuring. While unfamiliar sights or sounds may momentarily give them pause, they quickly recover.

Play

Surprisingly, play is as essential to maintaining a balanced life as eating and sleeping. Dogs engage in play only when they feel secure in their environment and with the company they keep.

Three key indicators of anxiety are a reluctance to eat, play, and interact with their people. Conversely, a clear indication that your dog's anxiety is improving is renewed interest in food, play, and interactions.

Fear

Fear is at the root of all anxious behaviors, prompted by a situation, person, or object posing as a potential threat, whether real or imagined. Most dogs choose to run away, hide, or retreat into their den (your home), although when a dog is enclosed or on a leash, they may cower, buck, or even show aggression. While you can do much to relieve your dog's fear, understanding the causes and modifying time and proximity can help alleviate and redirect their fear responses.

Frustration

Frustration erupts when a dog cannot attain what they expect or desire. It's easy to recognize when a ball rolls just out of reach; however, frustration also plays a role in anxiety. It becomes more complex when a dog with anxiety barks at passersby or feels trapped at the end of a leash.

I've left out the two emotions related to reproduction: lust and maternal instinct.

Peer just below the surface

Underlying your dog's emotions is their nervous system, which is composed of two parts.

>> The **parasympathetic nervous system** (PNS) conserves energy and prioritizes bodily functions such as eating and elimination. It's known as the *rest and digest* state.

>> The **sympathetic nervous system** (SNS) provides the energy necessary to cope with the needs and stresses of everyday life. Whether real or imagined, it increases blood flow and respiration. It is also known as the *fight, flight, or freeze* state.

TESTING YOUR KNOWLEDGE

Let's test your new knowledge. See if you can guess which need state these situations stem from:

1. Your dog pounces on you when you sleep in on Sunday morning.
2. Your dog backs up when a stranger reaches out to pet them.
3. Your dog barks at a toy stuck under the couch.
4. Your dog leaps to the window when a squirrel or bird is flitting about.
5. Your dog eagerly drops a ball in your lap.

Answer key: 1. Seeking; 2. Fear; 3. Frustration; 4. Curiosity; 5. Play

TECHNICAL STUFF

Ideally, the sympathetic and parasympathetic nervous systems should work harmoniously to regulate energy and relaxation. For dogs with anxiety, however, this system is often imbalanced. Stressful events throughout the day flood their bodies with stress hormones, such as cortisol and adrenaline, which are necessary to provide energy and alertness. While these physiological responses are crucial for survival, especially in threatening situations, many anxieties are irrational and can cause chronic activation of the sympathetic nervous system. This persistent state of heightened arousal can overwhelm the parasympathetic nervous system, which is responsible for promoting relaxation and recovery.

Alternatively, isolated or neglected dogs can experience an imbalance in their parasympathetic nervous system. Over time, any imbalance can lead to physical and psychological health issues in dogs, on top of their chronic anxiety.

HORMONES

Cortisol, known as the stress hormone, is at the core of your dog's anxiety. It can be constantly present in cases of severe generalized anxiety or released suddenly in dogs experiencing periodic anxiety. In mild cases of generalized anxiety, cortisol may drip steadily, especially when factors arise that predict an unpleasant or dangerous outcome.

Adrenaline is the hormone responsible for the body's immediate reaction to stress or danger. When your dog encounters a perceived threat, adrenaline floods their system, triggering the fight, flight, or freeze response. You might notice their heart rate increase, pupils dilate, and muscles tense, preparing them to react swiftly to the situation.

Serotonin is known as the happy hormone. When dogs experience a surge of serotonin, it elicits an enthusiastic response, such as during greetings or play. Think of the dog who jumps for joy! While you can redirect this behavior, the happy mood isn't cause for concern.

Oxytocin is another prominent hormone contributing to the loving bond between you and your dog. Gentle petting (which I refer to as "the soothing effects of the mother tongue," as it mimics the comforting touch of a nurturing mother) significantly contributes to improved health and reduced stress, partly because it releases oxytocin into the dog's bloodstream.

Emotional reactions vs rational responses

Recognizing the difference between your dog's emotional reaction to a situation or stimulus and a more measured rational reaction is essential to understanding your dog's anxiety. When your dog reacts impulsively to an unpredicted event, such as your leaving, hearing an unfamiliar noise, or seeing a stranger suddenly approach, their body floods with adrenaline and cortisol. These hormones provide a jolt of energy necessary when there is a real threat. When the fear is imagined, your dog's reaction may seem out of place or even feigned. They might become destructive, run away, or lunge to fend off a perceived threat.

Consider a dog or puppy startled by a thunderbolt during a walk. If they were alone, they might run for cover or race home to their den. However, when we restrain dogs on leashes, it intensifies their anxiety, as they feel trapped. Many people try to soothe or distract their dog with treats and toys, not realizing that a dog refusing food and comfort is likely in a state of panic.

TIP

If you are unsure about the extent of your dog's anxiety, offer them a treat or favorite toy. If they don't take the treat or engage with you, their emotional reaction is too high.

A better reaction when a dog is startled by thunder or another unfamiliar noise is to lead them home or to a nearby shelter. Once dogs feel safe, they naturally calm themselves by shaking off, yawning, or sniffing about. Rewards and attention should be offered only after the dog seeks social comfort. The time to engage the dog with familiar directions, games, and reward-based interactions is *after* they've recovered from an emotionally stressful episode, not during it.

FUN FACT

While scientists are still researching a dog's ability to use rational thought, anyone who loves a dog knows they can use their behavior to achieve preferred outcomes and choose responses that get them what they want.

Listening When Your Dog Communicates

Communication is merely the expression of emotions. One of the biggest differences between dogs and people is our communication styles. We talk a lot, while dogs rely on body language. You may be *listening* to your dog instead of *watching* them communicate.

Your dog's five talking points

This section outlines your dog's five key talking points — their ears, mouth, eyes, tail, and posture. It's important to recognize that your dog isn't always anxious; their mood can vary depending on their surroundings, situations, and companions.

Ears

Your dog's ears are very expressive. They can move independently or together and rotate up, down, backward, and forward. Your dog's focus, concentration, or concern can be quickly understood by observing their ears. Since dogs have different types of ears, from floppy to upright, there is no universal standard for interpreting ear position, but some general rules apply.

Use your dog's resting ears as a starting point. Notice them upright when they focus intently, one up and one back when trying to track noises coming from various directions or tilted back together when zoning or focusing on something behind them. You can recognize your dog's anxiety when both ears are pinned back. See Figure 2-1.

Ears are up
and forward,
alert and focused

Attentive

Ears are
held back
or sideways

Appeasing

Ears are
flat against head

Fearful | Anxious

Ears are
carried
naturally

Relaxed

© John Wiley & Sons, Inc.

FIGURE 2-1: Your dog's ears convey a lot of information if you pay attention to them.

Mouth

Your dog's mouth conveys a lot of information as well. An open mouth signals a relaxed smile (unless overheating), whereas closed lips convey concentration, anxiousness, or frustration (see Figure 2-2). Dogs also close their mouth when resting. Check in with your dog now — how are they feeling?

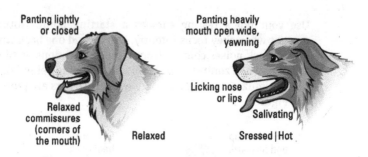

Panting lightly or closed

Relaxed commissures (corners of the mouth)

Relaxed

Panting heavily mouth open wide, yawning

Licking nose or lips

Salivating

Sressed | Hot

Mouth closed tight, commissures (corners of the mouth) are forward

May wrinkle muzzle or curl lip to expose teeth

Threatening | Aggressive

© John Wiley & Sons, Inc.

FIGURE 2-2: A dog's mouth tells us a lot about their current emotional state.

Eyes

Your dog's eyes can be difficult to read or get a clear fix on as you're not on the same level. Take a quick look at your dog's pupil — that dark circle in the center — when resting. The pupil will change shape in shifting light and in response to strong emotions. First, look at your dog's natural eye and pupil shape. Pupils get larger at dusk to let more light in and widen if a dog is fearful or startled. Ours do the same.

Dogs — like people — look at stuff that interests them. If you're wondering what has your dog's attention, notice what they're looking at — a squirrel, a garbage can, or the cupcake on the countertop.

Dogs signal discomfort, dismissiveness, and submission by avoiding eye contact. Should you even notice a stiff glare, with or without the white corners of their eyes showing, your dog is feeling threatened. Retreat or redirect your dog's focus with a toy or treat. See Figure 2-3.

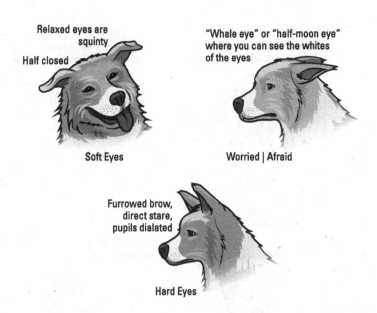

Relaxed eyes are squinty
Half closed

Soft Eyes

"Whale eye" or "half-moon eye" where you can see the whites of the eyes

Worried | Afraid

Furrowed brow, direct stare, pupils dialated

Hard Eyes

© John Wiley & Sons, Inc.

FIGURE 2-3: A dog's eyes show where their attention lies.

WARNING

Be mindful of dogs that show hard eyes: glassy, unemotional, and still, matched with a stiff posture. Back away immediately and slowly — whether this is your dog or someone else's.

Tail talk

A dog's tail is always talking; its movements and tempo convey wide-ranging emotions. Different tail positions indicate different emotional states: A relaxed tail is their default, a tucked tail signals anxiety, and a tail plastered against the belly indicates panic.

An uplifted tail suggests happiness, excitement, or curiosity, whereas an arched tail above the rump indicates frustration or defensiveness.

A side-to-side swing, paired with an open mouth and full body wiggle, signals friendliness, like a happy smile. Short arching sways can signify excitement, submission, or worry, depending on the tail's level. A vigorously twitching tip indicates emotional turmoil, while an arched tail suggests agitation. Contrary to popular belief, a wagging tail doesn't always convey happiness. See Figure 2-4.

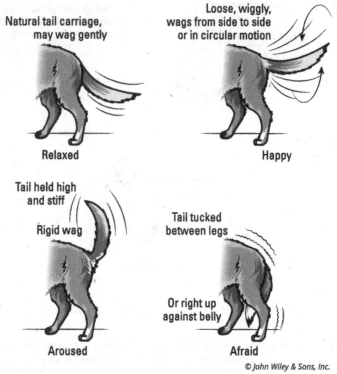

Natural tail carriage,
may wag gently

Relaxed

Loose, wiggly,
wags from side to side
or in circular motion

Happy

Tail held high
and stiff

Rigid wag

Aroused

Tail tucked
between legs

Or right up
against belly

Afraid

© *John Wiley & Sons, Inc.*

FIGURE 2-4: Tails convey a full range of emotions.

Overall posture

Your dog's posture is the clearest indicator of their emotional state; are they cowering in fear, bouncing enthusiastically, lying like a deflated balloon, leaning forward, stiff, or loose? Read all your dog's cues (ears, eyes, mouth, tail, and posture) together as they may sometimes convey conflicting messages, for example, when a dog wants to approach but feels apprehensive.

Take note of your dog's default comfortable poses (see Figure 2-5). Remember how your dog appears when resting — are they sprawled out on their side? This communicates trust — they're in a deep, nourishing sleep! Are they curled up in a ball? Dogs do this to conserve heat and protect their organs from potential threats. Dogs with generalized anxiety may struggle to relax anywhere other than their own home or safe place, like a crate or cozy bed.

FIGURE 2-5: Default, comfortable poses.

© *John Wiley & Sons, Inc.*

Happy, joyful dogs exhibit relaxed postures, moving freely without tension or distress. Their tail wags in a wide arc, and their mouth is generally slightly open, resembling a human smile. An alert posture indicates they recognize a sound or sight, even if it's not apparent. Their tail is lifted, their ears and eyes are directed toward the disruption, and their mouth is either closed or slightly open, especially in cases of generalized anxiety.

Vocalizations

While dogs can't talk, they use various sounds to convey their feelings and support their body language. There is a difference between a dog who barks from boredom, an alert barker, and one who barks for attention. Consider these various vocalizations:

>> **Alert barking** indicates territorial defense. Many dogs alert bark any time they sense something approaching. You'll know it's an alert bark if it's high-pitched and repetitive.

>> **Boredom barking** is low and spaced; dogs generally don't like quiet and will bark to fill the void. Boredom barks can also happen when dogs are crated or isolated and they hear someone in the home.

>> **Anxious barking** is frantic, single-toned, repetitive, and hard to ignore.

>> **Whining** expresses frustration or sadness.

>> **Growling** signifies fear or frustration. Belly growls are more severe than sounds that start in the throat or mouth, but all growls require immediate consideration.

>> **Howling** echoes in response to a high-pitched noise like a siren or loneliness and stress.

>> **Whimpering** communicates loneliness or distress. Injured dogs whimper when they're in pain.

>> Hound dogs will often **bay** — an alerting sound that lets everyone know they're on a scent or announcing a visitor.

As you can see, each vocalization is a unique expression, conveying their emotional states and needs.

TIP

The hair on your dog's back is another indicator of their mood. It will rise when they feel intense emotions like excitement, anxiety, joy, fear, or defensiveness. This is known as a *piloerection*. Dogs can also shed fur when scared or frazzled. This sign can be a harbinger of distress; you may also notice it after an altercation or routine trips to the veterinarian.

Tracking Your Dog's Anxiety

Setting realistic goals is essential as you and your dog work through their anxiety. Your first focus should be on reducing the intensity of their emotional storms. If your dog has a level 4 reaction when viewing other dogs on leash, reduce their fears using techniques like distancing and redirecting. If your dog suffers from separation anxiety, it can be weeks, months, or more before you can leave, confident knowing your dog's safe.

Table 2-1 illustrates the five levels of dog anxiety. Each level is accompanied by a posture, often with conflicting cues, reflecting the complicated nature of anxiety.

TABLE 2-1 **Five Levels of Dog Anxiety**

Level	Category	Behavior	Example Dog
Level 1	Subtle signs	Licking lips, averting gaze, yawing, pawing gesture, tail lowered with a slight wag, pupils slightly dilated, turning head away without moving.	
Level 2	Distress	May refuse food, toys, and direction. Tail down, possibly tucked, submissive grin, crinkled forehead. May refuse treats or grab quickly with hard bites, shallow breathing; pupils dilated.	
Level 3	Demonstrative	Locks eye with trigger, refuses treat or interaction, may retreat or threaten. Tail down (but not completely tucked), ears slightly back or to the side, furrowed brow, slow movements, fidgeting, panting with a tighter mouth, moderate pupil dilation.	

(continued)

TABLE 2-1 *(continued)*

Level	Category	Behavior	Example Dog
Level 4	Run away or freeze	*Runs away:* Ears back, tail tucked, mouth closed or excessive panting, tight tongue, whites of eyes visible, furrowed brow, dilated pupils. Attempting to escape by creeping or running. *Freezes:* Immobile, dilated pupils, ears back, tail tucked, hunched body posture, trembling, heavy breathing.	
Level 5	Reactive	*Offensive reaction:* Lunges forward, ears forward, tail up, raised hair on shoulders, rump, and tail, displaying only front teeth, lips puckered (lips pulled forward), tight and thin tongue, possibly dilated or constricted pupils. *Defensive reaction:* Raised hair on back and rump, dilated pupils, direct eye contact, showing all teeth including molars, body crouched and retreating, tail tucked, ears back.	

Keep an anxiety log

Start by jotting down when your dog is anxious and how they act, using Table 2-1 as your guide. This is called a *anxiety log*. To fully appreciate your dog's rational thinking skills, observe how your dog:

>> Navigates obstacles throughout the day, such as objects, doorways, gates, stairs, spills, and more.

>> Memorizes routines such as feeding, potty, and playtime schedules.

>> Uses clever ways to get rewards, such as learning cues and playing reward-based games.

>> Demonstrates problem-solving skills when faced with challenges like inaccessible toys or puzzles.

>> Communicates verbally and non-verbally to cue you into their needs and desires.

BOOKMARK

You'll help your dog utilize these rational thinking skills through training and playful engagement, even as their anxiety is activated. The goal is to strengthen your dog's cognitive abilities and social referencing skills. They will look to you for direction and support before reacting to unexpected events. Chapter 3 outlines thinking games and lessons that accomplish this.

TIP

Creating an anxiety log helps keep track of your efforts and progress. Each part of this book starts with a log tailored to that type of anxiety. You'll be proud to track your dog's progress! Share your efforts with everyone involved in the rehabilitation plan, and don't hesitate to reach out for help.

Regardless of the type of anxiety your dog is experiencing, they will exhibit similar symptoms. Whether you're dealing with separation anxiety at level 3 or social anxiety at level 1, it's important to record both the type and level of intensity. If you're addressing multiple forms of anxiety, consider creating multiple charts for each type.

Red zones, safe zones, and turning points

For conditions like leash reactivity, social anxiety, or sensitivities toward sights and sounds, it's important to note your dog's red zone and safe zone. Sometimes, their trigger is obvious, be it a person, animal, truck, or fireworks. Other times, you may not know what triggers your dog — and that's okay. The most important thing is to get your dog to a safe place until they calm down. See Figure 2-6.

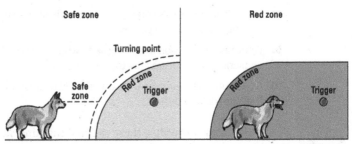

Safe zone   Red zone

Turning point

Safe zone   Red zone   Trigger

Red zone   Trigger

© John Wiley & Sons, Inc.

FIGURE 2-6: Red zones and safe zones.

The red zone

Think of the area close to the trigger as your dog's red zone. This no-go range stresses your dog to the point that they cannot think about anything else. The closer you get and the longer you remain within this zone, the more their fear level escalates.

The safe zone

Now, imagine your dog has a comfort bubble — far away from the red zone to a distance they feel safe, relaxed, and ready to interact. It could be around 10, 20, or even 30 yards/meters away from what upsets them. This is their safe zone.

The turning point

The turning point is the boundary where your dog first exhibits signs of distress. It could be just a few feet or even inches. At that moment, you can either guide them back to safety or push them past this threshold into their red zone, triggering an emotional tornado.

Why Anxiety Can Lead to Aggression

Many people view aggression as a sign of dominance, so it can be confusing when an aggressive dog is diagnosed with anxiety. Think of aggression as the bodyguard of fear. Dogs resort to aggression only when they've exhausted all other means of communicating their feelings. Dogs with anxiety may display aggression when protecting a resource, defending their personal space, experiencing injury or pain, or being coerced into unwanted situations. Aggressive behavior tends to escalate, so it's critical to be able to recognize the early signs.

Hard staring

When dogs feel anxious, they may resort to hard staring to convey their discomfort or apprehension. This intense gaze is a warning signal, indicating the dog feels threatened or stressed. Hard staring is a dog's attempt at communicating agitation and establishing boundaries. If it's not recognized or respected, it will lead to a more dramatic reaction, such as a lunge, snap, or bite.

Vocalizing

Dogs may growl, whine, or bark to express their anxiety when faced with unfamiliar situations, loud noises, or perceived threats. These vocalizations serve as a form of communication, signaling distress or discomfort or warning another dog, person, or animal to "back off!"

Lunging

In response to perceived threats or triggers, dogs may lunge forward to create distance or defend themselves. Lunging behavior can be a reactive response to fear or anxiety, as the dog seeks to assert control over their environment or avoid perceived dangers. This defensive posture may escalate into further aggression if the dog feels cornered or threatened.

Snapping and other warnings

As anxiety escalates, dogs may resort to snapping or other warning signals to communicate their discomfort and attempt to ward off potential threats. Snapping is often a last-ditch effort to establish boundaries and protect themselves from perceived harm. Other warning signs may include showing teeth, raising their hackles, or exhibiting tense body language, all indicating that the dog feels threatened and may escalate to aggression if the situation persists.

Biting

Biting is the ultimate expression of anxiety-driven aggression in dogs and typically occurs when all other warning signals have been disregarded or ignored. Dogs may resort to biting as a means of self-defense or to assert control over a perceived threat. It is essential to understand that biting is a last resort and often stems from a place of fear or insecurity.

Dogs are in control of the intensity of their biting. While some bites may serve as a quick warning, others can require immediate medical attention.

Calming Your Dog

The good news is that you can control how your dog processes, reacts, and directs their emotions. When their anxiety is most intense, you can take action. Whether it's by creating distance, providing a loving touch, a safe space, or a familiar object or bed, you play the most important role in helping your dog feel secure and comforted.

By understanding your dog's triggers and responding with patience and compassion, you empower your dog to navigate fears more confidently. Remember, their fears didn't come out of the blue; it's about discerning their behaviors and being their voice when they feel most insecure. Your dog can overcome their anxiety and lead a happier life with your guidance and support. Their happiness will be your reward.

CALMING SIGNALS

One of my favorite dog trainers is Turid Rugaas. She writes beautifully about canine calming signals, advocating correctly that dogs far prefer working their differences out peacefully rather than using aggression to settle disputes. Her writing details over 30 calming signals dogs use to dispel tension and keep the peace. Here are some common calming signals:

- Averting direct eye contact by tucking or turning their head
- Yawning
- Licking their lips
- Wagging their tail below their rump
- Turning away to sniff the ground
- Sitting and lifting a paw
- Showing their belly
- Play bowing
- Walking slowly or in a curve

Even growling is an attempt to avoid battle. Rugaas underscores that while other dogs read, recognize, and respond to these signals, people often misread them. Our lack of understanding can cause dogs to feel anxious or aggressive around people and other dogs. How can we expect them to tune into us if we don't tune into their communication?

Chapter **3**

Building Confidence with Routine and Play

There is more to your dog than their anxiety! You may find emotions like fear and stress overshadowing joyful feelings like curiosity and play. The best path to a life filled with more contentment is to discover what makes your dog most happy. Through play training, adventure and fun, this chapter can help you discover games and interactions that inspire their positive emotions. In the pages ahead, you also learn how to structure their life with routines, habits, and positive associations, giving your dog a stockpile of happy memories.

Assuring Your Dog with Daily Routines

A good antidote to anxiety is to frame your dog's day around consistent routines that satisfy their everyday needs. Like you, your dog needs to eat, drink, potty, play, and rest. The more predictable their day, the safer they feel. Teach your dog that words have meaning by assigning a word, short phrase, or hand signal to these everyday interactions. Though your dog doesn't understand the word's definition, they can quickly pair the sound of a word or visual cue with an action or object. Use treat cups to alert your dog's focus and encourage their cooperation. Remember to isolate and enunciate your words clearly — it should sound more like a happy bark than a question.

Table 3-1 assigns a word and routine to each need. While you can change the word or words, be consistent, create your own chart, and share it with all your dog's familiar people so everyone is on the same page.

TABLE 3-1 Assigning Directions and Routines to Needs

Need	Words	Routine
Eat	"Time to eat"	When bowl feeding, have your dog sit before lowering the dish. When hand feeding, use new and familiar words before dolling out a portion.
Water	"Water"	Assign 1-3 water stations so your dog knows where to go when they're thirsty. Ask your dog to sit before lowering the dish.
Sleep	"Go to your room" or "Place"	Assign a place for your dog in all the rooms you share. Place a mat and a chew toy to help your dog learn where to go and what to do in each area.
Elimination	"Outside" or "Papers" "Get busy"	Until your dog is house trained, follow similar routes to one door and potty area. Use words to organize and instill your dog's habits, directional cues as you walk, followed by toileting cues.
Play	"Ball," "Toy," or "Bone"	Satisfy your dog's play and chewing habits with appropriate toys, placed in easy-to-access locations.

TIP

Dogs love having a framework for their day: Think of yourself as your dog's parent and social director. As you develop a schedule and routine, communicate your plan in a confident, clear voice. If you want to get a handle on the tone, check out my videos on Instagram and TikTok (@SarahSaysPets).

Dogs and puppies can get as dysregulated as toddlers when their needs aren't met, especially when they need to potty or are over-tired. Instead of crying, they nip, fidget, and pace about. They have an unmet need, but pups don't cry. For more on puppies, see my book, *Puppies For Dummies*.

The following sections include ways to make everyday activities feel safe and consistent for your dog.

Eating

The fastest way to bond with your dog and teach them words/hand signals is to feed them by hand or portion their meal in a dish. Before offering your dog food, ensure they're sitting calmly. Hold the bowl above their head and wait until they stand or sit on all four paws. Should your dog jump in anticipation, lift the bowl up. Wait to present their food until they are calm. If you're using their food in games or training, portion out what you'll use before giving them each meal. Food is a universal motivator (well, for most dogs), and your dog will love playing games to earn their meals.

If your dog is a fast eater, buy or make a busy toy. Dispense their food in one of these contraptions, so they must work (think hunt) a little to get to it!

Drinking

Dogs hate being thirsty. Panting is a big clue, as is standing by the water dish. Always keep clean water out. If you're housetraining your dog, keep track of their drinking habits. What goes in comes out!

Going to the bathroom

Good potty habits are central to a happy household. To get your dog using the same potty place, get them on a consistent schedule and take them out after every rest, eating, or play period. Use specific words to direct them to their area, such as "papers" or "to your spot," and be sure to follow the same route each time.

If you've got a stress pottier, that's a different issue. Stress pottying has little to do with needing to go; it's all about nerves and heightened awareness. It's a common symptom of separation and containment anxiety, covered later in this book. As you work through these issues, stay consistent with your potty routine!

Assign words or hand gestures to other everyday routines. The more words your dog recognizes, the more they'll perk up and listen when you speak. Hearing familiar words will become the highlight of their day! Assign phrases like "upstairs and downstairs," "inside and outside," "kids are home," and "car," as you do these actions. Reward your dog with treats and praise for participating. You can even assign words to objects like balls, toys, and bones. Dogs are clever — you'll be surprised how quickly they learn!

Sleeping

Sleep is essential for dogs, just like it is for humans. They need intermittent rest throughout the day and a solid night's sleep. While specific sleep requirements vary based on age and breed, adult dogs generally need around 14-16 hours of rest. In their growth phase (two to nine months), puppies may need an additional four to six hours.

Overstimulation and inadequate rest can contribute to anxiety. Healthy sleeping habits are also a good indicator of overall health. Before addressing behavioral concerns, make sure your dog learns how to sleep well.

The first step is to create a calm environment for rest. This could be a quiet, darkened room or a crate. Playing sound-canceling music or white noise can help drown out distractions. Structure your day to include engaging activities in the morning and evening, with periods of rest in between. Avoid highly stimulating games close to scheduled rest times. Instead, focus on activities that promote self-soothing, such as chewing or puzzle toys.

Here's a sample schedule to help train your dog's sleep habits:

Morning

7:00 AM: Wake up, outdoor time, and feeding.

7:30 AM: Engage your dog in activities.

8:30 AM: Encourage self-soothing activities.

Mid-morning

9:00 AM: Rest period. Provide a quiet space for your dog to relax.

Midday

12:00 PM: Short wake cycle involving calming activities like a sniff and stroll or massage.

Afternoon

1:00-2:00 PM: Another rest cycle.

3:00-4:00 PM: Wake up for outdoor time and self-soothing activities.

4:00-5:00 PM: Second interactive cycle; consider socializing or free play.

Evening

7:00 PM: Reduce activity in preparation for the night.

10:00-11:00 PM: Final outdoor time before bedtime.

TIP

Visit SarahHodgson.com to download a free sleep and house-breaking schedule.

Training Lessons for Your Anxious Dog

Training strengthens the bond between you and your dog. By teaching them the meaning of a few basic words, they learn to prioritize your direction, especially when life becomes unpredictable. These interactions leave you both feeling included, recognized, and clever.

WARNING

Don't use fear tactics to train a dog with anxiety; that only creates a fear of the one person they need to trust. If your dog loves to eat or play, use treats and toys to excite them.

REMEMBER

When training, treats should only be given as or immediately after your dog behaves the way you want them to. Otherwise, you might inadvertently reward the very behavior you are trying to extinguish.

This section contains a list of cues and a step-by-step routine for teaching them. Use a building block approach — teach one word, then use that word to teach another, and so on. For example, you might teach "sit," then "sit and watch," then "sit and stay," and so on.

TIP

It's best to practice two to four times daily, keeping the lessons short, upbeat, and fun. Each lesson should be no more than three to five minutes. Be sure to use food and fun to keep your dog engaged. Avoid forcing your dog to listen if they're stressed or tuned out. Introduce all new lessons in a safe place, generally inside your home. Progress at a pace that is comfortable to them. Most of all, be loving, patient, and kind.

Teaching your dog to sit

Sit is a smooth move you can practice throughout the day. I teach it as an equivalent to saying please. To teach your dog a reliable sit, the first time you ask, follow these steps:

1. **Show it.** Initially, say nothing. Hold a treat or toy above your dog's head. If they jump, lift the treat above their head; when they're standing on all four paws, lower to the spot above their head. Reward your dog when their bottom hits the floor. When your dog is consistent, move on to Step 2.

2. **Label it.** Repeat the process in Step 1 but say "sit" as their bottom hits the floor. After two days, say "sit" as they maneuver into position.

3. **Prompt it.** After two more days, say "sit" as you offer your dog a treat or toy. Give them three seconds to respond. Reward and praise them instantly if they do it. If your dog jumps, lift the reward out of reach. Once your dog sits, reward them instantly. If they ignore you or refuse to sit, walk away calmly with the reward and try again later.

After this three-step learning process, follow this new direction for everything your dog finds rewarding, including treats, toys, food, and chews, before letting them out of the crate, car, or house.

Teaching sit-watch

Once your dog has mastered "sit," you can add "watch." This is a critical step in teaching your dog to refer to you in situations. Follow these steps:

1. **Show it.** Once your dog sits, quickly bring a treat from above their nose to your eyes. The second your dog's eyes lock on yours, reward them! Say nothing. Once they're consistent with this behavior, move on to Step 2.

2. **Label it.** Direct your dog to sit. Then say "watch" as your eyes lock.

3. **Prompt it.** After a day or so, begin to say "watch" as you direct their eyes to yours.

REMEMBER

Some people still refer to the words we teach dogs as "commands," but I believe that term implies a sense of bossiness that doesn't belong in a loving relationship. You wouldn't command your friend, your child, or your students. Training is more like teaching English as a second language. I prefer to think of these as directions or word cues.

Teaching your dog to stay

After you've got "sit-watch" down, you can introduce "stay," which means be still and calm down. Practice off-leash on a non-slippery surface and play calming music to drown out distractions. Break up 20-30 tiny treats, which you'll dispense throughout each lesson. Use whatever it takes (hotdogs are not off the table) to keep your dog's attention.

1. **Show it.** Take five to ten tiny treats or food kibbles. Instruct your dog to sit and watch, then sequentially reward them with three to five treats without saying a word. Space the treats no more than a second apart. Say "good job" to release them. Now, ignore them for 30 seconds before calling them over and repeating this quick sequence. Gradually increase to ten treats in one sitting. Remember to release and ignore your dog: They'll learn they only get rewards when they're still!

2. **Label it.** Direct your dog to sit, watch, and add stay as you distribute the treats. Vary the number of treats between each release and ignore your dog until they sit still. Gradually vary the time between treats from one to three seconds to one to five seconds to increase your dog's ability to hold still for prolonged periods.

3. **Prompt it.** After a day or so, say "stay," then dole out the treats. Remember to ignore your dog between stay segments. Vary the location you practice, the time between the treats, and the number of treats between each segment.

TROUBLESHOOTING YOUR LESSONS

How do I get my dog to listen when they're on a leash and/or in a distracting environment?

Your dog is an individual, and there is no predicting how soon they'll prioritize your direction. Keep practicing in low-distraction rooms, where they can perfect their understanding. Then, slowly perfect their associations by moving your lessons into more distracting areas.

Why do I start off-leash, and when should I practice on-leash? How do I know I can use these directions in everyday situations?

Many people think holding their dog's leash tightly gives them control. Leashes used like this confuse training, making dogs feel trapped and resistant. Training should feel more like being in school than in the military. Begin in an quiet room, using treats and toys to reward cooperation. After your dog has learned the meaning of a word, use a loosely held leash to reinforce the lesson in increasingly distracting places. Directions should feel engaging, not punitive.

What should I do — my dog listens and cooperates when I have treats, but the second we're on a walk or see someone passing by our window, all bets are off, and they are back to barking furiously.

When your dog's anxiety spikes, their ability to prioritize food or anything else (including you) will diminish. Don't take it personally. To soothe their stress, move away from the trigger and give them time to calm down. For everyday occurrences like barking on walks and at passersby, bring them away from the window or the other dog and wait until they calm down to direct or engage them.

Some trainers suggest using food and directions to calm a dog in a state of reactivity. This can't work; your dog is too worked up to think. Don't be discouraged if you've tried and failed. Wait until the distraction passes, or move the dog away and give them time to return to reality.

Teaching down

Getting your dog to relax in a down posture can be difficult, but play training can make it more appealing.

TIP

Down is a vulnerable posture. Anxiety aside, dogs won't lower themselves unless they feel safe or trusting. Once their anxiety is triggered, however, a dog is nervous, feeling neither safe nor trusting. Down is a good benchmark for your dog to feel more relaxed.

1. **Show it.** Take something your dog wants (a treat or a toy). Ask your dog to sit, then take the object from your dog's nose to the floor right in front of your dog's feet. Hold still for five seconds and wait; if your dog goes down, reward them.

TIP

If your dog follows the treat but doesn't go all the way down, reward them for a half-down ten times over the course of a couple of lessons, then hold the treat still to see if your dog will go completely down before rewarding them. Most will do it right away; some take a few days.

2. **Label it.** After they're willing to go down reliably, say "down" as they move into position.

3. **Prompt it.** Once your dog is comfortable going down, direct them down before petting, greeting, and playing their favorite games.

As your dog becomes more comfortable sliding into this relaxed position, use this direction in more distracting situations and practice it with other directions, such as "place" and "under."

Teaching place

Dogs often get anxious because they don't know what to do with themselves. Providing your dog with a mat, bed, or blanket in each room you share and teaching them to settle down at your side can provide relief and comfort, especially when you have visitors or are away from home.

As you learned in Chapter 2, anxiety causes a rise in energy. Teaching your dog to go to a place and providing them with a savory chew will focus their attention and energy as they learn self-soothing skills.

1. **Show it.** Take something your dog wants (a treat or a toy). Hold the object just above their head and walk toward their designated mat or bed. Release the reward the second their four paws are on their blanket, mat, or bed. Do this for all their rewards!

2. **Label it.** After they're willing to put all four paws on their mat, say "place" just before rewarding them.

3. **Prompt it.** After a day or so, say "place" as you show your dog their reward. Initially, stand near their area, then slowly direct them farther away.

Soon, your dog will go to their place on their own. Place chews and toys near the mat or in a basket. Calmly reward them with loving attention or treats when they go to their area undirected. Gradually phase off rewards in place of comforting praise.

TIP

Share this mantra — all good things happen to my dog when they're in their place (see Figure 3-1). Ask family and familiars to send your dog to their mat before rewarding them with anything your dog considers positive, such as treats, toys, attention, and freedom.

© *Grace Choo Photography/Getty Images*

FIGURE 3-1: Teach your dog that all good things happen when they're on their mat.

Teaching your dog to follow

Walks can be more stressful than enjoyable when your dog is anxious. When unfamiliar distractions surround them, your dog may tune you out as they scan the horizon for signs of danger. Unless you're acutely aware of your dog's mood, it can shift on a dime, sending them into a whirlwind of reactivity that can set you both on edge. As your dog likely feels most safe at home, being away from it can be unsettling. Whether they suffer from social, sensory, or generalized anxiety, a walk can be an overwhelming experience.

BOOKMARK

The leash skills outlined here will be useful in Chapter 10, which delves into leash reactivity. Remember to "dog-ear" this page and flip to Chapter 10 for more leash games.

Teaching your dog walking words can help you direct them in good times and more stressful times. Teaching a word like "follow" (the new version of "heel") encourages your dog to prioritize your voice; using rewards keeps it fun! Most important, however, as you work through this lesson, work on loose-leash walking skills, lest your dog feel trapped when with you and away from home.

FUN FACT

Dogs only stare and vocalize at each other if they're playing or fighting. When teaching your dog to come or follow, you must direct your voice where you'd like them to go, not at them.

1. **Show it.** Start indoors and off-leash. Bait your dog with a toy or treats and call out their name as you step forward. Walk five to ten steps, then say other cues your dog is familiar with, such as "sit and watch." Once your dog plays along, hold the leash lightly as you move around the house together. Should your dog get distracted, calmy turn, call their name, and head in the other direction. Have you mastered that step? You're ready to start labeling the behavior!

2. **Label it.** Repeat the same moves outdoors, adding your walking word: "heel," "follow," or "let's go." Turn in the opposite direction if your dog gets distracted. If they're pulling too hard, stop and be still. Walk away from the distraction and don't proceed until they're calm and able to focus.

3. **Prompt it.** After a day or so, prompt your dog to follow you by using your walking word. If your dog races ahead, calmly turn and move in the other direction or stop in place. Reward their interest in your whereabouts.

If your dog stops dead in their tracks, calmly stop and assess the situation. If your dog is terrified and wants to return home, go with them. Sit calmly once you're inside and reassure them by petting them lovingly or giving them a favored chew in their favorite room. If they need a minute to regain their composure, you'll know, as they will resume walking with a little encouragement and positive reinforcement. For more techniques to use when your dog gets triggered on a walk, turn to Chapter 10.

Teaching hurry, hurry

This game is fun, great exercise, and should be played often so when you need it, your dog will be excited to leave their troubles behind. On- or off-leash, suddenly say to your dog, "hurry, hurry," and pick up your pace to a healthy trot or run. Run ahead 10 to 30 yards and toss out treats or a toy as you encourage them. Repeat "find it" often. It's like stepping on the gas — as you use "hurry hurry," you're telling your dog to speed up!

Teaching your dog under

Dogs with anxiety welcome this direction; they will learn to lie under your legs, which can comfort them in unpredictable situations. You can use it when you have company, are out and about, or are in the waiting room at the animal hospital.

1. **Show it.** Sit on the edge of a chair or sofa, making a big space under your legs. Next, take something your dog loves, such as a treat, toy, or chew. Guide them under your legs or use a helper to guide your dog. Reward them when they are standing still under your legs. If they know "down," give that direction, then reward them.

2. **Label it.** Say "under" when your dog maneuvers under your legs.

3. **Prompt it.** After you've mastered Steps 1 and 2, position yourself at the edge of a chair or sofa and say "under" just before you lure them with the treat or reward. Begin to swap out food rewards and, in place, offer pats and chews. Encourage them by using "down" and "stay" if your dog knows these directions.

Teaching touch, come

Play this one inside or out. The goal is for your dog to touch their nose to your hand. Hold treats in your left hand as you extend a flat palm for your dog a few inches from their nose. The second your dog touches their nose to your palm, reward them with the treat (see Figure 3-2). If they ignore your hand, hold it closer, right before their nose. When they catch on, assign the word "touch" to the action. Slowly move your hand around and encourage them to move with you by touching their nose to your hand. This can keep a dog with social anxiety focused on you and encourages them to look to their hands for treats and reassurance rather than face staring.

FIGURE 3-2: Touch, come.

Teaching your dog to come

Come is often a dog's favorite word — togetherness is better than being alone. I like to think of "come" as the equivalent of "huddle!" It's the ultimate reconnection.

Of course, if you've faced off with your dog as they refuse to come closer, you may disagree with me. If your dog runs when you say "come," consider whether it could be from fear. Dogs only face off in moments of confrontation, so if you've stared your dog down, repeating "come, come, come" in a threatening tone, reconnecting might be the furthest thing from their mind. Dogs with anxiety (like people) are allergic to angry emotions. When teaching or retraining your dog, make sure you check your frustration before interacting.

Start the "come" lessons indoors, where your dog is least distracted and feels most safe. Gradually extend to more distracted areas, but don't rush it. Keep the lessons fluid and fun, so that your dog associates this cue with togetherness, not separation.

1. **Show it.** Take something your dog wants, like a treat or a toy; use your treat cup! Stand in another room and call to your dog as you run in the other direction. When your dog gets to you, reward and pet them.

2. **Label it.** Repeat this process, and this time, say "come" as your dog gets to you. Say "come" as you reconnect physically. Come should mean togetherness, not separation!

3. **Prompt it.** After a day or so, say "come" as you shake their treat cup or squeak their favorite toy. Practice standing six to ten feet from your dog and run away from them as you call out their name — like a game of tag, you're it. Gradually vary the distance and call them from other rooms in the house.

Perfect this cue inside off-leash before practicing outside on a six-foot leash or 10- to 30-foot line. Make the exercises more simplistic as you progress to more distracting areas until your dog catches on. Slowly progress to greater distances and more distracting environments, always using a long line to ensure your dog's safety.

When communicating with your dog, it's not just the words but the tone that matters. Imagine you are the coach of a middle school soccer team. Your tone should sound confident and strong! The goal in training is to reassure your dog that you're walking through this world together. Anxiety is an isolating emotion. It can be a lonely path no matter what your species. By recognizing this and engaging your dog playfully, you can help them feel more secure while bridging the communication gap between you.

For a list of directional words, visit SarahHodgson.com for free downloads.

Adopting Relaxation Techniques

The link between mind, body, and anxiety has long been understood by people; studies now show the same in dogs. Heightened and prolonged levels of cortisol (the stress hormones) have been shown to affect behavior and stimulate poor health. Cortisol can take up to 72 hours to dissipate in your dog's system, and routine stress takes its toll. One of the best things you can do when your dog's been upset is to calm them down. These relaxation techniques are transformative in helping your dog release their tension and regain a sense of calm.

Synchronized breathing

Find a quiet space and get comfortable with your dog. Gradually adjust your breath to synchronize with the length and pace of your dog. Take slow, deep breaths, matching their rhythm. Maintain synchronized breathing for several minutes.

Massage

Gently massage your dog's body using slow, circular motions. Focus on areas where your dog holds tension, such as the shoulders, back, and hips. Massage can help release muscle tension and promote relaxation.

TIP

TTouch was created by Linda Tellington-Jones, who is leading the way in using massage to calm many animals, including dogs. You can learn about her massage techniques by visiting her site at https://ttouch.com/.

Music therapy

Play soft, calming music or white noise in the background to create a relaxing atmosphere. My dogs love soft rock and classical music!

Aromatherapy

Use calming essential oils such as lavender or chamomile in a diffuser or diluted in a carrier oil for massage. These scents can have a soothing effect on both you and your dog.

**TECHNICAL
STUFF**

After birth, a naturally occurring calming pheromone is produced in a dog's mamillary glands. *DAP*, a synthetic reproduction, can reassure puppies and help them relax. It can be diffused like an air freshener and sprayed on bedding.

Anxiety wraps

Many dog with anxiety respond well to body wraps, which can be bought or made. DIY wraps are created from modified t-shirts that are tied securely around a dog's underbelly. Store-bought versions cling more tightly to a dog's torso, providing constant tactile pressure.

FUN FACT

These wraps work on a principle advocated by Temple Grandin, who originally noted that cattle are calmed when held securely in the chute. This theory was applied and found to lessen anxiety in stressed and reactive dogs.

Overcoming Anxiety with Play

Play provides an enriching outlet to escape worries and boost joy for you and your dog! In fact, throughout the book, I stress the importance of play training to increase your dog's joy and give them more agency in their decisions. The ability to choose their own reactions has proven to be the most effective and healthy way to bond and boost a positive association with your everyday interactions. This section delves into the two main types of play:

» **Thinking games** are designed to be mental challenges for dogs, like puzzles or chess for humans. Dogs, like young children, are more engaged when there's a reward involved, such as a treat or a favorite toy. These games operate on the "learn-to-earn" principle.

» **Energy busters,** such as competitive sports or swimming, require high energy output and are more instinctually driven. Engaging in active games and providing mental stimulation can help channel a dog's energy positively and strengthen the bond between you and your dog.

As with anything, balance is key. A dog provided only with thinking activities can become out of shape, overly fixated on people, and may develop anxiety due to a lack of freedom and routine play. On the other hand, when a dog is constantly engaged through physical exertion or forced interactions with other dogs and people, the dog may enter a state of hyperarousal and struggle to relax.

Dogs only play when they feel safe. Playing is a great way to gauge your dog's frame of mind. If your dog feels too unstable, they won't engage with you and will refuse treats and toys. Lucky for them, they have you!

This is a condensed list of games — there are enough games to fill a whole book! Refer to my book titled *Dog Tricks and Agility for Dummies* for specific tricks. Check out the online reference section for other books and articles on tricks, fun, and play!

Thinking games

Some people think that high-energy activities are all that will tire a dog out. This is not the case! Overstimulating a dog often leads to their needing more arousal to calm down. A dog with insatiable energy and a restless nature makes it impossible for anyone to relax. Fortunately, thinking games are exhausting, interactive, and fun. Each one encourages your dog to use their mind in new and exciting ways. Some of these games require teamwork, others inspire problem-solving skills, and more challenge your dog to think on their feet (ah, paws).

You'll encounter many of these games again throughout the book. Be sure to bookmark this section — you'll probably want to return to it often!

Find It

This game is a surefire winner everyone can enjoy. Follow these steps:

1. **Take your dog's food or a handful of yummy treats.**

2. **Toss a treat on the floor by their feet.** They'll catch on quickly!

3. **Once you have their attention, hold the treat two to three inches above their head.** If they jump, lift it out of reach.

4. **Drop the treat when they stand or sit calmly.**

Repeat this as often as you want throughout the day. Dropping treats also helps curb jumping and nipping habits. Once your dog knows directions like "sit" and "down," cue them before dropping the treat.

Feed the Chickens

Another version of Find It involves a jackpot of treats! Throw a handful of treats and say a fun expression like "feed the chickens" or "champagne for everyone." Your dog will soon associate this expression with a motherlode of goodies and quickly shift their focus from fear or frustration to fun!

Treat Cup game

This game has simple and more challenging versions. Follow these steps for the simple version:

1. **Get a plastic cup or flip-lid container (like a gum or toddler cup).** Fill half the cup with treats or food if your dog eats kibble.

2. **Shake the cup and reward your dog by tossing a treat on the ground as described in the "Find It" section.**

3. **Once your dog connects the sound to rewards, use it to call your dog and to teach "drop," as explained in the next section.**

Treat cups can also be used to teach impulse control and focus and help engage your dog as you desensitize and counter-condition more positive associations to stressful circumstances. Check out the Approach-Avoid game described later in this section.

Alligator Island

Follow these steps to play the Alligator Island game:

1. **Using your treat cup, climb onto a countertop or table. This is a great game for kids too!**

2. **Call your dog over and wait to toss food (or toys) until your dog has all four paws on the floor and behaves respectfully.**

3. **You can add multiple players and call your dog back and forth.**

TIP

Use this technique when people visit, in order to curb any jumping and teach your dog to calm down quickly.

REMEMBER

The opposite of anxiety is calm, reassuring confidence. Playing thinking games helps to develop a can-do spirit, inspiring self-confidence!

Catch

It might seem silly that many dogs need a hand in learning to catch, but the truth is it takes as much coordination as catching a ball. Try this:

1. **Gather some high-value treats and call your dog over.** Ask them to sit on their mat, facing you on the ground, or on a non-slippery floor.

2. **Hold the treat above their head.** Wait until they're calm and focused.

3. **Initially, don't toss the treat to them.** Instead, mimic the motion of tossing it, following the path as if you threw it without letting it go.

4. **Once your dog follows the treat with their eyes and opens their mouth in a timely manner, drop the treat in and reward them.**

5. **Gradually increase the distance you toss the treat until your dog learns to watch the treat and your hand.** Eventually, switch over to a toy or ball.

Got that? Remember to direct your dog to stay calm while throwing treats or toys from various distances and directions. This game teaches them focus, impulse control, and the ability to respond to hand signals.

Nosework

Dogs naturally rely on their sense of smell to identify other dogs and people, reveling in various scents that enrich their world. Nosework is an exercise that allows your dog to hone their scent skills. You can create DIY busy toys tailored to their scent perception. Try these toys:

>> **Egg carton excitement:** Repurpose old egg cartons for your dog's entertainment. Fill a few compartments with your dog's favorite kibble or healthy snacks. Close the carton and watch as your dog eagerly investigates and extracts the treats. Try

hiding the carton around the house or incorporating it into your dog's play routine to keep the challenge fresh.

» **Muffin tin treat box:** Using a muffin tin, fill some of the cups with small pieces of kibble and cover them with tennis balls. As your dog learns the game, you can increase the difficulty by baiting only specific cups, encouraging your dog to rely on their sense of smell to uncover the hidden treasures.

» **Creative hollow dispensers:** Raid your recycling bin for cardboard tubes or tissue boxes to create engaging treat dispensers. Seal off the ends of the tubes and cut holes large enough for the treats to fall through. Your dog will enjoy the challenge of moving, tearing, and tossing these homemade toys to reveal the delicious rewards inside.

» **Goodie bag:** Collect your dog's favorite treats and toys, pack them in a paper bag or box, and let your dog have at it. You can also use a recycled box. Cut holes on each side, fill it with treats or food, and watch your dog knock it around.

» **Recycled plastic bottles:** Using thick plastic bottles, fill them with treats or food and watch as your dog bats them around to free the food.

You can also purchase ready-made busy toys designed specifically to challenge and satisfy your dog's scent perception. Some may be more challenging than others. Look for these toys under categories such as Busy, Enrichment, and Puzzle Toys for your dog's enjoyment and mental stimulation.

Person, Place, or Thing

Dogs love to learn words — the easiest way to light up their brain is to teach and use more words, not fewer! You can assign words to people, places, and things:

1. **Label it whenever you're walking to a familiar room or destination.** For example, "kitchen," "upstairs," "outside," "Jackie's room," and "car." The list can go on and on! Remember to speak clearly and call in the direction you're headed, not down like you're talking to your dog.

2. **Next, teach your dog to identify toys by name.** Pick up a toy and name it. The second your dog taps the toy, mark and reward them!

3. **Now place the toy on the floor and call its name: Reward your dog for picking it up or tapping it.** Mix the item with unfamiliar items. Does your dog single it out?

Try mixing it with other toys as well. As they learn one toy, teach them another, and another, and so on.

The Guinness Book of World Records recognized Chaser the Border Collie as the dog who learned the most words — she can identify over 1,000 objects!

Name game

Dogs can learn to identify familiar people by name. Follow these steps to teach your dog:

1. **Call your dog back and forth across the room using a treat cup. The say, for example: "go to Lindsay."** Lindsay should call the dog's name as she shakes the treat cup.

2. **When your dog reaches the intended person, encourage them to stop, sit, or stand calmly before rewarding them with a treat.**

3. **As your dog catches on, challenge them. Add more people or hide between rounds.**

Treasure Hunt

Dogs love a treasure hunt as much as kids do, but while kids look around, your dog will sniff to locate the goods. Try this:

1. **Start by telling your dog to stay, tethering them, or having someone hold them on a leash.**

2. **Walk ten feet away and let your dog see you hide the treat in an obvious spot, like around a corner or behind a piece of furniture.** Say "treasure hunt" as you release them and watch them make a beeline for where you left it.

3. **Once your dog seems to catch on, increase the difficulty of the hiding spots, giving them enough time to locate the treasure.** You can stand near the location but resist pointing it out.

4. **Add more treats gradually, cueing your dog with, "there's more," until they've found all of them.**

CLICKERS AND WORD MARKERS

A *clicker* is a handheld device that produces a distinct clicking sound when pressed. Markers can be verbal cues like "yes!" or "good!" or any other distinct noise, even a kissing sound! Clickers and sharp marker sounds can be paired with treats to highlight when your dog does something right, even if they're apart from you. You'll see their use suggested throughout the book, as in the I Spy game.

You can also incorporate a hide-and-seek version, encouraging your dog to find you in different spots in the house or yard. Instruct your dog to "stay" as you hide, or have a partner hold them and release them when it's time to find you. Gradually hide in more difficult spots.

Scatter feeding

Another version of the treasure hunt is scatter feeding, which makes mealtimes more exciting. Tell your dog to hold still as you hide their food in various rooms or out in the yard. You can hide a handful at a time. Release your dog to find their food as you celebrate each find.

I Spy

The I Spy game is a great way to help address your dog's triggers. Before you start, take 20 tiny treats and assign them a clicker or a word, such as "yes!" Say or click once and toss a treat to your dog, saying, "find it!" You're ready to begin once your dog associates the sound with looking for the reward.

1. **Start by using a familiar dog toy.** Play in a quiet room. Hold the toy in one hand and treats in another. Bring both the toy and the treats behind your back.

2. **Call your dog and ask them to sit in front of you.** Bring the toy out and pause until your dog looks at it. The second they do so, say "yes" and reward them when they look back to you.

3. **As your dog catches on, you can move the object around, and your dog will look at it and then return to you for the treat.**

4. Now move on to another item; once they target that, try another object that you can hold in your hand.

5. **Next, try for a person or another sensory object, such as a wind chime or mixer.** This step teaches them to be mindful of changes in their sensory world. Once they look at the stimulus, say "yes!" and reward them for looking back at you.

In the real world, I Spy can be very helpful in many scenarios, including these:

>> **Use I Spy to deescalate your dog's fascination with household objects like socks and paper towels.** Initially, hold these objects as you did in Steps 1 and 2. When your dog sees the items as objects in a game, put them on a table (less distracting) and then onto the floor (more distracting). If your dog grabs the item, start the I Spy game at a greater distance. A helpful hint in this game is to toss the treats away from the distraction.

>> **Practice with people, visitors, and neighbors if your dog is weary of them.** Walk into a room where someone is sitting. The moment your dog looks at the person, say "yes" or click immediately and reward them instantly! Make the challenge harder by asking the person to eat something irresistible. Next, ask them to wander about the room or walk in and out of the door so your dog can resist going to them. A helpful hint: If your dog doesn't immediately respond to your marker word, they may be too close to the distraction.

>> **Over time, you'll be able to play this game with things that trigger your dog's anxiety, such as vacuums, other dogs, and distressing noises.** I reference this game throughout the book, so you might want to mark or fold this page. The key is finding the precise distance: not too close to the fear that your dog will implode and not too far away that your dog loses interest. This game is central to your dog's recovery, as it takes something dreaded and stress-inducing and makes it a prop in a game.

Operation Cooperation

Operation Cooperation, originally known as the Bucket Game, is the brainchild of trainer Chirag Patel. We often only listen when our dogs "yell" at us, that is, they use aggression to make their point, instead of listening when they whisper. In this game, your dog can communicate through their behavior when they feel positive about an interaction versus when they feel distressed. Here's how it goes:

1. **Take out a small bucket or container. Let your dog see you place treats in it.** Your first goal is to get them to sit still one to two feet from the bucket without getting up or jumping on you. To do this initially, stand and hold the bucket on a stool or table. If your dog jumps at the bucket, lift it up and wait until they're calmly sitting to place it back down and try again. Once the dog looks at the bucket calmly without jumping up, give them a treat directly from the bucket.

2. **The next step is to prove that your dog knows to look at the bucket.** Take the bucket and hold it out to your left or right side. When your dog looks at the bucket, reward them with a treat from the bucket. Remove the bucket between each sequence and encourage your dog to sit calmly.

3. **Now work on duration, getting your dog to stare at the bucket for gradually longer durations.** Initially, vary the time from one to three seconds, making it different each time: reward after one, then two, one, one, three, two. Increase the time until your dog can hold their stare for ten seconds.

4. **Next, practice simple arm movements with the arm farthest from the bucket as your dog focuses on the container of treats.** If they look away, stop moving; only continue when they look back at the container. If your dog continues to stare at the bucket, reward them with treats from the bucket.

5. **The final step is to touch your dog's ear while they stare at the container.** If they look away at any point, stop. If they stay focused on the container, touch their ear. Once they allow you to touch different parts of their body while staying focused on the bucket, you're ready for Operation Cooperation!

Your dog's eye contact with the container signifies a *green light*, indicating they're comfortable with the situation. Glancing away serves as a yellow light, signaling caution. A hard turn away acts as a red light, signifying a stop.

Use Operation Cooperation if you're prepared to exit a situation should your dog become too stressed to focus or eat. When your dog consistently maintains eye contact with the container, you can utilize this game during grooming sessions and veterinary examinations. It's great for desensitizing and counterconditioning a dog with anxiety, because it addresses issues such as social anxiety, sensory sensitivity, and resource guarding.

FUN FACT

Your dog's learning is unlimited! Your dog can easily be taught to understand simple words, differentiate colors, and even do simple math. Check out the online reference section for links to videos and books on the topic. Perhaps simplest is a move called "do as I do," where you model specific behavior you want your dog to mimic. I've listed a book by that exact name: Look for it!

Teaching energy busters

There's a common misconception that a dog becomes tired only when you physically exhaust them. Interactive play does release some energy, but note the word "interactive!" Robotically tossing a ball for an hour or taking your dog on a speed walk to boost your step count may be one way to exercise your dog, but it doesn't engage their mind and is lacking the best kind of social interaction. Instead, opt for fun and engaging activities that strengthen your bond while providing energy release — you'll be pleasantly surprised at how quickly they catch on! This section explains some activities to get you started.

Two Toy Toss

Two Toy Toss is a simple way to engage your dog in interactive play while reinforcing cues like "go get it," "bring," and "drop it."

1. **Gather at least three toys or balls that excite your dog.**

2. **Go to your free play space, inside or out. Hold the toy before your dog until they stand or sit calmly and give them a light toss while watching you.** As they run to retrieve it, say, "go get it," and quickly get their other toy ready.

3. **Show your dog the first ball and give it a short toss.** Praise your dog for going to the toy, but when they turn back, show interest in the toy you're holding. They might not return with the first toy. It doesn't matter. Wait until your dog is calm and sitting patiently before tossing the second toy.

4. **Praise your dog when they grab the first toy.** When they alert to the sound of your voice, however, ignore them and start playing with the other toy.

5. **If your dog runs to you with the first toy in their mouth, you can say "bring."** If they drop their toy and run to you, have them sit before you toss the second toy. Say "drop it" only if you see them dropping the first toy. Then, have them sit or stand calmly before you toss them the second toy.

Structured Tug-of-War

Dogs adore tugging and are very cooperative when taught how to play fairly. As you play this game, you'll teach "tug" and "drop," too. Unstructured tugging simulates high arousal, holding on for dear life as if the toy were prey and a vice grip hold that isn't wise to use around people. Play this way instead:

1. **Pick a good tug toy — a long rope, fabric, cloth Frisbee, or squeak toy.** Ensure that it's long enough to avoid accidental bites. Keep treats on hand to encourage and reward "drop it."

2. **Entice your dog by wiggling or waving the toy several inches before them.** Praise any interest and encourage them by lightly pulling on the toy.

3. **Now that you're engaging with them, teach two prompts: "you win!" and "drop":**

   You win! Let your dog win at least half the time. After a few good tugs, say, "you win!" as you release the toy.

   Drop: Get them to release the object. Bring a savory treat to their nostrils, saying "drop" as they release the toy. When possible, return the toy for another round.

WARNING

Avoid playing this game with children under ten. Before any child plays, ensure your dog understands self-restraint and a release cue like "drop". If your dog is possessive or still nips, consider skipping this game. Your dog must reliably listen to the children's cues before they play.

Predatory Play

Many dogs are born hunters. Even breeds you'd consider poised come alive like mighty warriors when they see a squirrel, a scooter, or a slipper move past them. Lucky for you, there's a game you can play to satisfy your dog's insatiable appetite for chasing. Try this:

1. **Purchase or make predatory play poles for your dog. You can tie any toy to a four to ten foot rope to drag about like a cat toy.**

2. **You can simulate the chase inside and out by putting the game on a cue: "get your toy!"** Let your dog win occasionally and reinforce "drop" by initially baiting them with a yummy-smelling treat.

3. **If you have children over seven, use a 10- to 20-foot rope and tie a favorite toy to the end.** Supervise play as your dog learns to run *with* you and your kids, not *at* you or your kids.

Many dogs get overstimulated, so keep these play sessions short and remind your dog to sit and watch between each "drop" pause!

Red Light, Green Light

Red Light, Green Light teaches your dog many new behaviors: moving together, impulse control, and basic directions, like "sit," "down," or "wait." Your dog will associate fun with listening. Play solo or ask a friend to call the shots.

1. **Grab a treat cup and pick a room or enclosed area outside to play.**

2. **Start by saying "green light." As you move about, say, "follow me!"**

3. **"Red light" means you slow to a stop.**

4. **Next, your narrator should call out a direction your dog knows, like "sit down" or "sit-stay," so when they say, "red light," you'll be ready.** You can also play solo and vary the directions between sprints.

Lily Pad game

Gather your treat cup and three to five resting mats, beds, or towels. The goal is to randomly send your dog to various mats, rewarding them once they sit or lie down. Once they catch on, vary the order you send them and keep them guessing on how many rounds they have to do to get the reward.

1. **Place three to five mats in an open room with treats or cups in hand.**

2. Point and look at a mat and say, "place."

3. The moment your dog has all four paws on the mat, praise them.

4. Next, either send them onto another mat or give them a treat.

5. Once they catch on to the game, add other directions they recognize, such as "sit," "down," and "stay."

Vary your demands and sequence to keep the game exciting.

Catch Me if You Can

Catch Me if You Can is a fun way for your dog to burn off some energy while learning that it's fun for them to run *with* you, not at or away from you.

1. Use a treat, toy, or other high-value item.

2. Entice your dog with the treat or toy.

3. Turn and run, calling, "catch me if you can!"

4. **Stop frequently to ensure your dog runs and stops with you.** Reward their cooperation by playing "find it" or giving them a toy if that's what you're holding.

5. Gradually extend your distance as you run sprints to focus your dog's attention and tire them out.

Treat-Retreat

Not only is this game fun, but it's also a great way to support your dog's fear of approaching their triggers. Suzanne Clothier, a respected dog trainer, originally developed it. In this game, you offer your dog a choice and reward them regardless of whether they choose to approach or avoid.

1. Begin by tossing a treat at your feet and saying "find it, treat" in a positive, happy tone.

2. Next, toss the next treat over your shoulder and say, "find it, retreat!"

3. Repeat this one-for-one treat-retreat pattern until your dog catches on.

4. Next, vary the sequences, sometimes doing two retreats, then one treat at about 12 inches away and another treat at three inches away.

5. Gradually phase out the "find it" indicator as you coach your dog to respond to these new directions.

Initially, when you use this around stressors, a dog will only approach so far, choosing to wait for the treats to be thrown away from the trigger. This activity acknowledges their fears and avoids the common mistake of rewarding them only when they cooperate, which overlooks the underlying fear causing their hesitation.

Parcourse

Parcourse is a fun activity designed to help your dog focus more on moving from point A to point B during leash walks rather than getting distracted by their surroundings.

1. Begin by identifying three to five stopping points along your route, called "stations." Plan to pause at each station and engage in a variety of activities.

2. You can play a leash game like silly circles or leash squares, practice hide-and-seek with treats or treat pouches, or even play a game like catch with your dog's favorite toys. The key is to vary the interaction at each station so your dog is excited to see what they'll do next.

REMEMBER

It's like parcourse for humans: The dog will walk from one station to the next and engage in a specific activity for one to two minutes.

Groundwork

Groundwork is a great way to engage your dog in exploring environments while keeping them connected to you. It was originally developed by Linda Tellington-Jones, creator of TTouch. The approach is summarized here, so check out the online reference section or search YouTube for more about this transformative activity.

1. Design an open area ahead of time with various obstacles, such as cones to weave around, a low seesaw to maneuver, low tables, benches, and so on. Hurdles can be made from logs or sticks across to objects of similar height. If your

dog can explore it, use it! Old carpets or plastic mats can be laid down — as many of your dog's sensory neurons are in their feet, they will be alert to the surface change.

2. **Place your dog on the black clip of their harness and bring them to the field on a long, lightweight leash that's six to ten feet long.** Stay close and let them explore the scene without your interference. As they grow more comfortable in their surroundings, you can show them how to work the seesaw and traverse around the cones.

3. **Your role is to observe which obstacles or treasures excite them.** This activity is meant to build your dog's confidence. Triggering dogs, objects, or people can be present but in the distance — far enough away so your dog doesn't give them more than a passing glance.

Anything goes here. Groundwork is geared toward stimulating their brains. The sky is the limit: boxes, ladders, or items that might stimulate caution but can be explored together. Consider using balloons or a pool filled with empty balls or bottles.

WARNING

If an item causes your dog anxiety, don't use it. Introduce one trigger at a time, placed off far in the distance.

Tricks

All training is a trick to your dog. What we consider "tricks" are unique moves we teach our dog to inspire adoration and joy. Since your dog loves both, the sky is the limit! Choose tricks your dog can do comfortably, pairing a word to actions they do naturally. For example, many little dogs love to prance on their hind legs, big dogs love pawing things, and all dogs love rolling on their back — a move I call belly up. Here are three universal favorites to get you started:

SPIN

I do this one when my dogs come in, as an equivalent to wipe your paws. To teach "spin," work on a non-skid surface like a carpet or outside on the lawn.

1. **Standing next to your dog, slowly bring a treat from your dog's nose to their tail.** Once they follow the treat, toss it behind them for a few rounds.

2. Once they have that down, bring the treat around the other side of their nose and toss it out so they run forward to get it.

3. After they master the full turn and look forward to the game, add the word "spin."

4. Gradually ask for more turns and always toss a treat to keep the game exciting!

ROLL OVER

This involves two great tricks rolled into one.

1. **Start by teaching your dog to belly up.** Call your dog over to their bed and use a treat to lure them on their back for a belly scratch. If they're not in the mood, practice another time!

2. **Once they willingly roll over for a belly scratch, add the phrase "belly up!"** Many dogs do this naturally, so no treat is necessary. Once they learn this skill, you only have one more step.

3. **Once they're on their belly, take the treat and gradually guide it from their nose to the opposite floor.** It may take them a minute to nail the coordination, but praise them mightily once they put it together! It's a fun, celebratory move. Once they've got it down, add the cue "roll over!"

HIGH FIVE

If your dog is paw expressive, using their paws for everything from opening doors to getting attention, they're a shoo-in for this trick. If not, you can teach them this skill in three easy steps:

1. **Teach them to offer their paw.** Ask your dog to lie down, then hide a treat between two fingers and move it slowly between their two paws. When they bat it, open your fingers to reveal the treat. When they've got this move down, add the word "paw."

2. **Practice this from a sitting position, gradually prompting them with an open palm and rewarding them with the opposite hand.**

3. **Slowly rotate your palm as you continue to reward them for offering their paw.** Once your fingers are facing up, pair the words: "paw-high five," eventually dropping "paw" when they've nailed this step. See Figure 3-3.

Compassionate Eye Foundation/Jetta Productions/Getty Images

FIGURE 3-3: The high five is great for dogs that are is paw expressive.

PLAYING WITH HIGH-DRIVE DOGS

Intense, repetitive activities can cause an endless release of adrenaline (the energy hormone) and cortisol (the stress hormone), which linger in the bloodstream, making it hard for a high-drive dog to calm down. To that end, the following activities may be too stimulating, especially if your dog is over-anxious or aroused:

- **Unstructured tug-of-war:** While structured tug-of-war encourages impulse control and fair play, unstructured, body-swinging, prolonged tug-of-war can stoke a dog's predatory behavior, leaving them more revved up than relaxed.

- **Repetitive fetching:** Fetching can be an interactive game that teaches learned cues and retrieving exercises, but tossing a toy repeatedly can push an eager dog over the brink.

- **Rough wrestling:** People love wrestling and think their dogs do too. However, rough interactions can inspire fear and dysregulation. There are many other games to choose from; avoid games that pit you against your dog, even in play.

- **Chasing games that end in mouthing:** While having your dog chase you can inspire focus and impulse control, chasing your dog can often backfire, especially when you're trying to rescue a stolen object or call your dog from a distance.

- **Overstimulating predatory play:** Dogs love chasing moving objects, whether you're pulling a toy on a string or dragging a scented rag through long grass. Some dogs, not all, short into overdrive, frenetically chasing, grabbing, and mock killing the "prey" once it's caught.

- **Excessive play with unfamiliar dogs:** Another fallacy is that playing with other dogs is a good way to tire a dog out. Playing with familiar dogs can be a good way to let your dog engage in species-specific activities. But pairing your dog with unfamiliar dogs is stressful and can end in more stress and anxiety. Imagine you're going to dinner with a group of childhood friends versus a bunch of strangers.

FUN FACT

Dogs love mind-body activities that involve you. If you have the time and inclination, explore sporting events like agility, flyball, freestyle, and other breed-specific activities that channel your dog's instincts. There are many options, including herding and dock-diving trails to lure coursing and cart pulling. Explore your options. You'll also meet people who are just as excited as you are, and you can all enjoy spending time with your dog!

IN THIS CHAPTER

» Recognizing the role of genetics

» Exploring the impact of early
  socialization

» Managing illness and age-related
  anxieties

» Addressing lifestyle changes

Chapter **4**

Addressing the Many Causes of Anxiety

Dogs are born with various personality traits, from confident and comic to reserved and sensitive. Anxiety is shaped by many factors, including, but not limited to, genetic predisposition and early upbringing.

This chapter explores the factors that influence your dog's experience of anxiety. Whether your dog has struggled with anxiety from day one or has developed anxiety seemingly out of the blue, their behavior isn't random. You can best help your dog after determining why they act a certain way.

Considering Genetic Factors

It is easy to grasp genetics when you observe how your dog's parents contribute to their physical attributes, but what about beneath the surface? Genetics also plays a crucial role in shaping your dog's sensory skills and personality traits. While this might contradict the "no anxious dogs" statement, consider this situation: If two highly noise-sensitive dogs were bred, their offspring would likely be similarly aware. If one went to live in the country and the other in the city, which pup do you think would be more prone to develop sensory anxiety?

The answer could go both ways, as your dog's personality comprises their genetics and puppyhood experiences. Though the city dog might seem the obvious answer, a dog's life is influenced by more than just their parent's life experience; nurture also plays a role. The next section explains the timing and influences of early socialization. If the city pup was heavily socialized to various sounds and the country pup was less socialized, the country pup might suffer sound reactivity — a topic I dive into in Part 5.

FUN FACT

A recent study showed that, while breeds can provide some indication of a puppy's inclinations, parental genetics have more influence on temperament than individual breeds.

Mother's disposition

Dogs are significantly influenced by their mother's disposition. Ideally, they should remain with their mother and littermates for their first eight weeks, which provides a foundation for their worldview. While human influence and nurturing continue to shape this initial foundation, their early guidance profoundly molds their worldview. When a puppy's mother is securely attached and lovingly interacts with humans, the puppy develops a sense of safety around human caregivers. Conversely, if the mother is free-ranging, neglected, secluded from human interaction, or even fearful of humans, she will serve as the puppy's role model.

Mother's health

When a mother's health is compromised due to lack of nutrition, injury, or congenital defects, her anxiety level will spike and her ability to focus on her puppies will be jeopardized. The puppies will suffer alongside her. For mindful breeders and those who care for abandoned dogs, it becomes apparent that there's much more involved in ensuring the early survival of a young puppy than meets the eye. When a mother's health is nurtured, and her sole focus is her puppies' well-being, it gives them an ideal environment to flourish.

Recognizing the Role of Socialization

Early life experiences play a significant role in shaping a well-adjusted and socially adept dog. Socialization refers to experiences in their early puppyhood — between 3 and 14 weeks — imprinting on their brain and cataloging them as familiar. I like to think of early puppyhood as an open funnel — sounds and other stimulations float in, are permanently categorized, and are recognized as normal. For an under-socialized dog, however, anything unfamiliar is suspect. Whether your dog's anxiety is generalized or pronounced, consider a lack of early life experience as a possible culprit.

Although socializing an older dog is more challenging, it's not impossible. Reconsider my funnel metaphor — instead of a wide-open funnel, the funnel inverts once a dog ages six months. However, the ability to encode new experiences is still possible, with patience and persistence (see Figure 4-1).

FIGURE 4-1: Taking your dog out into the world helps them become well-adjusted and socially adept.

Lifelong adventures

Don't despair or feel guilty if your dog is past this critical social stage and often stresses in social situations or around unrecognizable sensory stimuli. Even well-socialized dogs can experience something new and startle unexpectedly.

Of course, you can't change your dog's past, but you can improve their future. As you'll learn throughout the book, the way to calm your dog is first to distance them from whatever is causing them distress. For example, if your dog is afraid of a grate in the street, instead of dragging them over it, retreat with them and show by example that there is nothing to fear.

FUN FACT

Even if you've missed the ideal socialization window, there's still hope. Dogs' brains are in a constant state of growth and renewal. Use treats, toys, praise, and patience as you expose your dog to the nuances of your world and help them create more positive associations.

Trauma

When a once social, happy, and friendly dog has been traumatized by an unpredicted experience, their mood in similar social situations can shift from openness to guarded. Consider the once-friendly dog, Lucy, who was attacked by another dog while on a leash. Suddenly, leash walks create anxiety. Lucy becomes reluctant to leave the house and shows signs of stress (lip-licking, tail tucked, belly exposed) whenever the leash goes on. Although it might seem tempting to coddle, soothe, or force a dog like Lucy out, don't do that. When dogs are forced, their fear can grow exponentially and becomes panic. Instead, Chapter 10 about leash reactivity explains how to go at your dog's speed and embrace small victories.

Handling Medical Issues

Pain affects us all, regardless of species. It leaves us feeling vulnerable and lousy, overshadowing joy and paving the way for anxiety to take hold. Before you assume that your dog's anxiety is psychological, it's imperative to rule out medical causes. Consider the following medical issues that may influence your dog's mood and well-being, now and in the future.

Injury and pain

Even simple actions like wagging their tail can be agonizing if your dog has muscle, joint, or bone pain. If your dog is already prone to mild anxiety, this discomfort is likely to intensify it. Pain or injury can also make your normally cheerful dog anxious; they may develop social anxiety around other dogs, children, and people as their movements are compromised. If you have other pets, you may encounter confrontations due to your dog's localized pain.

Cardiac/respiratory issues

Respiratory and cardiac conditions can exacerbate your dog's metabolic functions and directly influence their anxiety levels. Among the diseases contributing to these issues in dogs are heart congestion, obesity-related breathing difficulties, dyspnea (shortness of breath), viral infections, and various respiratory illnesses like pneumonia and bronchitis.

Cushing's disease

Anxiety triggers the production of cortisol, a stress hormone released by the adrenal glands. When the adrenal gland malfunctions, it can lead to the overproduction of cortisol, causing a disorder known as Cushing's disease. The question arises: Does stress cause Cushing's disease, or does Cushing's disease exacerbate your dog's stress? Either way, the treatment of Cushing's disease directly affects anxiety, and the goal is to reduce cortisol.

Thyroid issues

Both hypothyroidism (underactive thyroid) and hyperthyroidism (overactive thyroid) can contribute to behavioral changes and increased anxiety levels in dogs. Symptoms of thyroid conditions may include lethargy, weight changes, hair loss, skin problems, and changes in mood or behavior.

WARNING

If you suspect your dog's anxiety is clouded with other symptoms like excessive panting, restlessness, increased heart rate, excessive thirst, or hunger, consult with your veterinarian, as proper diagnosis and treatment can help alleviate their anxiety and improve their overall quality of life.

Digestion problems

Digestive issues can also influence your dog's anxiety levels. Discomfort from digestive problems such as gastritis, gastrointestinal infections, or food sensitivities can lead to heightened stress and agitation. Symptoms may include vomiting, diarrhea, abdominal discomfort, or a loss of appetite. It's essential to address any digestive issues promptly to alleviate your dog's discomfort and reduce their overall stress.

Parasites

Internal and external parasites thrive on draining the life out of your dog. An excessive infestation can prove fatal, and even a few parasites can make your dog feel unwell. Symptoms include fatigue, vulnerability, itchiness, or persistent abdominal pain. It's crucial to ensure your dog is healthy and parasite-free before attempting to address any underlying anxiety issues.

Grooming/skin irritations

Pain or discomfort from skin irritations, ear infections, or injuries sustained during grooming sessions can cause your dog distress and anxiety. The fear or discomfort associated with grooming procedures, such as nail trimming or ear cleaning, can also lead to heightened stress levels. Paying attention to your dog's behavior before, during, and after grooming and promptly addressing any injuries or irritations can help alleviate their discomfort and reduce anxiety-related behaviors. Appendix C has much more about normalizing visits to the groomer.

TIP

Helping your dog develop positive associations with grooming tasks through rewards, games, and attention can reduce their anxiety about these activities. The Operation Cooperation game explained in Chapter 3 is an great way to achieve this.

Adapting to Aging Woes

Aging is tough no matter what your species. We sag, we ache, we droop, we dribble. Whether or not your dog has suffered anxiety throughout their life or is developing symptoms in their twilight years, there are many things you can do to make them feel safe and comforted. Aging is inevitable, but your relationship with your dog is everlasting; happy times may need to adapt to their limitations. Being together will always get their tail wagging.

Sensory decline

As dogs age, the senses that they've relied on to define their days and color their world decline. It's part of life's natural cycle, but you can't explain it to your dog. Suddenly, the sound of the doorbell or car fades to the point of startling your dog. Even the unpredictable appearance of faces becomes a cause for concern. When their sight fades, you may notice your dog stumble and tip, or they might lose their balance when they suddenly bump into a new armchair or antique. Daily adventures filled their nostrils with excitement and drive now are diluted to match the decline in their athletic prowess. Their interest in treats and food may also decline.

WARNING

Of course, age is not the only cause of secondary decline. Illness, ailments, and disease can also arrest your dog's awareness, including, but not limited to, cancer, diabetes, inner ear and eye diseases, and more. If you think aging is causing your dog's anxious state, start by bringing them to your veterinarian to diagnose any treatable condition that could be causing their mood shifts. It's important to eliminate any medical conditions first, especially with older dogs.

The most important attribute to your dog's graceful aging isn't how they decline but how you ease their transition and highlight the time you have together. Calming sprays can be used to guide visually impaired dogs and scent games — many of which can be found on my Instagram (@SarahSaysPets) and on blogs from the AKC or ASPCA — can enrich their days. Hearing-impaired dogs can also learn new tricks and enjoy hand-signal lessons that replace spoken language.

Cognitive Dysfunction Syndrome (CDS)

As dogs age, they can experience Cognitive Dysfunction Syndrome (CDS), a condition similar to Alzheimer's. You may notice symptoms such as disorientation, irregular sleep patterns, accidents, and inconsistent interactions with you and their other familiar pets and people. A diagnosis of CDS can occur as early as nine years of age.

Dogs with CDS require patience and grace. Try to avoid expressing your frustration. Studies show that dogs recognize changes in our chemistry and respiratory and cardiac patterns — in other words, they can sense when we're upset. The goal is to reinforce your bond and enrich their lives with safe places and experiences, elevating your and their oxytocin levels.

TIP

Early intervention through stimulating enrichment, dietary adjustments, and medical management can significantly improve the quality of life for dogs affected by CDS. For lots more about CDS and other issues affecting elderly dogs, check out Appendix B.

Arthritis

Aging dogs often experience arthritis, especially in overworked joints. This gradually leads to reduced mobility and the loss of the joy from long adventures. Pain becomes a constant, and the very dogs who felt confident and in control of their world may now be dependent on others due to their limited mobility and discomfort.

To help alleviate their discomfort, consult your vet about medication and continue their routines while simplifying adventures. For example, instead of high-impact activities like hiking or agility, focus on simple sniff-and-strolls on easy terrain.

Focusing on Human Reinforcement

Recent studies have shown that dogs can smell our moods and judge our emotions by the subtle changes in our heart rate and breathing patterns. Even when you try to mask an emotion (like fear or frustration), you can't fool your dog for a second.

Here is where it gets tricky, however. While your dog can identify what you feel, they can't identify *why* you're feeling it. If you get frustrated when they bark at the mailman, they sense your frustration but will associate it with the mailman, not their behavior. If you worry when you leave for work, your dog will associate worry with your separation, not their behavior. Your dog's anxiety, which motivates their reactions, will worsen instead of improving. This section discusses how to use your emotions to help your dog instead.

Mirroring instead of modeling

Do you mirror your dog's reactions throughout the day or model how best to act in certain situations? While it's critical not to mirror your dog's anxiety by becoming anxious, be mindful not to mirror other moods, too. Do you get excited with your dog when you come home or get frustrated when your dog barks at another dog? Do you feel guilty when you leave or your dog jumps on visitors? In these situations, your stress level mirrors your dog's anxiety.

Instead, be the confidence model for your dog, providing self-soothing toys or chews when they are nervous or removing them from overwhelming situations. The most important element in dog training and rehabilitation is a steady mood — nothing over-excited or worrisome. To a dog, emotions are contagious!

Targeting the wrong emotion

Sometimes, we reinforce our dog's anxiety instead of encouraging their confidence. When a dog is avoidant or fearful, your impulse might be to force them, repeat directions, or try to snap them out of it by offering them a treat. While a lack of interest in treats can sometimes indicate digestive upset, often it's because the dog is stressed or anxious. When training, treats should only be given as or immediately after your dog behaves the way you want them to. Otherwise, you might inadvertently reward the very behavior you are trying to extinguish.

REMEMBER

Anxiety can affect your dog's thought process and natural instincts, including their appetite. If your dog's eating habits suddenly decline, seek veterinary attention immediately. Without addressing underlying physical health issues, alternative strategies may not yield results. Additionally, consider varying the treats you offer to gauge your dog's preferences.

Changing Lifestyle Habits

Most dogs are very habitual and dependent on their daily routines. Changes don't go unnoticed, and while some dogs adapt without missing a beat, most take notice. If your dog already experiences anxiety, it may worsen or expand to new situations. Even a once secure dog can develop nervous tendencies when they experience unwanted change, such as pacing, lick-lipping, inability to settle down, defensive reactions, or hyperarousal.

Consider these new situations from your dog's perspective, remembering that dogs recognize environments, objects, and other beings through their sense of smell.

New baby, new pup, new pet

Dogs are highly attuned to changes in their environment, particularly when a new baby — of any species — enters the picture. Your dog may pick up on shifts in your mood, the schedule, or new daily habits caused by the new addition. Here are some tips to help ease these transitions:

>> Play the I Spy game, explained in Chapter 3.

>> Introduce your dog to the smells of the new addition before bringing them home to familiarize them with the scent (using something that has the scent of the new addition on it, like a blanket).

>> Initially, introduce your dog to the new addition in a neutral location to reduce territorial or anxious behavior. See Figure 4-2.

>> Structure your schedule to ensure your dog's pathways, playtime, and routines remain consistent.

>> Consider asking for or hiring help to maintain your dog's routine until they fully accept the new addition as part of the family.

New pet parents often underestimate the importance of keeping their new addition on a structured schedule, leading to a riff and increased anxiety levels for the resident pets and the family.

Changes in work and school schedules

Prepare your dog for changes in your schedule, such as returning to school or work, by gradually acclimating them to longer periods alone and mirroring the new schedule gradually over a couple of weeks. Sudden, unpredicted changes can cause tremendous anxiety for even the most stable dog, leading to issues like containment anxiety and separation stress. Implement a feeding schedule using an automatic feeder to maintain consistency. Consider hiring help to assist with your dog's care.

FIGURE 4-2: Introduce your dog to a new family member gradually.

Moving

Before moving, consider how the change will affect your dog's lifestyle. This includes factors such as transitioning from the countryside to the city or vice versa, which can drastically alter your dog's daily routine and surroundings. Will your daily outings suddenly involve leashed walks? What about pottying surfaces? Consider whether your dog will have more or fewer socialization opportunities with other dogs after the move. The moving process can be disruptive for dogs, so preparation is crucial. Conditioning your dog to the various factors they may encounter in their new environment can help ease the transition and ensure their well-being during the move.

Changes in relationships and roommates

As you have hopefully learned by now, anxiety in dogs is soothed by a consistent routine and familiar faces, including family, friends, and helpers. If you anticipate a change, such as someone moving in or out of your home, it's beneficial to make new introductions outside your home well in advance.

Encourage new roommates to interact with your dog positively by rewarding the dog whenever they respond to cues like "sit" or "paw." Consider your new roommates your dog's animated Pez dispenser for treats and ask them to reward your dog the instant they approach or look at them.

When people prepare to move out, gradually reduce their daily interactions with the dog. This can help minimize the void left when they depart. This gradual transition can help ease any potential anxiety your dog may experience due to the change.

Understanding and addressing the factors influencing your dog's anxiety is crucial for their rehabilitation. Now that you have a broader perspective on your dog's experience, the next chapter explores ways to help your dog with their anxiety.

Chapter **5**

Finding Help When You Need It

A saying in couples therapy rings true in dog training, too: It only takes one to change the relationship! As you'll soon discover, the key to rehabilitating a dog with anxiety lies more in your willingness to modify *your* behavior than in altering your dog's.

Sometimes it takes a whole village. This chapter offers guidance on finding qualified professionals to support your dog's rehabilitation. Additionally, you'll find a comprehensive guide to prescription medications, holistic supplements, and useful products.

Finding People Who Can Help

If you feel overwhelmed at any point, talking with a trained professional can help. Many individuals, like me, dedicate their whole lives to studying behavior and coaching people while staying current with the most effective training techniques. The following list explains many of the credentials, associations, and professionals who can help.

- » **Veterinarian (DVM or VMD):** A licensed medical professional specializing in animal health, including diagnosis, treatment, and prevention of diseases and injuries in animals.

- » **Veterinary Behaviorist (DACVB):** A veterinarian with specialized training and board certification in animal behavior, focusing on diagnosing and treating animal behavior problems.

- » **Associate or Applied Behaviorist:** A professional who has studied animal behavior and may specialize in applying behavior modification techniques to address pet behavior issues.

- » **Certified Dog Behavior Consultant (CDBC):** An individual who completed comprehensive training and certification to provide behavior consulting services to dogs, addressing various behavior problems.

- » **Certified Professional Dog Trainer (CPDT):** A trainer who meets specific standards for knowledge, skills, and ethical conduct in dog training.

- » **Certified Behavior Consultant Canine (CBCC-KA):** A professionals who has demonstrated expertise in canine behavior modification and training through rigorous examinations and evaluations.

- » **Certified Dog Trainer (CDT):** A trainers who completed training and testing to demonstrate proficiency in dog training techniques and principles.

- » **Certified Applied Animal Behaviorist (CAAB):** An expert in animal behavior with advanced degrees and experience in diagnosing and treating behavior problems in various species, including dogs.

- » **American Veterinary Medical Association (AVMA):** The largest professional association representing veterinarians in the United States, providing resources and support to veterinary professionals.

>> **American College of Veterinary Behaviorists (ACVB):** A specialty organization that promotes excellence in the practice of veterinary behavior medicine through education, research, and certification.

>> **International Association of Animal Behavior Consultants (IAABC):** An organization dedicated to promoting the field of animal behavior consulting through education, certification, and professional development opportunities.

>> **Association of Professional Dog Trainers (APDT):** An organization committed to promoting positive dog training methods and providing education and resources for professional dog trainers.

>> **Certification Council for Professional Dog Trainers (CCPDT):** An independent certifying organization for professional dog trainers, offering certification programs and continuing education opportunities.

>> **International Association of Canine Professionals (IACP):** A membership organization for professional dog trainers, behavior consultants, and other canine professionals, promoting ethical and effective training methods.

Many professionals, including myself, offer virtual counseling on anxiety and other behavioral difficulties. While virtual help might seem less effective, it fosters your relationship with your dog rather than your dog's connection with their trainer (see Figure 5-1).

WARNING

Sending a dog with anxiety away for training, often called *board and train,* is not ideal. Your home is their safe place, and their anxiety may worsen without you.

FIGURE 5-1: A virtual or in-person trainer can provide lots of guidance.

PROFESSIONAL JARGON

You may hear terms you don't recognize when talking to dog professionals, leaving you lost in conversations. I've listed the important ones in the online glossary, and here are a few here you should be aware of:

- **Positive reinforcement** involves adding or giving something to your dog that strengthens or maintains their behavior, such as rewarding them with a treat or toy when they sit calmly. However, it becomes complicated when you inadvertently reinforce less desirable behaviors, such as giving them attention when they bark or paw at you.

- **Negative reinforcement** involves removing something to strengthen or maintain a behavior. For example, if you're petting your dog and they jump, taking away your attention will discourage the jumping. Likewise, if they bark at a delivery person, resulting in their departure, the person's absence reinforces the likelihood of the dog barking again in similar situations.

- **Counterconditioning** is the process of redirecting your dog's emotional response from fear or frustration toward playfulness or seeking behavior. Emphasizing distance and time, this technique uses food, fun, freedom, and attention to create positive associations between your dog and the triggering events or sensory stimuli.

- **Desensitization** can occur when you slowly expose your dog to distressing stimulations or events in a way that is less triggering for your dog over time. For example, if your dog fears children, you might take them to the far edge of a playground rather than standing in the middle of the action.

- **Redirection** is the process of using words, games, and activities to focus your dog on a more positive coping skill when a triggering event occurs. For example, if a dog barks when someone walks by your home, you might redirect it to a chew toy.

Turning to Prescription Medications and Over-the-Counter Supplements

The medications, supplements, and products discussed in this chapter are referenced throughout the book.

BOOKMARK There is a ton of skepticism surrounding the use of prescription medication in cases of dog anxiety. However, relying on medication to address mental health concerns is quite common.

In addition to your training efforts, long-acting prescription medication (when properly prescribed and used, of course) can effectively stabilize generalized anxiety in dogs. Short-term medications can also offer stability to dogs experiencing periodic anxiety, such as fear of vet visits or storms. Natural supplements and calming products also benefit many dogs.

It's crucial to consult a veterinarian behaviorist before using prescription medication. Do not self-dose your dog based on information you get from friends, ads, or the Internet.

Prescription medications

In 1976, the American Veterinary Society of Animal Behavior (AVSAB) was founded, bringing together veterinary professionals and researchers to delve deeper into animal behavior and various behavioral challenges.

As discussions on human mental health and prescription medications gained momentum in the late 20th century, there was also a growing appreciation for dogs' emotional complexity. This shift in perception toward dogs and our own mental health, alongside veterinary advancements, brought the emotional needs of animals to the forefront and contributed to the development and adoption of prescription medications for managing behavioral issues in dogs.

Whether your dog is showing generalized or episodic anxiety, medication may be considered to soothe and support efforts to rehabilitate them. Anti-anxiety medications are available in two categories:

» **Long-acting medications** are administered daily to address generalized anxiety and they target issues such as separation, social, and containment anxiety. Examples include Fluoxetine (Reconcile or Prozac), Paroxetine (Paxil), and Sertraline (Zoloft).

» **Short-acting medications** can be used for event-specific triggers like thunderstorms, travel, and veterinary visits. In some cases, dogs may be prescribed both long-term and short-term medications. Examples of short-acting meds include Alprazolam (Xanax), Diazepam (Valium), and Lorazepam (Ativan).

If you are considering medication for your dog's anxiety, follow these preliminary steps and share your experiences should you decide to pursue pharmaceutical support with a veterinary behaviorist:

1. **Keep track of your dog's behavioral and health symptoms.** Share these symptoms with your veterinarian to explore if a physical illness might be contributing to your dog's anxiety. If your vet identifies a correlation between your dog's reactivity and a health condition, follow a treatment plan to address your dog's physical health to determine if helping your dog feel better solves their mental anguish.

2. **Once you've received a clean bill of health, educate yourself on the causes and manifestations of dog anxiety.** Reading this book is a great start!

3. **Consult a trainer or behaviorist for guidance.** Your vet can recommend someone, or you can check the IAABC or the other associations listed earlier in this chapter. Many trainers provide virtual guidance, which can be very helpful and less disruptive to your dog.

4. **Once you've made the decision to explore medication for your dog's anxiety, consult a veterinary behaviorist.** While your regular veterinarian may be able to prescribe psychotropic medication, it is wise to see a specialist. Certified veterinary behaviorists have extensive training and experience determining the most effective medication for each case. They can provide further insight into strategies to support your dog's rehabilitation.

5. **Introduce everyone on your dog's health and mental care team.** Get everyone involved and swap notes. Sometimes, anxiety gets better, and other times, you'll need lifelong support.

TIP

Don't underestimate the use of pharmaceutical support for dogs suffering from anxiety. In some cases, curing persistent anxiety without supportive pharmaceutics can be like trying to fix heart conditions with exercise alone.

Supplements

Many people rely on holistic supplements to help their dogs recover from anxiety. They can be very effective or at least have a placebo effect on you to lessen your concern, which alone will lighten your dog's mental load!

Be sure to consult your veterinarian before changing your dog's diet or using any of these supplements. Your veterinarian can help you determine the appropriate dosage, assess interactions with other medications, and ensure the safety and effectiveness of the treatment. Results may vary, and individual responses should be monitored closely.

CBD

CBD, short for cannabidiol, has gained popularity for its potential calming effects on dogs. Many pet parents turn to CBD as a natural alternative to traditional medications. While research on CBD for dogs is still evolving, anecdotal evidence suggests it can help. However, the purity of the oil or treats is critical, as the psychotropic element, THC, can be very toxic! Consult with your veterinarian for approved products.

Melatonin

Melatonin is a hormone naturally produced by the body that supports sleep patterns. It is sometimes supplemented to alleviate anxiety in dogs, promoting restfulness and calmness.

Probiotics and prebiotics

Boosting your dog's digestive health can also positively affect their mood and potentially reduce anxiety. Probiotics, prebiotics, digestive enzymes, and fiber supplements are readily available in stores. The same benefits can be gained by incorporating whole foods into their diet for natural probiotics, prebiotics, digestive enzymes, and fiber.

Bach flower

Bach flower remedies have been used to calm anxiety in dogs for decades. These remedies are made from dilutions of flower essences and are believed to restore emotional balance and alleviate stress. While research on Bach flower remedies is limited, some pet parents report positive effects on their anxious pets.

L-theanine

L-theanine is an amino acid found in green tea. It's believed to promote relaxation without causing drowsiness. Many pet parents find L-theanine supplements beneficial for calming their dogs during stressful situations, such as thunderstorms or vet visits.

Tea or tea leaves should not be given to dogs. In addition, acet-aminophen, ibuprofen, NSAIDs, antidepressants, oral contraceptives, and ACE inhibitors are all toxic to dogs. Don't diagnose and treat your dog with home remedies. Consult with your vet before you give your dog any medication.

L-tryptophan

L-tryptophan, another amino acid, is commonly associated with promoting relaxation and sleep. It's a precursor to serotonin, the happy hormone. Many people have used L-tryptophan supplements to help alleviate anxiety in their dogs, particularly in situations like separation anxiety or travel-related stress.

Supporting Your Journey with Helpful Products

Plenty of products are available that can help alleviate your dog's anxiety and come in handy during the rehabilitation process. This section covers just a few.

The ThunderShirt

The ThunderShirt applies gentle, constant pressure to your dog's torso, creating a calming effect like swaddling an infant. Many dogs find comfort and reassurance when wearing the ThunderShirt during stressful situations like thunderstorms or fireworks.

Calming caps

Calming caps are specially designed to limit your dog's field of vision, reducing visual stimuli that may trigger anxiety. By blocking out excessive light and movement, calming caps help dogs feel more secure and relaxed in stressful environments or during activities such as car rides.

Indoor pet cameras

You'll soon discover that staging departures is key to rehabilitating separation anxiety and monitoring your dog's behavior while you're away. It's easy with indoor pet cameras. You can also use these devices to evaluate your dog's stress when dealing with confinement anxiety. Just avoid using devices with treat-dispensing, voice conferencing, or remote training features, as they often further confuse and stress dogs. Alternatively, you can use services like Zoom or Skype to evaluate their behavior when they're left alone.

Music

Studies show that certain types of music, such as classical piano, reggae, or soft rock (my dogs like Bob Marley and James Taylor) have a calming effect on dogs. Calm music can help lower your dog's heart rate, reduce stress hormones, and promote relaxation. Playing music, especially during episodes of anxiety or stress, can create a peaceful environment for your dog and contribute to their overall well-being.

Snuggle Puppy

The Snuggle Puppy is a plush toy designed to simulate the presence of a littermate. It features a heartbeat simulator and heat pack, mimicking a mother dog's warmth and rhythmic heartbeat. This comforting toy can provide a sense of security, claiming to reduce separation anxiety in puppies or adult dogs.

Dog-Appeasing Pheromone (DAP)

DAP is a synthetic pheromone designed to mimic the natural calming scent emitted by mother dogs to comfort their puppies. Available in various forms, including sprays, diffusers, and collars, DAP can help reduce stress and anxiety.

Muzzles

Many people are convinced that muzzles are cruel and punishing. They're not; they can be necessary and even lifesaving in situations of leash reactivity, social anxiety, and vet visits. To help your dog fall in love with their muzzle, take it slow and follow these steps:

1. **Introduce your dog to the muzzle with treats.** Reward them the instant they look at the muzzle — all they have to do is glance at it!

2. **Next, encourage your dog to approach and touch the muzzle before giving a reward.**

3. **Wait for your dog to put their nose into the muzzle before rewarding them.** Lure them in by sliding a treat between the front opening, gradually increasing the duration they hold their nose steady in the muzzle.

4. **Practice pretending to put the muzzle on by briefly holding the straps behind the dog's head.** Reward your dog inside the muzzle. Gradually extend the duration of holding the strap until your dog is completely comfortable.

5. **Attach the straps for short periods; during these times, do engaging things like massage or favorite tricks and games that don't involve their mouth.** Reward them as you've practiced and slowly increase wearing time.

6. **If your dog paws at the muzzle or fusses, redirect them with a frozen treat or games like Find It.** Have them wear the muzzle in different locations and around distractions. Once your dog is ready, attach the muzzle to the collar and engage in regular activities.

REMEMBER

Dogs are smart, so avoid doing unpleasant things after engaging with the muzzle. If every time you muzzle up, you drive to the groomer and you drop them off, they will quickly associate the muzzle with being abandoned, even if you come back in a few hours. Eventually, you'll be able to use the muzzle in necessary situations (see Figure 5-2).

FIGURE 5-2: Muzzle training should be a slow and steady process.

DO PRONG, CITRONELLA, AND E-COLLARS WORK?

The short answer — do not use any of these devices on a dog with anxiety. They usually react negatively to anything that causes them additional pain or confusion. I feel these devices represent a shortcut for trainers to get quick results and impress their clients rather than providing genuine solutions. Ten countries, including the UK, have banned the use of e-collars. Studies show that e-collars risk animal welfare and are less effective than positive reinforcement training methods. It doesn't take a genius to understand that for a dog with anxiety, experiencing pain, fear, and intimidation will only heighten their sense of threat rather than fostering a sense of safety.

Do not be fooled by other e-collar names, including remote training, stim, static correction, impulse control, vibration, tens, and citronella collars. Celebrity trainers may endorse indoor and outdoor usage solely for their financial interests, touting that shocking your dog is a valid way to gain cooperation. The first goal of training is to prioritize your dog's emotional well-being and to motivate learning with joy, not fear.

Finding the Right Approach

There isn't a one-size-fits-all approach to soothing or even curing your dog's anxiety. Fear has its place in preserving life, but it can become overwhelming and difficult for some dogs. While it may be challenging to empathize with your dog's intrusive worries, it's essential to acknowledge that these feelings are real.

TIP

Keep a behavior diary to track the methods you choose and the duration you've stayed the course. Medicines and many supplements have an internal threshold to meet before they become effective. Trainers and behaviorists may need to try multiple approaches to find what's most helpful to you and your dog. Be patient with your dog and the people helping you. Time spent loving, showing compassion, and concern for your dog's well-being is never wasted.

2

Soothing a Dog's Separation Anxiety

IN THIS CHAPTER

» Recognizing separation anxiety

» Debunking common separation
anxiety myths

» Understanding the symptoms of
separation anxiety

Chapter **6**

Understanding Separation Anxiety

Coming home to a happy, carefree dog might seem improbable at this point in your dog's journey. You might be dealing with chaos, noise complaints from neighbors, or a frantic, dysregulated companion greeting you as if you'd been gone for ages. Or perhaps your beloved dog seems scared and sad, and you're unsure how to help. Fortunately, separation anxiety is a problem you can fix.

This chapter examines a host of behaviors dogs exhibit when they're left alone. Surprisingly, there are many misconceptions about separation anxiety. Behaviors symptomatic of this disorder, such as barking or chewing, may be present for other reasons. This chapter looks at the root causes of separation anxiety and explains how unrelated triggers can provoke anxiety, too.

Recognizing What Separation Anxiety Is and Isn't

Many dogs dread separation from their loved ones, much like young children. They're team players, prioritizing their family's well-being over individuality or independence. Being apart would never be a choice in a group of free-range dogs — they opt to eat, sleep, play, and hunt together. Being alone would pose a danger. However, the reality for people is that we must go out sometimes, which inevitably means leaving our dogs behind.

Until recently, the term "separation anxiety" was typically applied to dogs exhibiting an extreme attachment to one family member. Other terms like "isolation distress" or "separation-related stress" were supposed to be used by everyone other than behaviorists to identify every other category of this anxiety. After a while, the world began confusing all the terms, and separation anxiety became the catchphrase for every sad-faced dog who misbehaved when their people went missing.

The overarching term, and the one I use in this book, is *separation anxiety*, which applies to all dogs who exhibit extreme panic and who are physically distraught when left alone.

FUN FACT

Ever wonder what other dogs, without separation anxiety, do when left home alone? Most sleep. When given access, they might spend most of their day staring out the window, lapping up some water, or busying themselves with a toy, but most rest.

Pain-related distress

Dogs who are unwell or in pain may show sudden signs of separation anxiety. It's natural for a person to stress if left alone or feeling unwell, but since our dogs can't share their discomfort with words, we sometimes overlook that they're just as susceptible to disease and discomfort. If you observe a sudden change in your dog's behavior or the emergence of separation anxiety, first schedule an appointment with your veterinarian to rule out any underlying medical issues. Once you know it's not a physical issue, you can find and address the behavioral root.

Common misconceptions

There is a lot of bad advice and many misconceptions surrounding separation anxiety. This section addresses a baker's dozen. Have you found yourself thinking or believing any one of them? It's time to put these ideas to rest.

"Dogs behave out of spite."

Dogs do not possess the cognitive ability to behave out of spite. Their actions are driven by instinct, and their behavior during separation is never a deliberate attempt to punish the people they love (and miss).

"Adopting another dog will cure the problem!"

Having an extra dog won't resolve your separation anxiety problems, and studies show it may exacerbate the situation instead of improving it. Separation anxiety primarily involves the bond between you and your dog. Introducing another dog into the household adds stress by dividing attention and space, especially if the new addition is a puppy.

"Dogs get used to departures after a while."

Dogs suffering from separation anxiety do not suddenly get used to being left alone. Without proper intervention, their anxiety can persist and even worsen over time. As you learn in the chapter, there is a direct mind-body connection, and a constant state of arousal causes health problems. It's critical to address the root causes of separation anxiety through targeted interventions and training.

"Reassociating triggers like keys and purses throughout the day will reduce your dog's stress when you leave."

Manipulating things throughout the day, like keys and other associated activities, is ineffective in treating separation anxiety. Dogs are association masters and can quickly connect our actions with our departure. While making different associations to these departure cues isn't harmful, it won't directly address separation anxiety. Our activities are often time-sensitive, so if playing with keys throughout the day desensitizes your dog to the sound, don't be surprised if they associate all the morning events with your eventual departure.

While manipulating these environments can be part of a broader strategy, it alone does not cure separation anxiety. Dogs can quickly associate the time of day, our heartbeat, and our respiration with actions that lead to departure.

"Certain breeds are prone to separation anxiety."

Although certain breeds — such as shepherds, labs, border collies, and cavaliers — have been indicated as being more prone to separation anxiety, no studies have demonstrated that these specific breeds are *inherently* more susceptible to separation anxiety. One potential explanation for this observation could be that these breeds are among the most popular, resulting in more people having them.

"You need to be more of an authority figure for your dog."

If you're not already, transitioning to being an authority figure for your dog can be an odd and stressful process for you and poorly received by your dog. Studies have shown that adopting a domineering rule over your dog can induce more stress, not less. Recommendations to establish dominance by removing your dog from furniture and beds and restructuring feeding schedules to assert your "boss" status have long been debunked. The best approach? Be consistent — consistently loving, comforting, and confident in a way that feels most natural to you. Dogs feel safest and least stressed when they sense consistency and compassion.

"Crates are helpful tools to deal with separation anxiety."

Crates have often been found to exacerbate separation anxiety and can cause their own anxiety, and being confined in a small enclosure can compound the issue. Crates can make separation anxiety worse, not better. If your dog shows resistance and becomes frantic when placed in a small space or enclosure, refer to Part 3 on containment anxiety.

"More exercise and exhaustive play are the best cures."

The adage "a tired dog is a happy family" is always not true; a tired dog may be exhausted, but too much exercise can have unforeseen consequences, namely that you will create an athlete who needs a high level of stimulation daily to satisfy a routine you created. Being tired does not affect how they feel when you leave, and what about the days you're blindsided by commitments or are sick? Dogs are a restful species; limiting their physical stimulation to a level you can maintain is best.

"You can't fix their separation anxiety."

Contrary to popular belief, separation anxiety is not a hopeless condition. With patience, consistency, and the right interventions, many dogs can learn to cope with being left alone and experience significant improvement in their symptoms.

"'Spoiling a dog causes separation anxiety."

Spoiling a dog with love and attention does not directly cause separation anxiety. While inconsistent discipline or excessive attention may contribute to persistent attention-seeking and other behavioral issues, separation anxiety is a complex condition with many causes — including genetics, early experiences, and environmental factors — that extend beyond loving interactions.

"Leaving a dog with a chew, busy toy, or treats will help them link departure to good things."

While providing distractions such as toys or treats may temporarily alleviate a dog's anxiety when left alone, it does not address the underlying emotional distress. Once a distraction wears off, your dog's anxiety may resurface.

"Medicine or supplements should only be considered as a last resort."

Medication and certain supplements should not be viewed as a last resort, but as legitimate treatment options! Used with behavioral coaching, they can be invaluable tools to settle your dog's emotions, especially in severe cases. A veterinarian or veterinary behaviorist should oversee both. Don't self-dose your dog with information you read on the Internet or from ads.

"TV and specific animal channels will keep them company."

Watching TV is not a legitimate distraction that can replace being with your dog, and it does not address the underlying anxiety that dogs experience when left alone. Dogs rely on social interaction and companionship, which electronic devices cannot replace.

TVs can be alarming to dogs who find the sight or noise of other animals in their home distressing.

Common Reactions to Being Left Alone

Separation anxiety is a puzzling condition, as every dog has unique symptoms and varying thresholds of distress. Some dogs may get anxious when you shut the bathroom door or walk a few feet away, while others might only start to worry if you're ten minutes late. Most dogs can relax if someone's home, but a few become obsessively attached to one person and stress when they're missing. Certain dogs are fine tagging along to pick up the kids or run errands, but others get equally distressed when you step out of the car. Then, there are those with nighttime separation anxiety, stressing out as soon as their people head off to bed.

The various behaviors described in this section can all indicate whether a dog has separation anxiety. Bear in mind that all symptoms are considered equal. My colleague and expert in the field, Marlena DeMartini, emphasizes that separation anxiety cannot be neatly categorized regardless of your dog's symptoms. She likens it to people who fear spiders, noting that they may exhibit various reactions: One might cry, another might run away, and another might resort to killing the spider. Despite these varied responses, they all share the same underlying fear. The treatment, however, is similar regardless of the array of symptoms.

WARNING

Sometimes, as you'll learn in the pages ahead, a symptom of separation anxiety, such as destruction or house soiling, is indicative of something else, such as boredom or illness.

Potty accidents

Dogs experiencing anxiety may urinate or defecate indoors, even if they are typically house-trained. This behavior is often a result of stress and discomfort associated with being left alone.

Transition excitement

Transition excitement (see Figure 6-1) refers to excessive excitement or agitation displayed by dogs during departures and arrivals. Dogs may become overly excited when their people prepare to leave or return home, exhibiting frantic behavior such as jumping, barking, or panting. While this behavior may not always indicate separation anxiety, it can contribute to overall stress levels in the dog.

FIGURE 6-1: Transition excitement (left) versus a calm dog (right).

Household destruction

Another common sign of separation anxiety is household destruction. Dogs may chew on furniture, shoes, or other objects in the home to cope with their anxiety. This destructive behavior can be a manifestation of distress and frustration.

Hunger strikes

Some dogs with separation anxiety may refuse to eat their food while their family is away, even if they have shown no signs of appetite issues in the past. Emotional distress can lead to a loss of interest in food.

Excessive grooming

Excessive grooming, such as licking or chewing on paws or fur, can signify separation anxiety in dogs. Dogs may engage in this behavior as a self-soothing mechanism to cope with their anxiety and stress.

Vocalizing

Barking, whining, or howling excessively when left alone is a common symptom of separation anxiety. Dogs may vocalize their distress to seek attention or alleviate their anxiety. This behavior can be disruptive to neighbors and indicate underlying emotional issues.

Flight risks

Some dogs with separation anxiety may attempt to escape from their confinement when left alone. They may scratch at doors or windows, dig under fences, or even jump out of windows to find their people. This behavior can harm the dog and signal severe distress.

Self-harm

In extreme cases, dogs with separation anxiety may engage in self-harming behaviors, such as excessively scratching or biting their paws and fur. This behavior is a manifestation of extreme anxiety and can result in injuries that require veterinary attention.

Depression or hyperarousal

Dogs experiencing separation anxiety may exhibit signs of depression, such as lethargy, withdrawal, or decreased interest in activities they once enjoyed. Conversely, some dogs may display hyperarousal symptoms, such as restlessness, pacing, or an inability to relax when left alone.

FUN FACT

Negative bias describes the process of obsessively replaying bad memories instead of trusting in the possibility of better outcomes. It's an evolutionary layover that helped us avoid danger and survive. Dogs exhibit similar behavior, especially in cases of separation anxiety, with their mind catastrophizing their isolation no matter how short-lived it is.

Anxiety by association

Dogs are quick to correlate one action with another. They get excited when we grab a leash or a ball moments before use. They also equate other objects and routines with feeding and bedtime.

Dogs with separation anxiety similarly link various actions with an impending departure. For example, the appearance of a briefcase, the timing of an alarm, or even the choice of work shoes over sneakers. Dogs who have associated preliminary actions may begin to display stress signals before their people leave through a series of predictable responses, including:

>> Clinging

>> Panting

>> Pacing

>> Drooling

>> Door crowding/dashing

>> Whimpering

In each instance, dogs are preemptively stressed by the association even when the action might have other consequences, such as when you grab your bag to retrieve a note or a piece of candy. The result of associative learning is a chronic state of heightened emotional arousal that often leads to generalized anxiety throughout the day. With little time to relax and recover, these dogs have a lower threshold for arousal and stress-related illnesses.

But there is a silver lining. Dogs don't enjoy being in emotional arousal: It's exhausting. They'll cling to anyone, especially you if you lead them down a path to calmness and safety. And the best part? It only takes one to change a behavior.

The Mind-Behavior Connection

Separation anxiety isn't just your dog's reaction to your departure — it's a complex emotional state. Even the term *anxiety* can be misleading, as your departure does more than jangle their nerves. For dogs with this condition, your leaving causes a phobic response akin to a panic attack. While fear and anxiety are adaptive and necessary for survival, phobias are maladaptive states that hinder a dog's emotional and physical well-being.

In genetics, a *maladaptive trait* is more harmful than helpful. Unlike an adaptive trait, which helps a species survive, maladaptive traits hinder the species' ability to thrive.

The biology of separation anxiety

As detailed in Chapter 2, all dogs — and people, for that matter — have an autonomic nervous system that influences their behavior. The two branches include the *parasympathetic*, or the "rest and digest" response, which activates when your dog feels safe and content, and the *sympathetic*, or the "fight, flight, or freeze" state, which activates when your dog is distressed or stimulated. These systems work together to maintain a mental and emotional balance.

Ideally, these two sides live in harmony and balance each other out. When a dog plays fetch, for example, their sympathetic nervous system provides the energy to engage in physical activity. When they come inside for a sip of water, their parasympathetic nervous system helps them rest and recover from the exertion.

Chronic stress, however, like that experienced with separation anxiety, disrupts this recovery process, leaving your dog frazzled and distraught. Stress also affects your dog's physical well-being. Studies show that dogs with separation anxiety routinely have issues with digestion, immunity, the gastrointestinal tract, skin, respiratory system, and their heart.

The good news? Dogs can recover from states of chronic arousal — and they want to. Chapter 7 details how to treat separation anxiety. Like many other issues, modifying their behavior starts with modifying your own.

Is it nature or nurture?

Everyone wants answers to why their dog has separation anxiety. Why is my dog like this? What did I do wrong? Is there a quick fix? Most dogs are diagnosed before two years old, but separation anxiety can arise or recur at various ages and stages of a dog's life. The research is limited, but it's widely accepted that insecurities are influenced by three main factors — genetic predisposition, learned experiences, and current or past living circumstances. It's the age-old question: Is it nature or nurture? Well, it turns out that it's a little of both.

Genetics

Like people, dogs can inherit a genetic propensity for anxiety from their parents. Genetics alone doesn't overshadow other factors like early stress and human interaction, but inheritance does increase vulnerability to the condition.

Secondhand dogs

Many dogs experience stress and anxiety when moving to a new environment or when their routine is disrupted, especially when abandoned. Rehomed dogs often exhibit signs of stress, confusion, and clinginess. Dogs are creatures of habit, and sudden changes can be unsettling.

Age-related separation anxiety

As your dog ages into their twilight years, you may observe a decline in their physical and mental engagement. You may notice increased clinging behavior and separation stress, especially when you leave or at night. For more information on age-related anxiety, see Appendix B. There are many ways to enhance their quality of life at this stage.

Prey mentality

During their first eight to ten months, puppies are prey animals, relying heavily on their caregivers for security and protection. Small dogs may develop a strong attachment to their human family for protection throughout life, potentially making them more susceptible to separation anxiety when left alone.

Puppyhood influences

Ideally, every puppy would experience a safe upbringing with a loving and emotionally available mother. Unfortunately, this is not always the case. When a mother dog is bred in conditions resembling livestock or when she is ill, injured, neglected, or abused, she endures chronic stress, which can impact her behavior and her ability to nurture her puppies. These behavioral consequences are often passed onto her offspring. For more information on anxiety and puppies, see Appendix A.

Litter size

No studies directly link dog litter size to separation anxiety, but research in mice suggests a correlation between small litter sizes and increased anxiety. *Singleton puppy syndrome* can occur when a mother produces only one puppy. Without intervention, singletons may develop touch reactivity, frustration intolerance, and diminished social skills, leading to impulsivity, which is directly linked to elevated stress levels.

Sudden-onset anxiety

Being more sensitive and aware of their surroundings, some dogs can be triggered by minor changes, leading to clinging behavior and distress. Relocation, for example, disrupts their familiar routines and safe spaces, causing discomfort and anxiety. Life events such as new roommates or a new baby can also elevate a dog's stress levels and trigger separation anxiety.

Trauma-induced separation anxiety is also a reality. For instance, I once treated a beautiful husky mix who developed separation anxiety after being crated during a small electric fire incident. Even minor incidents, such as getting a foot, collar, or body part caught in a crate, can lead to sudden-onset separation anxiety.

Lack of socialization

Puppies who miss early socialization experiences during their critical imprinting phase, which is 5 to 14 weeks, will be more prone to anxiety and avoidant social experiences. Under-socialized dogs show reluctance to leave the safety of their home environment and display anxiety in social situations, fearing abandonment. While socialization during the critical imprinting period is very important, it is possible for dogs to be socialized after this period.

ATTACHMENT STYLES

Despite separation anxiety being the most studied dog anxiety, many mysteries still surround the cause, treatment, and prevention of the condition. Why do some dogs develop separation anxiety and others do not? Worldwide studies have done more to dispel long-held assumptions than to discover a cause or solution. It was long assumed that only "spoiled" dogs develop this condition — those given agency to eat from the table, misbehave, and sleep on the furniture. These theories have since been debunked. One hypothesis gaining traction is the influence of the attachment styles of a dog's primary caregivers: Studies suggest that the more comfortably attached a dog is to their people, the better their ability to cope with absences.

Misdiagnosing Separation Anxiety

As you've learned, separation anxiety isn't just a behavior; it's a distorted mental state that manifests when a dog is left alone or when a dog's favorite person has left the building. Sometimes, however, a dog may exhibit behaviors when left alone that can look like separation anxiety when they're not. This section covers common misdiagnosed behaviors, alternative motivations, and interpretations.

Illness, pain, and discomfort

REMEMBER

As mentioned, dogs who are ill or in pain have limited ways to communicate their distress, leading them to act out in various ways. An ailment might manifest as a housebreaking accident, destructive chewing, or attempts to escape. Before jumping to conclusions about separation anxiety, bring your dog to a veterinarian for a thorough checkup to rule out any underlying medical issues.

Destructive chewing

Dogs chew destructively when they're teething, a stage lasting up to 14 months. They also chew to relieve boredom. If chewing is your only frustration (and their only symptom), buy a selection of chew toys and busy toys to relieve your dog when you're out.

Excessive barking

Dogs bark for many reasons unrelated to stress. They bark if they're bored, if they need to go potty, and when stimulated by something outside. It is not uncommon for dogs to bark when left alone. Darkening your home, leaving on sound-blocking music or noise, and hiring someone to give your dog a potty run can be helpful when the barking is unrelated to separation anxiety.

WARNING

While it might be tempting to short-circuit your barking problem by purchasing a battery-operated shock collar or one that emits a repugnant-smelling spray, don't. These collars increase a dog's stress and may inspire separation anxiety where there was none before, especially if you're putting them on before you walk out the door.

House soiling

When dogs are left alone, accidents can happen. However, not all house-soiling accidents indicate separation anxiety. Here are some other interpretations to consider:

>> A dog might be marking your home with urine or poop in response to seeing or hearing passersby or strange noises.

>> Dogs typically avoid urinating where they live, but they may do so if the space is large enough compared to the dog's size. If your dog enjoys their crate, crating can help.

>> Some adult dogs and puppies, who don't have fully developed bladders until they're 8-14 months old, can't hold their potty for hours. When you gotta go, you gotta go!

WARNING

It's not uncommon to think disciplining your dog after the fact will lead to understanding. It doesn't, and it may trigger separation anxiety if your returning home consistently leads to confrontations. Cleaning up a mess takes less than two minutes, whereas becoming furious diminishes your dog's trust in you significantly.

Crate stress

Confinement anxiety is its own issue and can exist independently from separation anxiety. Many dogs with crate anxiety exhibit almost identical behaviors to separation anxiety. The key difference is that dogs with containment anxiety will display their reactions whether you're present or not. For more information on containment anxiety, see Part 3.

Trauma

Dogs can indeed experience trauma. This trauma might stem from something as seemingly benign as a fire truck passing by or wildlife on your property, or it may be as obvious as a challenging stay at the kennel or vet. Dogs can also experience trauma from various sources, such as inconsistent handling by someone unfamiliar with dogs, exposure to drugs, moving to a new location, or even the addition of a new baby or roommate. When dogs are traumatized, they may exhibit behaviors that resemble separation anxiety but should be viewed more as symptoms of PTSD. Chapter 2 talks more about unpacking the nature of your dog's anxiety.

Real-World Examples

Now that you have a deeper understanding of separation anxiety, this section delves into a few case studies. Many dogs with separation anxiety have secondary stresses that affect their rehabilitation. (Note that the names have been changed to protect the privacy of my clients.)

Sparky

Sparky, a ten-month-old Westie rescue, was found under an abandoned truck in a rural part of Texas and transported to a New Jersey shelter, where he was adopted a month later. While he adores his new family, he shakes uncontrollably when they leave. After watching them go out the window, he returns to the door, barking and scratching at the doorframe until they return. He shows no generalized anxiety inside the home but is leash-reactive outside the home with any dog larger than himself. Sparky's first thunderstorm sent him flying into the closet.

Diagnosis: Separation anxiety, storm phobia, and dog-to-dog social anxiety.

Jabba

Jabba, a rescued four-year-old Newfoundland-Husky mix, was relinquished to a high-kill shelter in NYC, then transported to a shelter in the suburbs, where he was adopted into a young family. A friendly, loving dog, his forever family called me to help with one issue: separation anxiety. His symptoms include staring out the window, pacing, and pooping in the upstairs hallway.

Diagnosis: Separation anxiety.

Lola

Lola, a Labradoodle aged ten, experienced a sudden loss of sight due to a condition known as *retinal detachment*. Disoriented and depressed, she became clingier and showed low-level isolation distress. An attempt to crate and then isolate her in the bedroom landed her with full-blown separation anxiety. Related sounds of metal or objects dragging across the wooden floor caused visible distress.

Diagnosis: Separation anxiety, containment anxiety, noise phobia.

Theo

Theo, a one-year-old Bernese Mountain Dog, was a confident, somewhat comical puppy who experienced a traumatizing event resulting in separation anxiety, confinement anxiety, and sensitivity to trucks and sirens. Resting in his crate, a small electrical spark set the house alarms off, and the smell of smoke lingered until emergency responders arrived. Left in his crate for 45 minutes, he was in panic mode when his mom finally arrived to soothe him.

Diagnosis: Separation anxiety, confinement anxiety, noise phobia.

Tank

Tank, a five-month-old French Bulldog, was brought home at eight weeks old. He spent his first month with an elderly English Bulldog named Rosie. Rosie and Tank slept in crates side by side, and Rosie mothered Tank. They were often together even when the family was home. After four months together, Rosie passed away suddenly due to a heart condition. Tank started licking his paws excessively when left alone and lost his excitement for daily walks.

Diagnosis: Separation anxiety, grief-related depression.

The End Result

Dogs are a sensitive, loyal, and thoughtful species, thriving in predictable, supportive environments. As you'll discover in Chapter 7, your goal is to encourage tolerance and impulse control when they're left alone. When certain routines, such as leaving home, trigger panic and constant emotional dysregulation, it becomes challenging to restore a sense of calm.

Now that you've learned about the complexities of separation anxiety and examined the contributing factors, including your role, you're ready to tackle the issue head-on and help your dog feel secure — whether you're at home or not.

Chapter 7
Treating
Separation Anxiety

I f your dog vocalizes in distress, has accidents, or outright destroys your house when left alone, it's not a deliberate attempt to make you stay or get back at you. Separation anxiety is an involuntary reaction that leads to panicked and erratic behavior. Your dog can't control their reaction any more than they could control the color of their coat or their personality.

With your help, however, your dog can overcome separation anxiety. Building their confidence, problem-solving capacities, and coping skills will build their resilience and strengthen your bond. Punishment or discipline have no place in this process, as they will only unsettle your dog and reinforce their fear of your departure. It may take weeks or months, but your patience will aid their sense of calm.

You'll be reminded of the confidence-building activities explored in earlier chapters in the pages ahead. A step-by-step rehabilitation process is also included. Remember, every small step forward is a victory worth celebrating!

Setting the Stage

Dogs with anxiety are by no means weak or foolish. They often have above-average intelligence. Until now, their hyperarousal may be laser-focused on getting your attention, and their behavior may be quite annoying: Do you love me? Do you love me? You were gone ten seconds — *do you still love me?*

WARNING

There's one catch to rehabilitating a dog with separation anxiety. They can't be left alone until they can handle it, which can take weeks or even months. If you need to leave them alone (and you will), prepare to leave your dog with a trusted caregiver or family member. Leaving them completely alone is out of the question. It will set them back and can even make their anxiety worse.

The goal is to build your dog's trust that when you leave, you will return. Through structured, incremental departures and interval training, you'll note changes within weeks, as your dog becomes more comfortable with being on their own.

Reassure your dog when you're home

If your dog constantly seeks attention when you're home— nudging you for pats, playing with toys, or wanting in and out — you might feel obligated to respond. Maybe your dog feels detached even when you're present but not accessible, like when you're busy cooking, using the computer, entertaining a visitor, and so on. Even these brief moments of separation can stress your dog, propelling them to interrupt you for reassurance.

If your dog can't cope with your going to the bathroom or into another room, you'll have to address those behaviors before you can dive into interval training. Here are a few tips:

>> Encourage your dog to stay before giving attention, food, or rewards.

>> Practice shutting doors and waiting before reentering the room. If your dog is anxious, stay in one place and practice synchronized breathing until they calm down.

>> Practice Operation Cooperation with a partner until your dog gets used to you (or a specific person) exiting the room. Chapter 3 includes detailed instructions.

Persistently seeking attention can resemble obsessive-compulsive behavior, where no amount of attention is enough. If this sounds familiar, consider what happens when you're not home. Use these tips to counteract frantic unease and chaotic behavior that overshadows their days.

>> **Structure their day:** Dogs thrive on consistent routines. Pairing words to objects and actions gives them a sense of belonging and direction. Your dog will learn to think ahead and reference you for the certainties of everyday life. Teaching them good manners, such as sitting calmly for attention, encourages impulse control and respect.

>> **Provide an area in each room you share:** Use comfortable bedding to give your dog a spot in each room you share. Place chews and toys within reach. Refer to the "go to place" direction to teach this skill and the "stay" direction to get them to relax there. These lessons are found in Chapter 3.

>> **Create a safe place:** Designate a calm, cozy area accessible to your dog, ideally with blackout shades and calming music. Spend time there doing relaxing activities like canine massage and synchronized breathing. This spot can be in a bedroom, kitchen, or mudroom; some dogs prefer crates or pens, while others find them stressful.

REMEMBER

Catering to your dog's every need can reinforce their chronic arousal and diminish their ability to stay calm. Teaching your dog to relax is essential. Like people, dogs prefer relaxing interactions over chaotic ones; persistent hyperarousal can jeopardize their health and well-being.

TIP

If your dog is comforted by being in a crated or gated area, continue doing whatever works. If you haven't tried gating or leaving your dog in a crate or pen, you may try setting up your pet camera and leaving them as you observe their reaction. Avoid repeating any sequence that triggers or intensifies their reaction.

Stay calm with the peekaboo solution

Correcting your dog dramatically not only fails to help them comprehend what you want but also guarantees a repeat performance. To dogs, our "discipline" is often translated as confrontational play. If it has any effect, it is due to fear, not understanding.

The best technique is what I call the *peekaboo solution*. It is a simple, no-drama solution based on the cause-and-effect principle. Here is how it works:

1. **Your dog approaches, wanting your attention.** Breathe calmly; wait to see what they do before acknowledging them.

2. **They will either act calmly, or try a rowdy behavior like jumping, pawing, or barking at you.** Do not respond immediately. Just continue with what you're doing and wait calmly.

3. **If they sit, pet them lovingly.**

4. **If they get rowdy, cover your face, as if you were playing peekaboo.** Wait until they've calmed down and are breathing normally, then request a "sit" or "place" before you reconnect lovingly.

5. **Acknowledge your dog only when they are calm and following the *four-paw rule* (four paws on the ground).** For some dogs, transitions can be particularly exciting, and it may take a while to calm down.

6. **If this process doesn't work, stay calm and redirect their enthusiasm to a favorite toy, chew, or activity like fetch.**

Encouraging Calmer Interactions

Chapter 3 introduces a series of games and lessons that, when taught cheerfully, have a magical effect on your dog's well-being. Review those lessons and begin using those words to direct everyday behaviors, such as going outside, getting into the car, or going for a walk.

When your dog understands words and/or gestures, their rational thinking brain becomes active, processing thoughts and performing behaviors to earn rewards. This engagement brings structure, routine, and added interest to your dog's life.

Lessons and play

Dogs, like people, love learning new things. Training is simply teaching them English as a second language. For dogs with separation anxiety, coming is rarely challenging, while waiting, staying, and going to places are all harder to master. Try to spend ten minutes twice a day, depending on the demands of your day, practicing the lessons in Chapter 3. Your dog will surprise you with their eagerness to learn and honor your expectations.

BOOKMARK

Play is another way to inspire joy in your dog. Flip back to Chapter 3 to find the games listed in the "Thinking Games" section, including the Operation Cooperation game, the Lily Pad game, and Treasure Hunt.

REMEMBER

Remember, you don't have to overstimulate or excessively exercise your dog to tire them out. Taking your dog out and allowing them to sniff and explore has a calming effect. Dogs love having the agency to explore!

Essential tools and resources

Tools, products, supplements, and medications can support your dog's rehabilitation journey. Certain things are necessary — a behavior diary to keep track of their progress, an indoor pet camera, a speaker, and blackout shades. If you don't have a cozy dog bed, buy one or use an old comforter or a smelly sweatshirt.

SELF-SOOTHING ACTIVITIES AND ADVENTURES

Busy toys and chews are designed to satisfy your dog's senses and promote mental stimulation. Giving your dog activities tailored to their sensory perception provides a constructive outlet for their natural instincts. While they may not address anxiety once you've walked out the door, chewing on appropriate items can also help soothe and relax your dog, reducing stress and promoting well-being. As your dog's separation anxiety diminishes, these activities provide stimulation when you're gone. You can find various toys and chews online and at local pet stores. Adventures, from a lengthy sniff and stroll or hike to a ride in the car, can also switch things up. Discover what lights up your dog's brain and think of things they would enjoy.

CONTAINMENT ANXIETY OR SEPARATION ANXIETY?

If your dog runs off when you attempt to crate or isolate them, you may not be dealing with separation anxiety, but rather containment anxiety (covered in Part 3). Sometimes, one can trigger the other, so your dog may have both conditions. Here's how to differentiate the two: Once you place your dog in their enclosure, do they immediately show signs of stress, even if you're still in the room? That's indicative of containment anxiety. Next, turn on your viewing camera as if you're leaving as usual. Monitor the camera feed. If your dog remains calm, you may be in the wrong chapter. However, if they start to exhibit signs of stress, and it escalates progressively, you're likely dealing with separation anxiety.

REMEMBER

Do not hesitate to use medication or appropriate supplements from the onset. I advise my clients to speak to their veterinarian or a veterinary behaviorist for recommendations and more information about supportive medication or supplements.

BOOKMARK

Other useful products include ThunderShirts, dog-appeasing pheromones (DAP), snuggle puppies, and calming caps. If you try any of these, track their efficiency in your behavior diary. For a full list of helpful products, see Chapter 5.

Rehabilitating Separation Anxiety

I wish a quick, surefire solution could help dogs with separation anxiety feel better overnight. This process, however, takes time. If you're like most people, you're thinking, "How on earth can I stay home with my dog? I didn't sign up for this!" And I get it. However, interval training is the only way to ease your dog's suffering long-term and restore the joys of living in harmony.

Interval training involves breaking down the process of leaving your dog alone into manageable steps, gradually increasing their tolerance for solitude. Imagine it like weight training, and their tolerance for being alone is a muscle. Just as lifting heavier weights builds muscle strength over time, practicing these departures bit by bit increases their resilience. Follow these steps:

1. **Identify their departure cues,** like touching the doorknob or putting on your shoes. These cues might initially trigger anxiety in your dog, so your first goal is to work on them until your dog can tolerate them without getting upset.

2. **Once your dog is comfortable with the departure cues, move on to the next step, which might be approaching the door.** Once they can "handle" that, you can progress further — try opening the door and stepping out.

3. **The goal is to build up your dog's tolerance for longer periods of separation.** You do this by gradually increasing the time you spend away from them, always at a pace they can handle.

Think of this process as a series of small victories, each bringing your dog closer to feeling comfortable alone. It's about taking baby steps and being patient — it might seem tedious, but it's the most effective way to help your dog overcome their anxiety. Repeating the separation exercises detailed in this chapter will teach your dog to trust that you'll always return.

WARNING

If you leave your dog alone for longer than they've shown you they can handle during this measured time, you'll very likely experience a setback. Starting over is hard, especially if you were well along.

When you must go

There will be times during this process when you can't be home and you cannot take your dog with you. Seek a trusted friend or family member to stay with your dog or provide temporary shelter. Alternatively, you can find a reliable dog sitter through online services, your vet, or your community. Be sure to check references when selecting someone to care for your dog. Dog daycare can also be a great option for dogs who enjoy socializing and interacting with other dogs.

WARNING

Choose your daycare or group classes wisely. Some facilities may use punitive measures to correct behavior and to prevent dogs from getting into confrontations.

THE ABCS OF DOG ANXIETY

A: Antecedents. The objects activities that cue your dog that you're leaving. Generally, these are independent events like putting on a coat or moving toward the door.

B: Behavior. This is what your dog does when stressed. Some dogs bark or howl, chew or scratch, and some run from window to window.

C: Consequences. This is how the situation plays out. Sometimes this consequence involves you, and other times, it does not; for example, perhaps their barking brings you back, or they claw at the crate enough to escape their confinement.

Departure cues

Departure cues are the actions you take just before leaving, such as picking up your keys or putting on your coats, and the rituals you perform after you depart, such as opening the garage and starting the car. The pros call these *antecedents*. Dogs have an uncanny way of anticipating our next move and grow attuned to noises that confirm an extended absence. Whip out your behavior diary and list things your dog associates with your leaving.

If you have a dog with separation anxiety, maybe you've tried to alter your departure cues — carrying your briefcase around, wearing your work shoes on a Saturday, or touching the doorknob without opening it. These techniques generally take a long time to work, so don't be discouraged if they haven't worked for you.

The best approach is to identify the objects and actions that trigger your dog and use the object or action as a prompting cue to calm your dog throughout the day and, eventually, when you leave. Here's how:

1. **Design or organize a behavior diary. Record each separation event and note your progress and setbacks.** Open the diary by recording how they act when you're home. Do they stress when you go to the bathroom, talk on the phone or to another family member, or stare at your computer too long? How do they act with other family members?

2. **List all the routines and objects your dog associates with your departure.** Dogs frequently associate our pace, tone, and accelerated breathing with leaving. Be very specific and note what your dog's picking up on.

3. **Choose two actions to repeat when you're home to stay.** Focus on maintaining calm breathing when preparing for the experience and during your interval training. For instance, if an early shower and blow-drying cause distress, practice this routine more calmly, concentrating on remaining relaxed as you go through the motions. Dial it back if your dog becomes anxious as you approach the door. Bring their favorite bed or blanket over, offer them a bone or busy toy, and then walk to and from the door to see if they can handle that. At another time, retrieve your keys, coat, and purse, then return to the couch while breathing normally.

REMEMBER

Your demeanor significantly impacts your dog's state of mind — if you're calm, they're more likely to be calm too! When practicing your separation anxiety interval training, check your own anxiety level and do whatever helps you model a relaxed demeanor.

Define their default behavior

By now, I'll assume you have an indoor pet camera in place, have created a safe space, and placed bedding, chews, and comforting toys by the door you leave from.

Before jumping in and practicing departures, get a handle on your dog's stress cues when left alone. Turn your pet camera on at least ten minutes before you leave so your dog doesn't associate this action as a departure cue. Leave as you normally would, then watch your dog's behavior once you're gone for two minutes, noting everything they do, from scratching at the door to pacing, vocalizing, and so on.

This will be the last time you mindfully initiate your dog's separation anxiety. Now, you're ready to begin the real work of curing your dog's separation anxiety.

What to watch for

In your behavior diary, re-create Table 7-1 or download a blank template from my website (www.SarahHodgson.com). When working through your dog's separation anxiety, keep track of the following variables. Based on your observations, these variables can be compared, scored, and noted:

>> **Threshold:** Your dog's capacity to tolerate a stimulus, such as witnessing your departure routine or being left alone, before exhibiting an emotional or behavioral response.

>> **Intervals:** A series of staged departures and other training exercises with recovery periods in between.

>> **Departure Cues:** List the departure cues included in each exercise, such as grabbing keys or putting on shoes.

As your dog's tolerance grows, departure cues can be added to each departure.

>> **Day's Events:** Note any novel activities, such as a trip to the veterinarian, experiencing storms or other loud noises, visitors, confinement, or discipline, that may have tipped off their anxiety when left alone that day.

>> **Prior Exercise:** Record your dog's activity on a scale from 1 (sedentary) to 3 (exhaustive).

>> **Seconds Between Exercises:** Monitor the seconds between these cues and your departure to gauge their impact on your dog's anxiety.

>> **Recovery Time:** Record how long your dog can relax after completing one exercise.

>> **Come and Go:** Track how your dog reacts to different people leaving.

>> **Reaction Level:** Assess your dog's initial response to separation on a scale of 0-5:

> 0: Accepts isolation
>
> 1: Calm until the one- to two-hour mark
>
> 2: Calm until the 30-minute mark

3: Calm until 15 minutes have passed

4: Calm until the five-minute mark

5: Not calm for any duration

When going through your interval training, don't push your dog too far too fast. The goal is to keep them below their threshold. It is a very slow process initially — I'm talking seconds.

After identifying your dog's stress signals, watch your pet camera to spot the moment they show distress. This could happen in 10 or 20 seconds, or it might be as quick as three seconds. It might even occur when you approach the door or your dog can't access you for attention. Here are some things to keep in mind:

>> Some dogs stress out when you put on your coat or shoes. Work to desensitize these cues by pairing them with calming interactions at various times of the day. When you must leave, space these departure cues out and sit with your dog calmly before bolting out the door.

>> Many dogs are mind readers and figure out you're leaving the moment you face the door and squeeze out the door the moment it opens a crack. Try initially leaving from a different door or start your interval training by simply facing the door. Do not proceed to a more difficult departure until your dog is more relaxed.

>> Family and helpers, with the best of intentions, can unintentionally derail your progress. Ensure everyone knows the plan and does not leave your dog, isolate them when under duress, or get upset with them for any reason. One prolonged isolation event can reset the clock and make their anxiety worse.

Day-by-day training

Devote 15-20 minutes to your interval training every day. Each session should involve three to seven predetermined departures or exercises related to your absence. Plan and outline each day's exercises in advance, varying the departure cues and duration for each exercise. Ease into the exercises by starting small and increasing the length at a pace that your dog can handle. As you plan your daily interval schedule, keep these points in mind:

» **Set up a camera and set the mood:** Turn on the indoor pet camera and set the mood long before starting your interval training (vary the time from 15 minutes to one hour before). Dim the lights, close the blinds, play sound-canceling music, and provide toys and chews your dog likes. Dogs sense patterns, so don't wait until the last minute!

» **Avoid predictable departures:** Shake up your 20-minute interval training by practicing it at different times throughout the day. In Table 7-1, observe how each exercise incorporates one or two departure cues — such as putting on shoes, locking or unlocking the door, or grabbing a coat — but no more than that. Initially, just the departure cue may trigger your dog's reaction, making the departure cues themselves the entire exercise.

» **Stay calm before, during, and after:** Model calmness and reassurance for your dog to mirror in every action, including departures, arrivals, and throughout the day.

» **Offer physical touch and rewards only once your dog is calm and breathing normally:** When returning after a separation, stay calm despite your dog's excitement. Prompt them to "sit," "down," or "go to place" only when they are relaxed, grounded, and composed.

Case Study: Helping Jabba with His Separation Anxiety

When I work with my clients, I engage them virtually throughout the week, shaping daily interval protocols based on the recorded results from the previous day. In Chapter 6, I introduced a few dogs I've rehabilitated for separation anxiety. This section expands on Jabba's journey.

In case you forgot, Jabba is a four-year-old rescue dog, a New-foundland and Husky mix. He initially ended up in a high-kill shelter in NYC before being relocated to a suburban shelter where a young family adopted him. Jabba is friendly, loving, and has an extreme case of separation anxiety. His symptoms include pacing, watching, and pooping one to two times in the upstairs hallway.

Before we could begin our separation anxiety interval training, we had to address Jabba's over-attachment to Jenny, his primary caregiver. During our first meeting, she shared that she could not leave the room without him shadowing her or closing the bath-room door for privacy. When visiting friends or meeting for coffee, Jenny was unable to walk away from Jabba without his vocalizing until her return. The first two weeks of working together were spent addressing these behaviors. Techniques we included:

>> Jenny would ignore Jabba's overzealous demands for affection by covering her face when he nudged or whined. She taught and asked Jabba to "sit-stay" before engaging him with pats, rewards, and meals.

>> Jenny would leave the room, shut doors, and count back from 5 to 10 to 20 seconds before reentering the room. If Jabba was anxious, Jenny stayed in one place and practiced synchronized breathing for up to three minutes or until he calmed down.

>> Peter, Jabba's secondary caregiver, would practice Operation Cooperation (see Chapter 3) as Jenny navigated around the room and eventually went in and out of rooms.

>> They also put Jabba on a long-acting medicine to ease his stress.

Once we had a handle on these day-to-day behaviors, we began to tackle the overarching issue of separation. Table 7-1 details three interval training sessions: one each from the beginning, middle, and end of Jabba's training journey. Although it took six weeks from start to finish, Jabba can now be left home without incident or stress. In fact, he has since become a therapy dog, bringing comfort and joy to children in hospitals in New York!

TABLE 7-1 Jabba's Separation Anxiety Behavior Log

Caretaker Name(s)	Time	Departure Cues	Session Details	Day's Events	Prior Exercise (1-3)	Reaction Level (1-5)	Seconds Between Next Exercise
Jenny and Peter	9:30 AM	Put shoes on	Approached the door and turned the knob	N/A	2	4	40s
Jenny	9AM	Put shoes on, grabbed purse	Unlocked the door and turned the knob	N/A	2	5	70s
Jenny	5:45 PM	Put shoes on, grabbed purse	Unlocked the door, turned the knob, stood there for 30 seconds	Daycare for 2 hours	1	3	55s
Peter	6:00 PM	Put shoes on, rattled keys	Unlocked the door, turned the knob, stood there for 1 minute	N/A	2	2	45s
Jenny and Peter	8:00 AM	Grabbed purse, put shoes on	Unlocked the door, paused 10 seconds, opened the door a crack then shut the door	Stayed home with grandma for 3 hours	3	3	60s

Caretaker Name(s)	Time	Departure Cues	Session Details	Day's Events	Prior Exercise (1-3)	Reaction Level (1-5)	Seconds Between Next Exercise
Jenny and Peter	5:30 PM	Put shoes on, said goodbye to Peter	Unlocked the door, paused 10 seconds, opened the door 2 feet and then shut the door	N/A	2	2	60s
Jenny	9AM	Put shoes on, grabbed purse	Unlocked and opened the door, stepped out with the door open for 10 seconds, then shut the door	Vet visit	1	3	60s
Jenny	5:45 PM	Put on shoes, grabbed purse, shouted goodbye to Peter	Unlocked and opened the door, stepped out, closed the door for 10 seconds, then stepped back in	N/A	1	2	55s

(continued)

TABLE 7-1 *(continued)*

Caretaker Name(s)	Time	Departure Cues	Session Details	Day's Events	Prior Exercise (1-3)	Reaction Level (1-5)	Seconds Between Next Exercise
Peter	6:00 PM	Put shoes on, rattled keys	Unlocked and opened the door, stepped out, closed the door for 30 seconds, then stepped back in	Had an altercation at the dog park	3	4	45s
Jenny and Peter	8:00 AM	Grabbed purse, put shoes on	Unlocked and opened the door, stepped out, closed the door for 2 minutes, then stepped back in	N/A	1	2	60s
Jenny	12:00 PM	Put shoes on, said goodbye to Peter	Unlocked and opened the door, stepped out, closed the door for 5 minutes seconds, then stepped back in	N/A	2	3	60s

Caretaker Name(s)	Time	Departure Cues	Session Details	Day's Events	Prior Exercise (1-3)	Reaction Level (1-5)	Seconds Between Next Exercise
Jenny	5:30 PM	Put shoes on, grabbed purse	Unlocked and opened the door, stepped out, closed the door for 10 minutes, then stepped back in	Stayed at home with dog sitter for 3 hours	2	2	60s
Jenny and Peter	5:30 PM	Ready to go	Left for 30 minutes	Stayed at home with dog sitter for 4 hours	3	0	60s
Jenny	12:00 PM	Put shoes on, grabbed purse	Left for 2 hours	N/A	2	1	N/A
Jenny and Peter	8:00 AM	Grabbed purse, put shoes on	Run through, left 3 hours and come back for the day	N/A	1	1	N/A

Slow and Steady Wins the Race

Remember to take your time, be patient, and allow your dog to progress at their own pace. Don't be afraid to ask for help when you need it — there are many qualified professionals, such as myself, to guide you — in person or virtually. Your dedication to your dog's well-being is a beacon of hope in their world of uncertainty. Together, you can rewrite the story of separation anxiety, turning fear into courage and dread into resilience! Your dog can overcome this challenge with consistency, commitment, and empathy, and your efforts will be their greatest reward.

3

Resolving Containment Anxiety

Chapter **8**

Soothing Indoor and Outdoor Containment Anxiety

Containment anxiety is heartbreaking to witness. Dogs with this condition typically panic with the intensity of a trapped animal, frantically pawing, spinning, or vocalizing their distress. In such moments, the only solution is to release the dog from containment, yet some people can't or won't do this, especially if their schedule necessitates leaving home.

Internally, if your dog stresses when placed into a crate or is otherwise confined, their adrenaline and cortisol levels skyrocket. Without relief, this can feed other issues, like separation anxiety and noise phobias. Your dog may associate being crated with your departure or, when left confined for hours, experience a loud event they can't escape from. While containment distress may resemble separation anxiety, there's more to the story.

This chapter delves into these various scenarios and provides solutions to help your dog feel less anxious when containment is necessary.

Understanding Containment Anxiety

If you've ever experienced claustrophobia or felt uneasy in the elevator, you'll empathize with dogs suffering from this condition. They feel antsy, have difficulty breathing, and if they can't escape, they will panic.

REMEMBER

Many people confuse containment anxiety with separation anxiety, and while it's true that one can often trigger the other, they are not the same. Containment anxiety and separation anxiety have distinct characteristics and should be addressed separately. For example, a dog experiencing separation stress may associate containment with being left alone, while a dog uncomfortable with containment may only exhibit distress when their family leaves.

To determine if your dog struggles with containment anxiety, check off the following scenarios that apply to you. If you check off several, your dog likely has containment anxiety.

❏ When confined, my dog exhibits excessive vocalization (barking, howling, or whining).

❏ My dog shows signs of restlessness, spinning, or pacing when confined.

❏ My dog shreds anything within reach, including blinds or blankets.

❏ My dog attempts to escape or shows frantic behavior when confined, including biting or scratching at the bars.

❏ My dog excessively salivates or pants when confined.

❏ My dog eliminates (urinates or defecates) inappropriately when confined.

❏ My dog shows other extreme signs of agitation or distress when confined.

Once you've identified that your dog is experiencing containment anxiety, take the time to observe the symptoms you see. Symptoms may include elevated heart rate, pacing, hiding, cowering, destructive behavior, excessive or frantic vocalization, tucked ears and tail, unusual alertness, and urination or defecation. Noting these symptoms helps you anticipate your dog's stress levels and soothe or redirect them.

SEPARATION ANXIETY, NOISE PHOBIA, AND CONTAINMENT ANXIETY

While these disorders share similarities — such as heightened stress levels and increased cortisol production triggering the flight, fight, or fear response — dogs don't necessarily experience all three simultaneously. A dog can have crate anxiety while comfortably roaming freely in shared rooms or the house. Similarly, dogs with noise phobias may develop intense fear reactions to loud sounds in their crate, but might not exhibit signs of anxiety when otherwise confined. Each dog's response to these triggering situations can vary based on their experiences, temperament, and environmental factors.

Containment anxiety can manifest in different ways. While one dog may only struggle with being in a crate, another might find fences and other barriers stressful. The goal should be to reinforce calmer behavior when your dog needs to be confined.

Crate stress

Dogs and puppies who dislike their crates often show resistance from the start. Due to past trauma, lack of socialization, or insufficient exposure to a crate, resistant dogs tend to avoid it altogether, even when enticing food and toys are placed inside or nearby. They may flail about when placed inside, attempt to back out or escape as you secure the latch, and engage in keep-away behavior when they sense you're about to put them in. Enforcing their isolation can lead to intensified containment stress, strained bonding issues, social anxiety, and even aggression when forced out of a hiding spot or into the crate.

WARNING

If your dog has crate anxiety, do not buy a stronger crate or padlock them in. Crates are not for every dog; check out the following solutions instead.

POOL PANIC

Pools should be off-limits to dogs until they are trained to swim safely. The issue is rooted in barrier panic — dogs who fall into a pool instinctively attempt to exit from where they fell in. Since pools are made of cement, they lack a gripping surface, leading to frantic clawing, flailing, and, sadly, drowning. In addition to monitoring your dog around the pool, teach them how to orient themselves and swim to the steps should they fall in. Investing in a session or two with a professional trainer can ensure your dog's safety around water.

Barrier frustration

Many crate-averse dogs exhibit barrier frustration when blocked from something they desire, such as following their family, chasing animals, or guarding their perceived territory. Common symptoms include barking at windows, clawing drapes and window trimmings, scaling pens or gates, and clawing or chewing at doorways or windowsills. When a dog feels trapped and cannot escape, they can develop learned helplessness, leading to these symptoms.

Fence and enclosure anxiety

Dogs experiencing actual containment anxiety may also display tension outside the home, often wanting to break free to explore or run off. Being confined triggers frustration, creating a lower threshold for reactivity. Adrenaline and cortisol levels skyrocket when the impulse to escape sets in. This behavior can extend to leash pulling and frantic racing along the fence line. This heightened state of arousal may result in targeted or displaced aggression.

Helping Dogs Overcome Containment Anxiety

Dogs don't like feeling panicked or anxious. Being in an impulse-driven, emotionally charged state drains a dog's energy and can lead to chronic health issues, most commonly stomach problems and overproduction of adrenaline. Being proactive can help your dog relax when you're together *and* when you're gone.

Determine the root causes

Barrier frustration is common with rescue dogs, especially those housed in kennels with other dogs. Chapter 9 is devoted to rescue dogs and others severely traumatized in containment.

REMEMBER

When a dog gets startled, their impulse is to move away. When a confined dog is startled, however, it can lead to greater fear of the original stimulus (the thunder or loud construction, for example) and the containment space by association.

Dogs can develop containment anxiety for various reasons, including these:

>> Prolonged periods of isolation

>> Experiencing a frightening event while confined, such as being confined during a storm or fire

>> An illness or underlying distress like separation anxiety that becomes associated with crates, gates, and barriers

>> Fear of entrapment, territorial frustration, and conditioned reinforcement (such as a person passing by)

>> Reliving past traumas, such as stressful shelter experiences

WARNING

If routinely locked up, some dogs will go to extreme lengths to break free, including self-mutilation or causing extreme levels of destruction.

Consider supplements, helpful products, and prescription medications

To help your dog overcome their containment anxiety, consult your veterinarian and consider adjusting their diet and utilizing calming products, supplements, or prescribed medications alongside the rehabilitation techniques outlined in this chapter.

BOOKMARK

Refer to Chapter 5 for more information on diet, supplements, prescription medications, and helpful products.

TWO TRUTHS

Consider the contrast between your perspective and your dog's. For instance, think about delivery people. While you see them bringing packages, your dog might perceive them as a threat. Similarly, when people pass by your home, you see neighbors and friends, but your dog sees something like a zombie apocalypse. Barking might be your dog's way of saying "stay away," which can be effective for delivery people and strangers since they eventually disappear, but it is not always based in reality. When visitors do come in, a dog with anxiety might react with aggression or mixed emotions, which results in the guest retreating.

To help your dog overcome their impulsive, reactive fears, use brain games and activities when they feel safe and eager to learn. Your dog will learn to balance their reactive nature by employing their thinking brain as you help unpack irrational fears with calm reactions.

Evaluate their stress levels

Dogs with containment anxiety exhibit stress when you call or lead them toward their containment area. Many deduce routines that proceed with isolation and respond proactively by running away. In this case, avoid chasing or grabbing your dog, which leads to more stress. Instead, leave your dog on a five- to ten-foot dragging leash to enable calm intervention and guidance. While working through your dog's issues, keep a behavior diary to plot your progress and their reactions each time you leave them.

TIP

One helpful tool for managing containment anxiety is a wireless monitoring camera. This camera allows you to observe your dog's behavior and gain reassurance while working on their rehabilitation. Avoid using treat-dispensing or remote-training features with these cameras, as they often further confuse and frustrate dogs.

>> In cases of crate panic, anxiety can start when your dog approaches the enclosure, with the panic spiking the moment they're shut in.

>> Like crate panic, barrier frustration generally occurs when your dog is enclosed in a pen or behind a gate, indoor pen, or closed door and will generally include trying to climb or escape the zone.

>> Some dogs panic even when given full house freedom. They claw at the blinds and chew the door frame or molding.

>> In cases of window, yard, or leash reactivity (covered in more detail in Chapter 10), the triggers are often predictable, such as the approach of repair personnel, utility workers, delivery persons, and passersby — especially those walking another dog.

Soothe indoor stress

Dogs with containment anxiety feel trapped, especially when they move, explore, or distance from a stimulus. Whether they experience anxiety, panic, extreme frustration, or, as is often the case, a toxic blend of each, their behavior — whether clawing, pawing, vocalizing, or attempting to escape — is the direct result of their body's response to an unpredicted trigger.

THE ROOT OF ALL REACTIONS

A dog's reaction usually mirrors their emotional state when confined, whether behind a window, door, in a crate, or on a leash (see Chapter 10). Dogs tend to become aroused when they experience:

- **Fear:** Dogs often startle easily at unexpected sights and sounds, exhibiting behaviors such as staring, vocalizing, or attempting to flee. They may cling to you, run away, or race home.

- **Frustration:** Dogs may become frustrated when they cannot reach or explore something they desire. This frustration can arise from various situations, such as wanting to engage with another dog or person but being unable to do so.

- **Anger:** Dogs may express anger when they feel their personal space is invaded. In such cases, they will direct their anger at the target. They may redirect their frustration onto another nearby dog or person if they can't reach the target.

- **Predatory impulses:** Many dogs have a high prey drive, wanting to chase and revisit areas when prey animals congregate. When the leash restricts them, they pull hard and may attempt to break free.

Containment stress is the one anxiety response that will worsen if left unaddressed. These dogs can get relief through calming techniques such as synchronized breathing, brain games, and massage and develop greater tolerance through mirroring, desensitization, and counterconditioning. Patience is the common thread.

WARNING

Don't punish your dog if their containment stress leads to household destruction. Remind yourself that they were having a panic attack, not plotting a hostile takeover. It's normal to feel frustrated with the situation, but punishing your dog will only increase their stress level.

Create a safe place

Dogs need a safe, comforting place to escape, like your bedroom or another cozy place in your home. Your goal is to make this area so reassuring that simply entering it will trigger their parasympathetic nervous system, inducing the rest and digest state, as explained in Chapter 2.

Consider your dog's favorite spots in your home to create this area. Choose one that is quiet, easily darkened with shades if needed, and situated in the center of your home, away from passageways, doors, and windows. If your dog sleeps in the bedroom with you or enjoys their enclosure, that's the perfect place.

Here is a checklist to keep in mind when creating a safe place for your dog:

- ☐ Darken the room as the inner sanctum of the den. I suggest using blackout shades or covering the windows with blankets to block light temporarily.
- ☐ Play comforting music, such as reggae, soft rock, or calming piano classical. There are even stations that stream dog music! Be mindful to learn what's most comforting for your dog.
- ☐ Clear the room of any valuables and make sure counters are free of anything enticing.
- ☐ Provide a comfortable bed made or embellished with clothes or blankets that carry your scent.
- ☐ Engage in fun training sessions and play brain games in the room to tap into their calm, thinking side. Remember, mental stimulation can be exhausting, too.

- [ ] Spend time in this location, whether feeding your dog, massaging them, or simply being present and calm.
- [ ] Consider relocating a desk to be present more often, though not always accessible.

Go into this room once or twice a day when your dog is not stressed. Cue the room by identifying it as their "happy place." When you're home, keep the room accessible so your dog can enter on their own if they desire.

REINTRODUCING THE CRATE

If your dog or puppy becomes distressed in the crate, be prepared to consider alternative options. Some dogs never acclimate to small, enclosed spaces. To assess whether your dog might eventually be persuaded, consider purchasing two crates: one placed in a quiet, dimly lit room, which you hope will become the permanent spot, and another located in the central area of your home.

Fill the crates with enticing items such as toys, treats, and your dog's water and food dish. Create a cozy environment by propping a pillow and resting your head in the opening while engaging in quiet activities like reading or texting. During this time, ignore your dog and show them *you* love the crate. If possible, involve a child in the process by having them enter the crate, closing it gently, and dropping treats and favorite toys inside for them to collect and play with.

Throughout this game, ignore your dog, allowing them time to observe and become curious. After a few days of this routine, see if your dog begins to show interest in the crate by entering to retrieve toys or simply spending time inside. If they do, don't close the crate or make a big fuss; instead, calmly approach and drop treats through the bars. Avoid dramatic engagement as it might hyper-arouse or agitate your dog and prevent them from settling inside.

Continue this process for about a week, consistently modeling your enjoyment of the crate while observing your dog's reactions. After this period, you can carefully attempt to close the crate door. Patience and observation are key; pay close attention to your dog's tolerance level and response throughout the process to ensure a positive experience.

Remain present but not accessible

To help your dog build confidence and self-soothing skills, teach them that, at times, you're present but not accessible. Start by offering them stimulating toys, chews, and solo activities. Spend time nearby without actively engaging them. When they seek attention, gently guide them toward their toys or chews by calmly saying, "get your toy." When you finish your work, direct your dog to their area and give calm, loving attention instead of riling them up. Teach them that good things happen when they're relaxing in their area.

Keep white noise or soothing music playing throughout the day to help them adjust.

TIP

If you want your dog to calm down, leave your emotions out of it. If your dog is pawing, jumping, or barking furiously for your attention, for example, and you shout or push them away, they might interpret this as confrontational play. Fun! Instead, cover your face with your hand, magazine, or pillow. Breathe calmly, waiting out their temper tantrum. When they give up, direct them to their bed (you can pull it close if you'd like) and pet them gently. Set an example!

Depart gradually

To help your dog become more comfortable with containment, practice short departures, briefly taking a few steps away while staying within sight and then returning. If your dog shows signs of anxiety, such as jumping on the gate, step back and ignore them until they calm down. It may take a few minutes to come back into the room. To help them relax, use synchronized breathing and cover your face should they try to get your attention. Refer to the peekaboo solution in Chapter 7.

REMEMBER

To your dog, staring is either a threat or an invitation to play rough. Repeating directions like "sit" over and over is more annoying than instructional. Imagine my asking you for the ketchup 13 times!

As your dog becomes more accustomed to your brief absences and stays calm when within eyesight, you can gradually disappear. Initially, duck out around the corner, keeping with your catchphrase, "be right back!" Using a Bluetooth camera, monitor their reactions and return if they show signs of stress. When you return, stay calm and wait until they are more relaxed to reconnect. Breathing calmly helps.

Little things can make a big difference. If your dog has trouble settling on their bed, move it closer to the exit door. Consider the music genre. Music should soothe your dog and block external noises that could excite them — many dogs like reggae, and some like classical piano or soft rock. Don't use sounds that include loud bangs or animal noises. Consistently reinforce calm behavior and track progress using your behavior diary.

Unpack their stress

Overcoming or curbing containment anxiety takes time, and it can worsen quickly. Because these conditions can arise indoors and outdoors and occur whether you're home or away, a dog with this diagnosis may find little relief from the intensity of their emotions.

When possible, limit the containment that is causing the stress. If they're unsettled in the crate, try leaving them in a room, perhaps with the crate door open. If the crate is in a well-trafficked area, you may try to put it in a quieter room, encircling the crate with a pen and leaving the door open. Your goal is to help your dog feel safe and restful.

CRATES AREN'T ALWAYS NECESSARY

While I view crates as cribs that provide security and ensure good rest, especially for puppies, they aren't necessary if they stress your dog out. If your puppy or dog resists entering the crate and becomes anxious when you return, it may be doing more harm than good. While you can attempt to create a more positive association with the crate, consider eliminating it if your dog continues to shows signs of stress when confined.

Instead, you can gate your dog into a comforting room or give them household freedom. To test these options, place your dog's bed near the door or area you're using, prepare to leave, and calmly say, "I'll be right back." You can leave a chew or puzzle toy. You can observe your dog's reaction using a Bluetooth camera.

Ideally, your dog will settle within minutes of your departure, especially if they've had exercise and potty time beforehand. If your dog paces, attempts to escape, or vocalizes, they may also have separation anxiety.

Calming Outdoor Reactivity

An outdoor dog pen is like a crate, especially in close containment. Dogs are socially intelligent animals and can experience enclosure stress like zoo animals. Dogs in pens may resort to digging, jumping, barking, and even self-mutating without stimulation. Dogs with these heightened levels of agitation are also more susceptible to injury and illness.

To address this behavior, consider the following tips:

>> Adjust the fence line to the backyard or plant trees or shrubbery to obstruct their line of vision.

>> Engage your dog in the I Spy game, rewarding them each time they look to delivery people or walkers. The goal is to turn a fear or frustration into a fun game. Flip back to Chapter 3 for a full description.

>> Supervise their freedom until your dog becomes more chill with comings and goings. If you have both a front yard and a backyard, feed and play with your dog only in the backyard. Take them out when foot traffic is minimal.

Reactive dogs can become overstimulated if they're left outside during the day. Remember, when your dog is allowed to stare at distractions, they can become consumed by them. All dogs need daytime rest to maintain their well-being.

While you might believe that assuming the role of border patrol provides a sense of purpose for your dog, their heightened response releases a continuous flow of adrenaline and cortisol. This can lead to difficulties in relaxation, wariness, or aggression toward visitors, and potentially the development of stress-induced illnesses.

BOOKMARK

If your dog's anxiety skyrockets each time they hear the doorbell, buzzer, or gate alarm, keep in mind that you're not alone. Many dogs are upset by unpredictable noises and routinely bark defensively or try to run or escape them. Noise-related sensitivities are covered in detail in Chapters 13 and 14.

Dogs displaying outdoor reactivity are often misjudged as aggressive, but they may be unsettled by strangers or other dogs approaching them. Their barking sends a warning, "don't come any closer." When the perceived threat retreats, it inadvertently reinforces their stress and the belief that their frantic reaction effectively deters potential intruders.

When You Can't Be There

Leaving a dog confined with severe containment anxiety will exacerbate the issue, potentially leading to unmanageable behavior. It is one of the more challenging anxieties to address, as it tends to escalate rapidly from mild discomfort to full-blown panic.

So, what can you do if you have to leave your dog alone but can't confine them? Surprisingly, many dogs with this issue do better when given freedom of movement. If you're open to trying this approach, set up a Bluetooth camera near the area you'll be leaving, provide a comfortable bed near the exit, and offer some engaging chews. Before leaving, take your dog for a calming walk, engage in training or brain games (refer to Chapter 3), and then spend three to five minutes practicing synchronized breathing or a gentle massage to relax them. Finally, calmly tell them, "be right back."

WARNING

Initially, monitor your dog's reactions during these departures. While some level of stress, such as whining, pacing, or watching out the window, may be expected, return immediately if their anxiety escalates to the point of excessive clawing, vocalizing, or escape attempts.

If you're uncomfortable granting complete house freedom or your dog can't handle any form of containment, you should consider alternative options like daycare or hiring a dog sitter. As you gradually expose your dog to extended periods of solitude, consider consulting a holistic veterinarian to discuss dietary changes and supplements or a veterinary behaviorist to explore medicinal options that can support your efforts.

Chapter **9**

Recognizing Trauma in Rescues and Other Dogs

Traumatized dogs are easy to spot. Some may be overly stressed, seeking constant reassurance. I refer to this as the "do you still love me?" syndrome. Others may struggle to form trusting relationships with people. Trauma differs from anxiety in that the triggering event — be it a dramatic rescue, a medical crisis, abandonment, or a puppy mill scenario — elicits a deep emotional response and leaves lasting psychological scars. Fortunately, I can teach you how to alleviate them.

Identifying the Root of All Trauma

The question of why some dogs are prone to panic attacks while others grow up emotionally unscathed likely has more to do with nature and nurture rather than one identifiable cause. Genetics weigh in, as does lack of socialization, unconscious reinforcement, neglect, abuse, and rehoming. Many incidents can spawn a traumatic reaction in dogs, and while some recover on their own, others need help. Having a role model — such as another calm person or pet — can make all the difference.

Are you able to pinpoint one event that may have contributed to your dog's trauma? If you've rescued them, can you learn more about their backstory? If so, it may shed more light on what they need help unpacking. On the other hand, you may have no clue about the challenges they've faced. Here are a few scenarios to consider:

- >> Prolonged confinement
- >> Neglect or abuse
- >> Abandonment or stress from sheltering
- >> Extended medical stay or treatment due to illness or emergency
- >> Exposure to severe weather events such as tornadoes, thunderstorms, floods, or earthquakes
- >> Trauma from fireworks or other loud noise events, such as construction noises
- >> Exposure to explosions, whether from police or military-style work
- >> Low interaction and lack of socialization in a free-range lifestyle
- >> Being used as a bait dog
- >> Involvement in an unsolicited dog fight, whether on or off a leash

Note that even lovingly raised dogs can experience one traumatic event that can have lasting effects. Consider Benny, an adorable Cavalier King Charles Spaniel whose family included a calm, loving child. When visitors came with their six-year-old twins, no one stepped in to save Benny as he tried unsuccessfully to avoid grasps, hugs, and tail pulling. When Benny bit a child two years later, no one had traced it back to this triggering event. Fortunately, Benny responded well to the techniques discussed in this chapter.

Should attempts to flee a threatening situation be thwarted, or if dogs are pulled out of a place of safety, such as a closet or cavern, they may show signs of aggression to warn off people who interfere with their survival attempts.

HUGGING AND STARING

WARNING

To any animal besides humans, a direct stare, gleaming teeth, and a direct approach are threatening; a locked embrace can be life-threatening. Hugs can be traumatizing for dogs, especially for puppies. Prolonged starting has the same effect. While some dogs may grow comfortable with these signs of affection, others may react dramatically. When dogs or puppies squirm or back away, people often persist, thinking they can override their escape attempts with more intense shows of affection.

When puppies are forced to endure this handling, they often flail, nip, or try to escape; when they can't, they may freeze and endure it. Enduring, however, is different from enjoying. As puppies emerge from these early inhibited months of development, they can become dogs who won't hesitate to use aggression to clarify their confusion. While some dogs can be conditioned to endure hugs and may seek out direct loving eye contact in moments of calm affection, do not attempt to stare down your dog in anger or hug them without consent and rewards.

When terror overwhelms a dog's brain, their other autonomic behaviors, such as eating, breathing normally, and playing, shut down. Some dogs may resort to biting family members. Other anxious behaviors that may indicate the onset of a total emotional shutdown include:

>> Freezing

>> Hiding

>> Social anxiety with people and other dogs

>> Hesitation in new environments or with new people or dogs

>> Destructive behavior

>> Excessive motion and hypervigilance or immobilized behavior

>> Jumping or pawing at their people in desperation

>> Uncontrollable shaking, urination, or defecation

>> Excessive digging

>> Persistent vocalization

>> Aggression when forced to engage or move positions

Get a full health check

Dogs don't act happy if they feel unwell. If your dog suddenly develops anxious behavior, their reaction may have a medical basis. Since your dog can't communicate verbally with you, it's up to you to interpret their behaviors. Your veterinarian is trained to interpret symptoms, and you can assist them by observing and logging what you notice. Here is a checklist of common symptoms to look out for:

- ❏ Limping
- ❏ Sleeping more than usual
- ❏ Refusing food
- ❏ Excessive drinking
- ❏ Irregular stool consistency
- ❏ Excessive scratching or licking
- ❏ Unusual aggression or irritability
- ❏ Changes in weight
- ❏ Coughing or wheezing
- ❏ Vomiting or diarrhea
- ❏ Difficulty breathing or excessive panting

Whether your dog's trauma response is sudden or prolonged, it's important to make an appointment with your veterinarian or a veterinary behaviorist for a comprehensive blood screening and checkup.

Veterinary trauma

Visits to the vet can be a challenging experience for all dogs, especially rescue dogs who may be triggered by forced containment or slight discomfort. For many rescue dogs, the vet visit marks their first interaction with people, because they are checked by a vet before entering a shelter.

Bring familiar objects, toys, and their mat or bed to ease veterinary visits or overnight stays. Offering treats can also help gauge their comfort level and alleviate anxiety. Dogs refuse food when they are stressed. Remember to stay calm, focus on breathing, and practice relaxation techniques.

Building Your Dog's Coping Skills

Nothing screams "forever home" more than consistent routines, loving touch, calm redirection, and synchronized breathing. Once your dog feels safe, they'll be more open to learning new words, playing games, and interacting daily. Eventually, they'll replace the old terrifying memories with the happy memories you create together, but you need to earn their trust first.

REMEMBER

When adopting a dog with generalized anxiety or who fears unpredictable events and reacts strongly to unrecognized stimuli, you need to be patient and calm. It will take time for them to let go of what they've known, and they'll need a calm, confident role model to show them the way forward. While babying a nervous dog comes easily, sometimes they may misinterpret your effusiveness as a sign of danger. Dogs with trauma may not recognize love when they see it; give them time to acclimate and trust.

Routines of everyday life

Like people, dogs have five basic needs: to eat, drink, sleep, potty, and play. Check out Table 3-1 (in Chapter 3) to see how to assign words and routines to each need. You can also print a template from my website at SarahHodgson.com. This consistency, plus linking words to actions, provides reassuring stability.

Often, a traumatized dog develops learned helplessness, a state in which they give up trying to escape or improve their situation. This can paralyze any hope of experiencing joy and forming loving connections. Dogs with learned helplessness usually only act to fulfill basic needs before retreating into their emotional shell.

TIP

Adopted dogs who have been traumatized generally follow what's known as the 3-3-3 rule. Plan for at least three days of nervousness and feeling overwhelmed, three weeks of gradually building trust in the routines (the more consistent, the better), and three months of coming to fully trust that this is their forever home.

Freedom, food, and fun

While you can't simply set them loose, you can give them room to roam on a long 10-30-foot leash. Taking your dog to a field, beach, or wooded path and allowing them to lead the way can be incredibly enriching. Many dogs, especially those rescued from hoarding situations or free-range lifestyles, may find leashes or harnesses triggering due to lack of exposure. By granting them the freedom to explore and positively reinforcing their behavior, you can help them associate the joys of exploration with the leash and your companionship. For more guidance on using long lines effectively, check out the instructional e-book available at SarahHodgson.com.

WARNING

Leash walks can indeed be traumatic if not handled correctly. Tightening the leash too much can lead to distress, and using neck collars that restrict airways or shock or prong collars that threaten pain can all contribute to learned helplessness, even in confident dogs. Instead, consider using a harness and incorporate high-value treats to establish positive associations with the leash. For more information on leash walking, refer to Chapter 10.

Confidence boosters

The first goal of bringing home a rescue dog is to uncover what excites them. While their breed mix can offer some clues, remember that hounds adore scents, retrievers are all about chasing, and terriers have a strong hunting instinct. Do you notice them looking around or sniffing? Do they like to chew toys or chase them? Once you discover what lights up their brain, create or buy objects to satisfy their desires.

BOOKMARK

Dogs love games like Hide-and-Seek with toys and scatter-feeding. Chapter 3 includes instructions on these games and more.

Comfort toys

Your dog may become deeply attached to a specific toy, such as a stuffed animal, bone, blanket, or puzzle toy. If this happens, consider purchasing multiples and keeping them readily available.

Years ago, I rescued a German Shepherd named Balderdash. He developed a strong attachment to one of my children's teddy bears. He carried it everywhere — on walks, in the car, even to bed. We affectionately dubbed it "Super Bear," as it seemed to be his confidence-boosting companion!

Supplements, medication, and other products

If you've recently welcomed a rescue dog into your home, allow them time to settle in and get comfortable before making significant changes to their diet or introducing supplements. Take a few weeks to observe and understand your dog's behavior, preferences, and potential health issues.

Consider scheduling an appointment with your veterinarian to discuss your dog's needs and develop a plan tailored to their quirks and concerns. Many professionals offer consultations online, providing convenient access to expert advice and guidance.

While long-acting serotonin-boosting drugs can be beneficial for traumatized dogs, it's important to wait a few weeks before introducing any medication. Fast-acting drugs can also significantly impact your dog's behavior, potentially leaving them feeling disoriented or out of control. These should not be considered until your dog has had the opportunity to feel safe and secure in your home environment. Remember — always consult with a veterinarian before considering any pharmaceutical interventions.

BOOKMARK

For more information on qualified professionals, supplements, medication, and helpful products like the ThunderShirt and dog-appeasing pheromone (DAP), check out Chapter 5.

Externalizing Your Dog's Focus

Dogs triggered by past events can panic at times that seem uneventful to you. Simple things can remind them of past traumas — someone in a hat, an odor you may not notice, the sound of keys, or boots on the cement. Play the detective as you determine the source of your dog's reaction. In severe cases, a traumatized dog may display aggression if provoked, forced to move, or reprimanded.

To address these behaviors, encourage your dog to seek guidance before reacting. Establish a strong bond and encourage your dog to check in with you so that you can redirect their focus and better manage their responses. The rehabilitation techniques covered in Chapter 10, such as counterconditioning and desensitization, work well in situations like this.

Teach them to watch

One helpful skill is encouraging your dog to check in with you using a word like "watch." Practice these steps in a quiet area in your home first, gradually extending to more distracted rooms, then outside.

1. **Select a treat or toy your dog finds enticing.** Promptly bring it to your dog's attention, then swiftly bring the toy to your eyes to establish eye contact with them. Reward them immediately upon making eye contact.

2. **While holding the treat or toy in one hand, use your other hand to guide your dog's focus using a finger gesture.** Once your dog is focused, say "watch" and deliver the reward from the opposite hand.

3. **If you notice your dog struggling to focus due to distractions, move away from the distraction.** Give them time to settle down as you take a few calming breaths to model relaxation. Once they relax, try to get their focus.

REMEMBER

As you learn throughout this book, space and time are the only things that can rescue your dog when triggered. Food, toys, and even your touch can't reassure them in the moment. First, they need to escape, then give them time to reassess, regroup, and reconnect with you.

Call them back to you

A simple and effective way to reassure your dog when fear takes hold is to teach them a cue that means, "let's evacuate!" When used in a crisis, this cue allows your dog to retreat gracefully from perceived threats rather than become fixated on them. Teach this direction on a leash and in a low-distraction environment before using it in real-time. You can use a treat cup too!

1. **While your dog is preoccupied with sniffing indoors or during a walk, position yourself behind them and call out, "come back!"** As you say this, run back about 10-20 feet.

2. **Turn to face your dog as they respond to your cue and reward them with food, toys, or verbal praise as positive reinforcement.**

3. **Incorporate two to three callback exercises per walk when your dog is calm, reinforcing the behavior so that they understand what is expected of them when triggered.** Remember, all dogs prefer reassurance over reprimand, so approach training with empathy rather than anger.

If they don't respond initially, wave a favorite toy or bait them with yummy food to get their attention before calling out "come back" and running away.

Helping Dogs Play Their Way to Joy

Fun and games are great ways to boost your dog's confidence and bond with them. Most games they'll enjoy depend on their personality and experiences; half the fun is discovering the ones they like best. Chapter 3 covers various games to try with your dog; this section discusses some special rules for playing with traumatized dogs.

Believe in their innate goodness

Dogs are genuine in expressing their emotions; they act happy when they feel joy, display fear when they're afraid, show panic when they feel helpless, and demonstrate frustration when they can't get what they want.

Believe in your dog and trust in their innate goodness. You might be their last chance at a better life. Once they've been given the chance to heal, dogs will often show their gratitude in countless ways that will leave a lasting impact on you.

Support their healing

Play may be uncharted territory if your dog lives without human interaction and love. Discover little things your dog enjoys, whether sniffing along a pathway, dancing on their hind legs, or playing fetch. Allow your dog to win and praise them warmly. When you want to teach them to "drop," prompt them with a treat. Keep the session upbeat and fun and stop playing when your dog loses interest.

WARNING

If your dog panics or becomes anxious during a game, stop and calmly remove them from the source of distress. Provide comfort through synchronized breathing and loving touch; if they relax entirely, you can try massage. Resume playing when your dog initiates a game or returns to a happy mindset.

Check your frustration

There's no room for human aggravation in a traumatized dog's life. Dogs do not understand what triggers our emotional ups and downs and can't connect our outbursts with their behavior. Though a dog might look guilty, that is a look of fear. Your dog looks to you for emotional support, kindness, and consistency; anger terrorizes them further.

If you have a rescue who has experienced trauma, it may initially be hard for them to separate past wounds from their current situation. I call this playing an old record. Feelings of joy and freedom can get clouded by reoccurring memories triggered by unexpected actions or stimuli. Be your dog's anchor — their friend and mentor — as you help them rebuild trust in their new, more stable environment.

Watching the Flower Bloom

I've cherished all dogs: rescues, abandoned puppy mill survivors, purebreds, and fosters. Love knows no boundaries or breed. I can tell you that when you love a dog, sacrifice your time for them, offer patience, and show empathy, few relationships on this planet can compare. Guiding them patiently toward healing is like watching a flower bloom in the desert.

Chapter **10**

Rehabilitating and Training Leash Reactive Dogs

D
ogs have a complicated relationship with leashes. On the one hand, most dogs enjoy the chance to venture outside. On the other hand, leashes are highly restrictive and, if not handled correctly, can be confusing, frustratingly confining, and even painful.

Rehabilitating a leash-reactive dog requires you to assume *less* control, not *more*. The goal is not to dictate your dog's every movement; it's to accompany them on a peaceful stroll or an exciting, enjoyable adventure.

This chapter explains how to use leashes of all sizes and for every purpose, from careful roadside walks to meandering sniff and strolls and free-wheeling romps in open spaces. Most importantly, you learn how to calmly redirect and soothe your dog when triggered by another person, animal, sight, or sound.

Understanding Reactivity

Many dogs behave better when they're off leash — after all, being tethered and forcibly controlled is typically an unpleasant experience! For dogs with anxiety, when their heightened awareness and sensitivities to stimulation pairs with compulsory leash control, the drama or, in some cases, panic quashes all hope of a peaceful outing.

Before the widespread use of leashes, dogs had a free-range lifestyle, with plenty of freedom to roam. They could forge friendships or avoid encounters. When a free-range dog became frighted, they instinctively distanced themselves or ran home. Despite the obvious issues of overpopulation, safety, and disease, dogs cherished their freedom and autonomy.

Fast-forward to today — dogs have transformed into surrogate children. We manage their eating habits, control the duration and route of their on-leash walks, and moderate the intensity of their play. While we've enriched their lives with structure, affection, and companionship, the question remains whether they feel stripped of their innate agency — the very essence of what makes them dogs. No, I'm not proposing that we release our dogs into the wild, but rather that we find ways to replicate the experience of freedom within their structured existence.

FUN FACT

We walk in straight lines, but for dogs, constrained, linear walks are unnatural. They prefer to meander and explore at their own pace. When a dog with anxiety pulls away or resists, continuous leash pressure increases their stress. Fortunately, there is an easier way.

Identifying Your Dog's Leash Personality

Take a moment to reflect on your dog's current relationship with their leash. Consider the postures covered in this section, which can help you understand your dog's emotions during your walks.

Fearful

Fearful dogs often resist walking too far from home, stopping frequently and refusing to move on. They may startle to unpredicted sights and sounds as well. Too often, people label these dogs stubborn; they yank on their dog's leash and get loud and frustrated. This poor dog is experiencing emotional abandonment, which increases their fears, sometimes to the point of panic. The result is that the dog's distress and generalized anxiety increase. Other signals include scanning the environment with their ears back and wide pupils. Tails are either tight to the body or low. Their tails may even wag — a sign of stress in this circumstance.

Frustrated

Frustration results from being caught between something your dog wants to explore but can't. This could be a desire to interact with another dog or person. Dogs who get frustrated stare intently at what they desire, often swiftly wagging their tails in excitement, vocalizing, rearing up, and pulling incessantly.

Angry

Dogs can get angry when they feel their personal space is being invaded. Their hair will stand up as they lean forward, tails erect. They might vocalize furiously at the object of their aggravation. Sometimes, these dogs will displace their frustration on another dog or on a person standing near them.

Predatory

On leash, predatory dogs constantly scan for things to hunt, pulling with force when they notice a prey animal. Their awareness is focused on the world around them as they are preoccupied with hunting. They are hard to focus on and often tense and aroused.

Cooperative

These dogs walk comfortably, engaging with their person and environment. The leash is held loosely with a soft tension, reassuring them to slow down and stay connected. Their ears flicker, displaying awareness of their surroundings and their person's movements, although they may be more focused on their person than the world around them.

Assessing Your Walking Style

This section discusses your role in these leashed excursions. Whether your dog stops dead in their tracks or is frantically pulling or running for home, you may also have a part to play in these anxious outings. Consider which of the following categories describes your outings:

>> **Dog walks person:** People laugh at the question, "Who is walking who?" but some dogs become so overwhelmed by sensory stimuli that their behavior shifts from being intensely excited when encountering squirrels and other animals to becoming extremely fearful or anxious, especially in response to loud noises and sudden or triggering stimuli.

Some people allow their dogs full agency to explore on a leash or flexi-leash. However, this pleasant experience can take a turn for the worse when encountering other people or dogs, especially off-leash ones. Dogs with anxiety often try to avoid face-to-face interactions and display calming signals (outlined in Chapter 2) to prevent confrontation. As a result, dogs may suffer while their people socialize, often leading to scuffles due to ignorance rather than aggression.

>> **Dogs on a march:** This person walks their dog in formation. Obedience is important for this group, and when challenged by their dog, they often resort to tools like prongs or e-collars to enforce compliance. As they are expected to conform to the person's idea of a good dog, constant corrections for unfocused behavior end the dog's autonomy. These demands increase a dog's anxiety.

>> **The multitasking outings:** Some people multitask while walking their dogs, casually holding the end of the leash or a retractable leash as they chat with friends on the phone or scroll through social media feeds. From the dog's perspective, lacking any clear direction or engagement, they become more attuned to the surrounding world. For dogs with anxiety, this is nerve-wracking. When forced too close to triggers, behaviors such as freezing, barking at strangers, and leash lunging become pastimes. As this dramatic behavior gets attention, their anxiety is reinforced.

>> **The communicative walk:** This is the ideal way to walk your dog. This excursion is more about enriching your dog's

experience and sharing time together. When possible, using a longer leash, ranging from 10 to 30 feet, grants your dog a sense of freedom while ensuring their safety. These walks encourage two-way communication, with your dog referencing you versus reacting to various situations. Later, this chapter explains how to craft this style of leash walking.

WARNING

Avoid using neck collars when working with a dog who has anxiety or hyperarousal. They're stressed enough without the added discomfort of being strangled or poked with prongs.

Starting with Preliminary Exercises

Before you can help your dog manage their fears and frustrations, you need to shift their focus to a happier interaction. While many dogs may become excited upon seeing the leash, eagerly racing out the door and charging through their walk, this enthusiasm doesn't always translate to a love for the leash. For these dogs, the leash symbolizes freedom from enclosure rather than togetherness, often resulting in a walk that lacks a shared experience. By associating the leash with freedom and fun, you can strengthen the bond between you and your dog, leading to countless enjoyable outings exploring the world together.

Reintroduce the leash

Out with the old habits, in with the new! To create new associations with the leash, start at the very beginning.

1. **Fit your dog for a harness; the best choice is one that offers both a front clip option and a back clip.**

WARNING

Choosing the right harness is all about the fit. It's essential to ensure that it doesn't interfere with your dog's natural movements or gait. I opt for step-in harnesses or one with no more than three to four straps. If your dog has not been fitted for a harness, ask a knowledgeable friend or pet care professional for help.

2. **Show your dog the harness and leash; reward them with treats and attention as they smell it.** When ready to place the harness on your dog, sit or stand beside them. Approaching them head-on can seem threatening. Use a

spreadable treat, like peanut butter, on the floor or on a licky mat, or ask a helper to distract them with treats. Slowly clip and unclip the clasp (does the sound frighten your dog?).

If your dog is okay with the sound, proceed to maneuver their legs through the openings. If at any point your dog stops to look back, stop. Proceed only if they turn back to the treat. Go at your dog's pace; getting your dog comfortable wearing the harness may take days. You lessen their anxiety by going at their pace. Flip to Chapter 3 and use the Operation Cooperation game if your dog struggles with transitions. Break the act into smaller steps, rewarding as you go, until your dog is happy to see their harness.

3. **Begin inside using a dragging leash, which you can create by cutting the end loop off a lightweight four-foot leash (to prevent it from getting caught).** When you can supervise, and only when you can supervise them, attach the lead to the back clip of your dog's harness and let them drag around behind them. Throughout that time, when they approach you for a snack or attention, pick up the leash gradually, for longer periods (one to ten seconds), then let it go and reward them.

4. **Still inside, pick up the leash and hold it loosely as you follow them around.** Any time they look to you, mark that moment with a word like "yes!" or a click from the clicker, then reward them with a treat. Practice following them for 20-second to 5-minute increments and end with a favorite game. Finally, unclip the leash and disengage from any fun activity for five minutes. Leash equals fun time and treats!

If your dog is too fixated on food rewards, mix in praise and use marking and treats for periodic reinforcement.

WARNING

5. **After following them about four-six times, your dog should enjoy the interaction. Still work inside and now practice calling them to follow you.** Continue to reinforce their cooperation with praise and treats. Your goal is a loose leash walk. Avoid dragging or jerking them even if they don't cooperate. Remember, from Chapter 3, the importance of calling in the direction you want them to follow instead of staring them down or repeating yourself. Use other words, too, like sit, watch, wait, and stay. If your dog freezes, stop with them, but don't look back to coax them. As you wait for

them, you can pretend to eat their treats or play Find It. When they approach, take a few steps forward before letting them in on the game.

6. **Now you're ready to go outside; begin working in an open environment with few distractions, swapping out your inside leash for a longer one.** Use 10 to 30 feet, as it gives your dog slack to explore. Go back to Step 5, simply following their lead and rewarding them for checking in with you. Log five to ten minutes of this routine before showering them with affection, play, or an adventure.

7. **Continue in a low-distraction area and begin using a shorter, six- to ten-foot leash as you direct them with familiar directions.** Call them back to you, encourage them to sit and watch, play some of the learning games, and use treats, praise, and loving pats to reward them.

8. **Before returning to normal walks, infuse leash time with a little fun.** You can even play games when your dog feels overstimulated.

TIP

An adventure for a dog with anxiety is relative and should be tailored to your individual dog's sensitivities. Do they love playing with other dogs? If so, find some trustworthy dogs and create a playgroup! Do they love a car ride? Many dogs do! Do they prefer people over dogs or love a solitary excursion with their favorite person? You know best what makes your dog happy.

Good form

As you work with your dog, remember that all animals, including humans, have an innate freedom reflex. It's the instinct to pull away from a tight grip. If someone were to grab your sleeve and pull forcefully, you would naturally jerk away and likely feel frustrated. Your adrenaline and cortisol levels would also skyrocket.

A dog's freedom reflex is severe. It is triggered when people grab them by their neck, jerk them on a leash, or hold them against their will. When this happens on a leash, dogs with anxiety become more stressed, often resorting to freezing or pulling to escape without any means to manage or calm themselves. If their efforts fail, they may resort to defensive aggression as a final attempt to distance themselves from the trigger. The only remedy for the constant tug-of-war is practicing a loose leash walk.

Before heading out on your next leash walk, take some time to familiarize yourself with the various types of leashes and the proper way to hold them. Understanding the correct form and knowing which tools suit different situations can greatly improve your walking experience.

Loose leash walking

The best way to walk with your dog is side-by-side and at a pace that works for both of you. Avoid a taut leash where you're being dragged by your dog or vice versa. Picture it like keeping a "smile" in the leash — a gentle curve indicates a lack of tension (see Figure 10-1). This form encourages your dog to walk comfortably by your side without feeling restrained or pressured.

Relaxed arms
Loose hand grip
Confident posture
Loose leash

© John Wiley & Sons

FIGURE 10-1: Loose leash walking.

Longlines

A *longline* is the ultimate long-distance learning tool. It's 30 to 50 feet long (see Figure 10-2). These leads allow your dog the freedom to play, meander, run, and explore to their heart's content while still allowing you to maintain control and ensure safety. Longlines allow you to work on distance control as you explore the world together.

© John Wiley & Sons

FIGURE 10-2: Longline.

Socialize on leash

Allowing dogs to socialize on a leash requires enough leeway to prevent stress. A ten-foot leash is ideal to prevent tangling. While being held on a short leash can create tension and inhibit natural posturing, a longer leash held slack will facilitate positive interactions, allowing dogs to approach or retreat at will. See Figure 10-3.

© John Wiley & Sons

FIGURE 10-3: Socializing on leash.

Leash games

Helping your dog love their leash requires food, fun, and companionship! The games discussed in this section make leash walking more enjoyable, reinforcing that walking together is a mutual adventure.

If you have a new dog or puppy, get a jump start on your walking skills. A lot of anxiety reveals itself at the end of the leash — the constant dragging, raising the levels of cortisol and adrenaline, and frightening realities of navigating a world they can't always comprehend.

TIP

If your dog is too nervous to focus in your neighborhood, take them to an open field, work on a longline, or start inside, where your dog feels safest.

>> **Hurry, Hurry:** Starting inside, grab a handful of treats and race across the floor as you say, "hurry, hurry." Let your dog choose to follow or watch you. If they follow (most do), toss a treat or two before you, prompting them by saying, "find it." Bring the game outside on a leash, practicing in a familiar area before using it around distractions.

>> **Callbacks:** Turn or walk backward 10 to 20 feet as you call your dog to back to you. Praise, pet, treat, or play a fun game to celebrate your togetherness.

>> **Crossovers:** Position yourself between your dog and any distractions using high-value treats to encourage your dog to ignore the distraction. Pass the leash behind you and cross your dog over to the opposite side of the sidewalk or street, ignoring triggers and reinforcing positive behavior. Apply the crossover technique for any distracting elements on the street to ensure your dog feels safe.

>> **Turnabouts:** When walking your dog, the goal is to keep their attention on you rather than worrying about the world around them. Initially, practice these turns before your dog gets distracted. Use your dog's name to alert them to your changing direction, and "wait," "watch," and "find it" before rewarding them. Avoid surprising them and jerking the leash; this is too startling. Call their name, shake a treat cup, slap your thigh, and do what you can to cue them toward change. Gradually call them away from distractions, starting with low-level distractions and moving to higher ones. Once your dog gets the game, increase the number of turns between rewards and phase-off, luring their attention.

>> **Silly Circles:** With your dog on a leash, call their name and turn away from them as you spin in gradually expanding circles. Give your dog as much leash as they'll take, and after a few turns, toss treats out and say, "find it."

The Silly Circles game can make you dizzy!

>> **Walking Squares:** This is another great way to excite your dog to follow you. It's a great warm-up before heading out for a walk. Walk in random square patterns, making crisp turns away from (not into) your dog as you call out their name. Reward your dog at unpredictable intervals, making the warm-up and the occasional walking square variable and fun.

KEYWORDS

This recap summarizes the keywords you'll find useful when helping your dog. If the brief descriptions here aren't enough to jog your memory, refer to Chapter 3 for detailed instructions.

Yes!: This one marks when your dog makes a good choice, such as turning away from something that triggers them or checking in with you. Another unique sound or a clicker can also mark moments.

Find It: Tossing treats on the floor is a great way to engage your dog while being anatomically correct (dogs are supposed to eat with their heads down) and to discourage jumping. A win-win is a great way to redirect your dog when they're aroused.

Follow: When you call your dog to follow, encourage them to change direction with you and follow your lead.

Wait: Teaches your dog to stop, look, and listen for another cue.

Sit: This is another great anchoring cue, and one that can be used to focus your dog in a moment. If your dog doesn't, respond that indicates you're too close to their trigger.

Watch: Encourages your dog to check in, reestablishing your connection.

Come Back: When out on a leash walk or practicing on a longline, your dog may be alert to a distraction. Cheerfully calling them back to you offers them a choice — get all in a huff or run back to their person and have some fun.

Settle: This instruction can calm your dog after they recover from an upsetting experience. Keep them at your side and stroke or massage them comfortingly.

Treat-Retreat and Parcourse are two additional games that work wonders for leash walking. See Chapter 3 for detailed explanations.

Since leash training is a treat-intensive project, buy a handy snack pouch. It's like an external pocket, so your treats will be easy to access.

Knowing What to Do When Your Dog Is Triggered

The goal is to help your dog process what's upsetting them and reference you rather than react. With the right mindset, this can be a fun process. Keep in mind that there are only two things you can do when your dog gets reactive on leash:

>> Distance them from whatever has their attention until they disengage.

>> Give them time to calm down. Some dogs calm quickly, within 30 seconds, while others may need three to five minutes to regain their composure.

Record each experience

Don't forget to log each experience in your behavior diary. Use it to track progress and note patterns in your dog's reactivity and responsiveness. Use the questions in this section and key details as you analyze your dog's progress. For a sample entry and access to a downloadable behavior diary, visit SarahHodgson.com.

What triggers your dog on walks?

>> Seeing people

>> Seeing people with dogs

>> Hearing or seeing children

>> Loud trucks or unfamiliar noises

>> Weather events

>> Unexpected motion or stimuli (e.g., bicycles, cars, skateboards)

How does your dog typically react when encountering these triggers?

» Freezes and stares

» Freezes and swivels head, looking away

» Ignores verbal cues and treat offerings

» Barks or growls at the trigger with ears pinned back

» Barks or growls at the trigger with ears and body leaning forward

» Retreats on leash; tries to run home

» Pulls on leash toward the trigger, such as lunging at a dog or trying to chase a car

» Whines or whimpers

» Cowers and tucks their tail

Is there a certain area where your dog is more reactive on a leash?

» Your neighborhood

» Daycare or veterinarian

» Sidewalks or roads

» City environments

» Rural areas — woods, fields, beaches, and so on

» All of the above

Is there a certain time of day your dog is more reactive on leash?

» Morning, before or after breakfast

» Midday

» Evening

» All of the above

BOOKMARK

Chapter 2 explains red zones, safe zones, and turning points. Review that information and remain mindful of each boundary during your leash exercises.

Consider triggers from your dog's perspective

Dogs with anxiety often freeze during walks. They may hear a sound in the distance that startles them, see another dog that you don't notice, or encounter any number of triggering events that are unnoticed by you.

I recall Taylor, a Newfoundland mix recently rescued from a shelter. During his walks, his people mentioned that he often froze and refused to move. Given his size, this presented quite a conundrum as they had to coordinate to coax him back home, sometimes pulling his collar, staring at him, or attempting to pull him along, all to no avail.

My approach with Taylor differed, and I recommend it to everyone facing similar situations. Instead of offering treats (which he would have likely rejected), we pretended to eat them ourselves. While maintaining a calm demeanor, we also engaged in synchronized breathing, taking deep breaths to help soothe his nerves. As we tuned in to the environment, we noticed various sounds: dogs barking in the background, passing garbage trucks, and crying babies.

After sitting quietly with Taylor for several minutes, we calmly changed direction and started walking away. After only 5 to 10 yards, we encouraged him to explore a patch of grass where we had scattered treats for him to find. Following this simple technique, which took mere minutes, we engaged in some slow, playful circles before continuing our walk.

By taking the time to understand the world from Taylor's perspective and letting go of demands that intensified his anxiety, we gradually helped him overcome his fears over a few months. Today, he's transformed into one of the most fearless, joyful, and affectionate dogs imaginable!

Soothing Your Dog's Leash Reactivity

Be sure to note the distances between the red and safe zones and to recognize the specific triggers that cause an on-leash disturbance in your behavior diary. Begin working at a safe distance, where they still see and are fully aware of their trigger.

Helping your dog feel comfortable in the presence of disturbances, such as another dog or traffic, begins with preventing the following unavoidable situations:

>> **Startle effect:** This happens when a dog with anxiety is caught off guard by the things they dread. Prevention is best; should this happen, retreat quickly, and when you're back in their safe zone, refocus their attention with affection, food, or play.

>> **Magnetic factor:** When dogs with anxiety are thrust up close to a trigger, they often lunge forward. This is a high-energy fight response from the sympathetic nervous system: fight, flight, or flee. Act quickly to retreat, as you do not want to practice a reaction you do not want them to repeat.

FUN FACT

Many people assume their dog is acting to protect them. For dogs with anxiety, this is never the case. Their reactions stem from fear, an internalized state of self-preservation.

Desensitization

Desensitization, as you learned in Chapter 5, involves helping your dog feel more comfortable in the presence of a trigger. Regardless of what upsets them, find a location you can observe from a distance while handling them on a loose leash. Here are some helpful tips:

>> **When possible, work on a longer leash, one that's 10 to 30 feet.** This can reduce stress and allow more natural exploration and movement.

>> **Practice an activity known as *groundwork*.** Before bringing your dog out to an observation point, place discoverable objects, like treat pouches, enrichment activities, favorite toys, and obstacles, out for your dog to discover while their trigger is off in the distance. Groundwork is explained fully in Chapter 3.

>> **Engage with your dog by playing games and using word cues they're familiar with.** Follow, wait, sit, stay, and watch are great cues for walking.

>> **Play the I Spy game, marking the moments they look to distant triggers and rewarding them when they look back.** For more details, flip to the "Thinking games" section of Chapter 3.

>> **Operation Cooperation is another game outlined in Chapter 3 that can work wonders as you desensitize your dog to distractions.**

>> **As your dog grows more comfortable interacting with you and engaging with the environment at a distance, practice on your everyday six-foot leash.**

>> **Gradually move closer to their trigger as you continue the lessons and games.** If your dog becomes too preoccupied with their trigger, move back until they feel more comfortable.

Counterconditioning

Counterconditioning is another important step in easing your dog's leash anxiety. This involves changing your dog's perception of the fear-inducing stimuli, encouraging them to reference you rather than react in the moment.

Consider a dog who is anxious about encountering other dogs on leash walks. This fear may arise from a lack of socialization or a past negative experience. Regardless, their initial reaction often comes from feeling restrained or forced against their will to engage with the very thing they fear.

Your new approach involves these steps:

1. **Acknowledge your dog's fear by maintaining distance from other dogs.**
2. **Use desensitizing paired with counterconditioning by engaging their mind and interacting with them at a safe distance.**
3. **Redirect their focus to toys, movement, and referencing you instead of reacting to the trigger.**

Let your dog know that you're doing this together and that you respect their anxiety. Dogs, like people, aren't perfect.

Handling Life's Unavoidable Situations

Life can be unpredictable, and your dog may encounter unexpected challenges or setbacks. I recall walking my pit-bull-boxer mix, Wahoo, on a leash in the woods; an off-leash dog bounded onto the trail and attacked him. It deeply frightened my sweet, gentle giant.

Despite avoiding injury, thanks to my spray deterrent, which I carried just for such incidents, he grew anxious about seeing other dogs on our outings. When another dog approached, he became aggressive. Most often, I could distance myself from the other dogs, but sometimes, I could not. To avoid his overreacting and practicing a pattern I did not want him to repeat, I muzzled him on our walks during the rehabilitation process.

It's essential to be prepared for such situations and have a plan. Be prepared to jump into action as you help navigate unforeseen challenges and ensure safer outings.

REMEMBER

Remember that leash training isn't about control but having a safe, shared experience with your dog. By engaging with your dog and crafting a fun experience, you'll promote a reciprocal dialogue on both ends of the leash.

4

Helping a Dog with Social Anxiety

IN THIS CHAPTER

» **Understanding social anxiety from your dog's perspective**

» **Recognizing how your dog looks when they experience anxiety**

» **Identifying your dog's triggers**

» **Building a toolkit to help your dog**

» **Using counterconditioning and desensitization to ease your dog's fears**

Chapter **11**

Easing Your Dog's Fear of People

This chapter focuses on dogs who experience anxiety around people. Whether it's a friendly visitor, a passerby, or professionals like veterinarians or groomers, these encounters can trigger a spiral of distress for dogs with social anxiety. What these dogs need most is an advocate, and that advocate can be you!

The Origins of Social Anxiety

Dogs are naturally social animals; they thrive in communities. When you bring a dog into your home, you become part of their group. Social anxiety in dogs can arise from a variety of factors. Some dogs are born with more sensitive dispositions, while others may be particularly affected by their day-to-day interactions. Studies suggest that through confidence-building exercises, shy puppies can learn to overcome their hesitancies. On the other hand, under-socialized or neglected puppies, regardless of their inherent temperament, may develop social anxiety at an early stage.

A UNITED FRONT

One of the biggest challenges for dogs with anxiety is our inconsistencies. We tower over even the largest dogs, often approaching with the direct swiftness of a predator, and while some dogs become conditioned to our effusiveness, many don't. Good manners start at home, so remind everyone, including strangers and friends, to approach your dog at an angle, sit or kneel to pat them, and keep their hands below their chin rather than looming over them and trying to pet the top of their head.

Another confusion involves inconsistent expectations. Confusion sets in when one person encourages their dog to jump up during greetings while another family member shouts and pushes them aside. This dog won't know how to handle visitors and friends — should they jump up joyfully or steer clear of each new person they meet? Anxiety often sets in.

A united front is easiest for your dog's emotional well-being. There are limited hours in a day and only so many boundaries to enforce, so come together, make a list, and enforce it lovingly. Simple changes can have an immediate impact.

Contributing factors

There are many contributing factors to the development of canine anxiety:

>> The well-being and health of the mother dog

>> Limited experiences and lack of broad social interactions during the dog's early imprinting phase

>> Punitive or rough handling during play or training sessions

>> Unsupervised interactions with children

>> Exposure to random threats from strangers or caregivers when their people are absent

>> Illness leading to a prolonged hospital stay

>> Extended boarding during a period of fear-impression or critical socialization phase

Like young children, dogs are highly influenced by their early experiences. However, unlike children, who can receive therapy, dogs are often left to navigate their world independently. Without nurturing guidance and someone who understands and interprets their emotions, a puppy's anxiety can escalate as they transition into adulthood. Luckily, they have you!

Early missteps

There are a few common missteps even the most loving households make that can impact their dog's social anxiety. In many households, the excitement of bringing home a new puppy, or even an older dog, builds for weeks, if not months. However, adoption day can be a mix of joy for us and apprehension or sadness for the dog or puppy. The puppy is leaving behind everything they've ever known, especially their littermates with whom they've slept, eaten, played, and wrestled since birth, as well as their mother, who has nurtured them from the moment they entered the world. A dog may be leaving behind a foster family, loving shelter staff, or a free-range lifestyle. While that realization may tug at your heartstrings, it's the reality of adoption.

Once home, there will be days (and nights) of acclimating. Puppies, unlike older dogs, don't do much more than eat, poop, and sleep for the first few weeks. Dogs need to learn the rhythm of your lifestyle and acclimate to your routines.

FUN FACT

Young puppies need up to 20 hours of uninterrupted sleep daily. Their brains are still developing and will continue to develop into adulthood.

In the best-case scenario, each new family member is patient and calm. They give their new dog or puppy time to learn the ropes and establish a sleep routine to ensure safe and comforting rest.

However, sometimes people don't understand the needs and sensitivities of their new canine family members. They make mistakes that can lead to social stress. Don't be discouraged if you've done any of these things; you can still help your dog trust people. It's important to understand where things may have gone awry:

>> **Overstimulation:** When a new dog arrives home, people are often excited, but the dog can quickly become overwhelmed by the new sights, sounds, and smells.

Many people find it hard to resist constantly interacting with their new dog. However, it is important to give them time and space to acclimate and let them rest when needed.

>> **Leash pulling and rough handling:** One of the first things you may try is fitting your new dog with a collar, leash, or harness. Dogs have a life-sustaining oppositional reflex, viewing any physical constraint as threatening, so initially, this can be traumatizing, especially for puppies.

>> **Prey animal mentality:** Until a puppy is around five to six months old and has been properly leash trained, they may not want to stray far from home. Puppies lack muscle development and hormones and have tiny, porous teeth, making them vulnerable prey animals. In the event of anything alarming, their instinct is to run back home, not necessarily to their person. Puppies undergo fear-impression periods, as discussed in Appendix A, which can make forced excursions terrifying for them. It's important not to force a puppy or dog to walk where they do not want to; their reluctance may be a sign of being overwhelmed or scared.

>> **Admonishing:** Do not admonish a dog or puppy. Routinely getting frustrated with your dog can lead to stress and generalized anxiety. Remember, dogs do not naturally know how to behave in our homes; it's our responsibility to teach them. It's much easier for dogs to learn what to do rather than be corrected for what *not* to do. For training tips and problem-solving strategies, see Chapter 3.

>> **Anthropomorphic interactions:** Humans are the only animals who view face-to-face greetings, toothy grins, dialogue, and tight physical contact as cheerful. We convey joy through enthusiasm, which is good if you're talking to another person, but dogs (and many other mammals) can find these overtures terrifying. Dogs never come face to face unless they are fighting; hugs can be predatory and confining; effusiveness is playful; and a toothy grin can be terrifying. Even for people who claim their dogs love these greetings, I'd argue against letting a stranger approach them this way (see Figure 11-1)!

© John Wiley & Sons

FIGURE 11-1: The right way vs. wrong way to approach a dog.

Understanding Your Dog's Social Anxiety

Not all dogs love all people, just as you probably don't gravitate toward everyone you meet. But not jibing with a stranger is different from feeling dysregulated and physically upset in the presence of unfamiliar people or terrified by the sight of someone in a hat or uniform.

Before easing your dog's social anxiety, assessing their triggers is important. Some dogs fear everyone, while others are haunted by memories of individuals who may have wronged them. If your dog is afraid of someone, even you, at times, it is for a good reason, although you might not always understand their motivations.

What does social anxiety look like?

When dogs sense danger, their bodies release adrenaline and cortisol, alerting them to stress and providing a jolt of energy. Left on their own, dogs will try to distance themselves from whatever is triggering their anxiety. Their goal is to avoid the threat to survive. When they're prevented from escaping, such as when they are leashed or enclosed, they'll assume postures or take desperate actions to defend themselves. This can include barking aggressively, growling, or even biting, especially when their early cues of discomfort are ignored.

Postures to look for include:

>> Tucking their tail between their legs

>> Pinning their ears back

>> Cowering or hunching

>> Avoiding eye contact

>> Rolling onto their back and exposing the underside and belly

>> Yawning or lip licking

>> Panting or drooling excessively

>> Showing whale eye (showing the whites of their eyes)

>> Trembling or shaking

>> Pacing or restlessness

>> Excessive barking or growling

Signs of escalation

When a dog fears a person's approach or interaction, and their avoidant signals are misunderstood or ignored, their fear can intensify into panic. Recall the sympathetic nervous system's fight, flight, or freeze response. Dogs who are fearful of people may first try to avoid engagement by fleeing or freezing, but if that doesn't yield a response, escalation may follow.

Just before they lash out, their bodies will tense up and become rigid, like a person flexing their jaw or muscles. Dogs fixate on the body part they intend to bite, signaling their intentions. While some dogs issue a warning growl, others may not, and the bite can happen swiftly if the growl or posturing is ignored. Since dogs communicate their emotions through body language and behavior, it's crucial to recognize such signs early and take appropriate action.

REMEMBER

Dogs bite people only when their initial signals are overlooked. By becoming more aware of your dog's sensitivities, you can significantly reduce the likelihood of dog bites.

Why sustained direct eye contact can confuse your dog

People are the only animals that view prolonged face-to-face staring as normal. Dogs often perceive direct staring as confrontation or an invitation to play rough. When a person focuses on your dog excitedly (often in the hopes of greeting, petting, or even hugging them) or your dog fixates on someone, the mood can shift from social engagement to stress and suspicion. Here are a few examples of how this comes into play with social anxiety:

>> Admirers and well-intentioned pet care professionals routinely stare at dogs in the hopes of winning them over, often grabbing or continuing to approach even as the dog is trying to back away.

>> Loving people often mistake their dogs for stuffed animals, especially children. By routinely interrupting sleep, quiet time, chewing activities, and feeding rituals, a dog or puppy can quickly become anxious when caring for their everyday needs and leery of social interactions.

> » Many people still believe in punitive, harsh punishment for what they perceive as bad or spiteful behavior. This is devastating for dogs suffering from anxiety. Their connection to people is often their only bridge to safety. When the people they trust suddenly and often without warning turn against them, their stress levels rise, and they grow wary of people's shifting moods.

> » Unsocialized dogs are especially wary of human interaction and quick to read a head-on approach as threatening. People are often completely oblivious to a dog's social cues, only exacerbating the issue.

REMEMBER

At the heart of your dog is one who longs to feel safe. In your dog's mind, their behavior is neither good nor bad; it's just a way to release the energy that builds up in their daily interactions with people. What you pay attention to is what you reinforce: If you don't want your dog to bark, think, what could my dog do instead?

There are two times dogs with anxiety will return a loving gaze:

> » When a trusted person is calm and provides undivided attention, dogs with anxiety often fall into a sleepy, loving gaze. When you pair your gaze with slow blinks, deep breaths, and gentle massage, you'll help to soothe your frazzled nerves.

> » Another time is when your dog enters a room and stares at you. When my dogs do this, I envision them saying, "What's next?" or "I'm bored." While we need to teach our dogs that sometimes we're present but not accessible, it's ideal to redirect them to a toy or activity.

WARNING

Of course, if you think they're prompting a bathroom break, attend to that immediately.

Assessing Your Dog's Condition

Before starting your dog's social rehabilitation, assess which category of anxiety they suffer from, as your rehabilitation plan will be tailored accordingly.

Dogs with *specific anxiety* are friendly and calm around most people but get anxious or act out in certain situations, such as when the delivery person approaches or during visits to the veterinarian or groomer. Certain sensory stimulations can also trigger anxiety, like seeing a person in a hat, smelling cigarette smoke on clothing, or hearing a chain. Another scenario under this classification is when a friendly dog becomes agitated or loses composure when an overly excitable friend comes over, determined to win the dog's affection.

Dogs with *universal anxiety* experience discomfort around all people except a select few. They may even fear certain members of their household. When forced to socialize or live in a busy household, these dogs often associate other non-stressful activities with seeing people, leading to the development of generalized anxiety that pervades their day. Related events may even trigger phobias, such as car rides, traffic, or even walks in general.

FUN FACT

Many dogs are nervous around men, especially if they do not live with them. To a dog, a man is a walking plume of testosterone — they can smell our hormones even better than they can perceive our features — which may seem suspect or threatening.

Identify the triggers and your dog's reaction

Now is the time to whip out your behavior diary and start recording each social interaction that involves your dog. Keep track of factors like the following ones and chart your dog's progress throughout the rehabilitation process.

Who triggers your dog's anxiety?

>> People wearing hats, glasses, or hoodies
>> A certain family member
>> Strangers
>> A pet sitter
>> Other dogs or pets
>> Delivery people or workers

Where is your dog most afraid?

>> At the window

>> At the door

>> The whole house

>> In unfamiliar environments

>> In crowded places

>> In confined spaces

When is your dog most afraid?

>> In the morning

>> In the afternoon

>> In the evening

You may have circumstances that aren't listed here. Add them to the list and be reassured that many of the rehabilitation rules are universal.

If you think your dog might bite

If you feel your dog might bite someone, inside or outside your home, muzzle them. Studies show that if your dog has bitten someone, they will likely bite again. Preventing the severity and frequency of your dog's reactions is critical. Wearing a muzzle protects possible victims and your dog, as dogs who cause damage repeatedly may be forcibly euthanized. At the very least, such attacks can be costly, as state laws and insurance companies have steep consequences for reports of even mild dog bite cases.

Start by attaching the straps for short periods and engaging your dog in activities like massage, nose work, or fun tricks. Then, gradually increase wearing time. Redirect any pawing or fussing with frozen treats or games.

BOOKMARK

Muzzle training is covered in detail in Chapter 5.

Three-fourths of reported dog bites happen to children under 20 years of age. Why? Because kids are impulsive and have a harder time understanding a dog's boundaries and distancing cues.

WARNING

TO HUG OR NOT TO HUG

As humans, we're adept at the art of hugging. It's a universal symbol of love that we often extend to our pets. However, many dogs aren't keen on this gesture, viewing hugs as more confrontational than comforting. You can generally discern a non-hugger from their demeanor when approaching them: A dog will stiffen up, avoid eye contact, or even issue a warning growl. If your dog isn't the hugging type, don't take it personally and let other people know — there could be various reasons for their discomfort, such as past trauma or sensitivity to restraint. Whatever their reason, respect it. If your dog exhibits growling behavior, seeking professional help is crucial. There are many other ways to show affection to your dog, from soothing, loving pats to discovering activities and games they love.

By the same token, refrain from approaching someone's dog without permission and never hug a dog you don't know. Teach your children these same guidelines.

Recognize and respect your dog's limits

One of the biggest mistakes I see in my private practice is people ignoring or disrespecting their dog's boundaries. Although a dog won't verbalize their stress, they are always communicating. Refer to the postures explained in Chapter 2 if you need a refresher. If, when working with your dog, you sense that they're distressed, move them out of triggering situations or distance from them if they're uncomfortable with your proximity. Remain calm until they regain their composure. You can then redirect them with a game or other activities.

Exploring Rehabilitation Techniques

Now that you know the details of your dog's condition, it's time to prepare the tools you'll need to help them. Make a list of all the things your dog loves most, starting with favorite treats and toys, then moving on to games, cues, and activities (like sniffing or jumping up and over obstacles). These will come in handy when you try out the rehabilitation techniques.

Treats and toys

Like people, dogs respond well to incentives! Since you can't offer them money, entice them with high-quality food rewards. If your dog is a picky eater, try warming up some turkey or hotdogs to see if they pique their interest.

Toys are another excellent source of comfort for your dog. Some dogs adore plush toys, while others prefer rubber chews or braided ropes. You likely already know what your dog loves — most dogs have a favorite toy they cherish.

Games

BOOKMARK

There is no better way to associate people with positive interactions than to pair the sight of them with fun and games. Chapter 3 details how to play them, but here are my top five games to use as you socialize your dog with people:

>> Find It and Jackpot Find It

>> I Spy

>> Operation Cooperation

>> Treat-Retreat

>> Groundwork

Be your dog's social director

As you work near and around people, your dog's anxiety may sky-rocket. When you sense their distress, use familiar words to help organize their thoughts and actions. Keeping a line of dialogue open between you and your dog is critical. Remember that your dog will communicate visibly through posture and movement. While they may occasionally yip, bark, or grumble, their auditory cues generally happen after their visual displays are overlooked.

Use the words you've taught them to clarify where they should go and what they should do when they get triggered. If you need help teaching your dog your dog these directions, see Chapter 3.

>> "Get your toy"

>> "Come back"

>> "Sit and watch"

- >> "Follow"
- >> "Wait"
- >> "Down and stay"
- >> "Place"

Try medication or supplements

BOOKMARK

Use anything that can safely alleviate your dog's anxiety, from anxiety wraps to supplements to prescription meds. These options are explored in Chapter 5. Always discuss medical options with your veterinarian to support your behavior modification efforts.

Counterconditioning and desensitizing

If your dog's social anxiety is triggered by specific events like visiting their veterinarian or groomer, addressing it will be more straightforward than if your dog has generalized anxiety. Either way, you'll rely on these two trusted techniques to help your dog develop more positive associations when seeing people both inside and outside your home.

REMEMBER

Before you begin, identify your dog's red zone, safe zone, and turning point. Recall that the *red zone* is the area around a person or people where your dog shows signs of distress. The *safe zone* is the distance from a person or people where your dog might be curious but doesn't feel threatened. The *turning point* is the boundary where your dog shifts their focus from you or the world around them to their trigger.

Desensitization, as outlined in Chapter 5, involves exposing your dog to people at a distance that does not trigger them (their safe zone). By creating a list of specific social triggers, such as the sound of a man's voice, the sight and vibration of boots, or a toddler's shriek, your desensitization process can target individual triggers, gradually building your dog's confidence to face what to you seems to be a normal interaction.

TIP

Before you begin the rehabilitation process, pack yourself like a piñata, filling your pockets (or treat pouch) with your dog's favorite food rewards (hot dogs, boiled chicken, turkey, etc.), as well as any special toys and chews — anything that helps them associate seeing people with their favorite things.

Counterconditioning works in tandem by pairing positive rewards and interactions with whatever triggers your dog in social interactions or events. The magic cure comes from determining how far away from frightening situations you need to be for your dog to feel comforted enough to engage with you and welcome the food.

Restructure people's interactions with your dog

You are your dog's only advocate; they rely on you for guidance and support. Dealing with your dog's fears may seem challenging, but remember, they won't be as difficult to manage as the people around you. Whether your dog is fearful of people some or all the time, it's essential to meet them where they are and acknowledge that their fears are real to them. Help them reevaluate their fears and work toward developing a new, more positive outlook in each social interaction with people.

Set boundaries

While I'm not the most passionate football fan, let's consider a football metaphor: Picture your dog as the quarterback and you as their lineman, the one who shields the quarterback from incoming attacks. It's wise to view life from your dog's perspective — especially when interacting with people, as they often feel like they're under attack. Setting boundaries for your dog is your responsibility; you're their lineman! Try these tips:

>> **Bring your dog behind you:** Calmly tell your dog to "come back" or "stay" as you step in between them and whoever is triggering them. By doing this, you're blocking the person's visual and physical access to your dog. Do this even when the person is your veterinarian technician or a pet care professional. See Figure 11-2.

>> **Come up with key zingers:** These are short statements that get the message across, like "My dog has some social anxiety." If your dog is easily won over with treats, invite your helper to toss a few and to stand and kneel sideways if it helps your dog relax. If you're at a loss, "I have the flu!" works well, too.

>> **Don't be afraid to walk away:** The only one you should be beholden to is your dog. While you can explain yourself if you feel the need, staying in a situation that causes your dog distress is emotionally painful for your dog, setting you both back.

© John Wiley & Sons

FIGURE 11-2: Bring your dog behind you in social situations.

Handling At-Home Reactivity

From your dog's perspective, your home is their den. Just because you're welcoming and friendly doesn't mean they'll feel the same way. Dogs with social anxiety read into everything — every inter-action, harsh tone, and every anxiety you feel. What they can't judge is that your anxiety is coming from their reaction. Dogs with anxiety hold tight to experiences that frighten them. While some dogs welcome all people like long-lost friends, dogs who experience social anxiety do not.

If your dog tends to overreact to any activity outside your home and can't disengage, try these tips:

>> **Block visual access to the window so your dog is less aware when company arrives.** Many people wrongly assume window-watching is a fun pastime; it's not. These dogs have the stressful job of homeland security and can develop severe social anxiety when they're forced to meet people in the flesh. In addition, chronic arousal can

negatively affect their health; these dogs have inadequate rest cycles to recover from heightened reactivity.

» **Redirect, don't correct.** Dogs with anxiety are laser-focused on your reaction. If their behavior worries you and you become anxious, you'll reinforce your dog's fear that the visitor is a threat. The best approach to helping them overcome their anxiety is to bring them far enough away (out of the red zone) so they can relax and then desensitize them to the occasional presence of people in the home.

» **Know your delivery, mail, garbage pickup, and cleaning helpers' schedules.** Keep your dog in their safe space or with you on a leash to prevent a reaction as you work to associate your their routines with positive rewards and interaction.

Create a safe space

If your dog is anxious with visitors or people at home, your first goal is to establish a safe space that is familiar and calming to them. If your dog loves their crate and it's positioned at an appropriate distance from the front greeting area (or you can move it there), that's an ideal spot.

If you don't use a crate or your dog is stressed when there is commotion in the home, find a comforting area or room where you can place your dog until visitors have come and gone or have transitioned into your home. Once the greeting drama has settled, introductions can be made.

For a dog experiencing social anxiety, having access to a calming room or crate equipped with a blanket and a chew or busy toy can provide reassurance. Everyone, including dogs, needs a safe place — a quiet corner to retreat to when the world becomes overwhelming.

Welcome visitors to your home

Before you open the door to a delivery person or welcome a visitor, consider the situation from your dog's perspective. If you've noticed they become frantically aroused, unresponsive to your suggestions, and won't calm down until you put them away, it might be best to put them away before you open the door. Remember that good manners start at home. If you want your dog to greet visitors and workers calmly, model that behavior in your own greetings. If you reciprocate a hyper-aroused greeting when you come in, your dog will likely become hyper-aroused whenever people come to the door.

Consider these tips for smoothing the transition of new people coming into your home:

>> **Discover a comforting introduction ritual.** Some dogs prefer to meet new people outside the home than inside. Others prefer to sniff people once they sit down and are more relaxed.

>> **Equip each person with a treat cup and favorite toy.** When visitors arrive, ask them to carry a treat cup and toss treats to them each time they approach. I call this the animated PEZ dispenser routine!

>> **Bring your dog closer as their greeting skills improve.** Over time, you may notice that your dogs are less reactive when people visit, perhaps even soliciting their attention now that your visitors are armed with their favorite goodies. Chapter 3 explains how to use a platform to teach your dog solid "sit-stay" skills, especially in heavily trafficked areas. As your dog's anxiety around people improves, practice directions like "down," "sit-stay," and "place," which increase their impulse control and social referencing, especially when triggered.

TIP

Teach your dog how to act by modeling calm, well-mannered emotions, especially when they are deregulated. Be the one to watch!

Let go of the expectation that your dog must be friendly and politely greet everyone in your home. When working with a dog with social anxiety, I remind my clients that no one comes over specifically to meet the dog, and they should not force their dog to approach anyone they're uncomfortable with in their home. Keeping your dog in a safe place while people are visiting, or workers are doing repairs is perfectly okay.

If you want to introduce your dog to visitors, here are three approaches to consider:

>> **Tether, crate, or gate your dog.** This involves gating, crating, or tethering your dog away from the main entrance

and waiting to introduce them until they've fully calmed down. Isolate them 10-15 minutes before your visitors arrive and leave them a favorite chew or busy toy to deflect their excitement when people arrive. Gradually bring your dog closer to the entranceway, working on "place" and "stay" until your dog learns to stay back from the door when people arrive. Place a chew and mat or bed within reaching distance and wait until they settle nicely or respond to "place" before introducing them.

>> **Use a dragging leash.** A dragging leash is simply a four-to-five-foot leash that your dog drags behind them as you supervise their interaction with visitors or helpers. Cut the handle off to prevent catching and discourage picking up. If your dog becomes triggered, step on it calmly and call them away from the person.

>> **Walk in together.** If your dog is comfortable with most people but gets upset when people come in from the outside, an alternative is to meet them outside first and walk in together. In this instance, stand apart from your guest and ensure your dog will sit and watch you calmly before allowing them to greet your guest. Ideally, your guest is willing to wait as you engage your dog in games like Treat-Retreat and I Spy, which will allow them to view visitors as in on your games versus a threat. Give your guests a treat cup or a handful of savory treats if they're willing to toss treats to your dog when they approach.

If your dog can't deal with social interaction, place them in their safe space with a toy.

TIP

In your behavior diary, note everyone's greeting manners. Track your dog's reaction when they come in and how many seconds it takes your dog to calm down. Record how the various techniques in this chapter work and try new approaches if necessary.

Counterconditioning and desensitizing at home

Enlist helpers to create a controlled environment when shaping a more positive association with people visiting your home. Decide ahead of time where your dog will be when company first arrives. Your goal is to help your dog settle down before introducing them or bringing them closer to the entrance. Try these steps:

1. **Identify various sensory triggers that set your dog off when visitors arrive.** Perhaps it's the sound of a car arriving, the car door slamming, or the doorbell. List all the things your dog associates with "stranger danger" and see if you can't re-create these situations by soliciting the help of a friend or family member.

2. **Choose one trigger to work on at a time.** Ask a friend or family member to re-create the scenario, such as driving up to your home or ringing the doorbell.

3. **Initially, stay with your dog and wait until they settle down to redirect them with a chew, treat, or toy.** After they are more settled, you can direct them to a place and work on "stay." If they have a hard time calming down, consider bringing them to a safe place or a more distant area.

4. **As your dog calms down, bring them closer to the entryway, perhaps in an enclosed area or secured on a tether, or leave them alone as you practice going to the door.** Your goal is for them to be easily redirected or calmed as people enter your home.

5. **After you've developed a system, ask your helper to play the role of the visitor.** Invite the helper in, stand with them, and wait until your dog is breathing normally and following the four-paw rule. Then, play games like I Spy or Treat-Retreat. You can review the instructions for these games in Chapter 3.

6. **Once you've welcomed your visitors, give them a bag of high-value treats.** Teach them to toss the treats on the ground and say "find it" each time your dog approaches. Once your dog is keen on this game, try it with someone less familiar and, eventually, with someone unfamiliar. Soon, just having the visitor dole out five to ten yummy treats will make them your dog's best friend.

TIP

In addition to this routine, record triggering sounds like a doorbell, elevator, or garage door opening. Play the recordings at a low volume to desensitize your dog throughout the day, pairing the noise with treats, toys, and rewards.

Change can happen quickly or take weeks or even months. Each scenario depends on many factors, including your dog's transitional excitement, breed, past trauma, and how long their reactions have been habituated or reinforced in your home.

A large part of this process involves changing your own habits, too. For example, if your dog gets hyper-aroused each time you walk through the door, they will experience the same emotional intensity with visitors, except they'll react out of fear or frustration rather than joy.

Their reactions may also vary based on the different personalities, appearances, and energies of the people they encounter. Go at a pace that is comfortable for your dog and celebrate every small victory. Some dogs might grow indifferent toward visitors, while others might grow more comfortable with certain people over time.

Easing Your Dog's Fear of People Outside Your Home

Most dogs become less reactive when away from home, as their confidence diminishes as they stray into unfamiliar places. Dogs with anxiety, however, are the exception to this rule. Reactivity doesn't stem from confidence; it stems from fear. Fearful experiences can add up, linking with other unrelated but routine stimuli, resulting in dogs being tense when they step out the door or are put in the car.

When they are frightened by someone they see or meet outside their familiar surroundings, these dogs may get spooked, terrified, or react aggressively. Empathy goes a long way in helping your dog regain their composure. They're not mindfully slowing down your walk or embarrassing you in front of the neighbors.

Your first goal is to encourage your dog to look to you for direction when they sense danger: what I coin as "referencing you before they react." This involves fun leash lessons (the ones you learn in Chapter 10) and rewards. Use engaging games, food, and lessons to convince your dog that the appearance of people predicts something good. When your dog makes this association, they will happily look to you for guidance and refer to you for positive reinforcement!

REMEMBER

If your dog is distressed by a person's approach, bring your dog behind your legs or physically step out to block the stranger's progress. Your only priority in this scenario is to your dog's emotional well-being. Likewise, if another trigger arises, such as a storm or another dog, exit the area promptly. Trigger stacking, which is the process of accumulating multiple triggers, can overwhelm many dogs and set back their progress.

The aim is for your dog to see people as a source of treats and enjoyment, associating their presence with the opportunity for attention from you and plenty of rewards. You can phase out food rewards over the weeks and months ahead, but continue to be mindful of your dog's reactions.

REMEMBER

The hardest thing to control isn't your dog; it's people! Someone, somewhere, may unnerve your dog for reasons you cannot predict. Just like you, your dog won't like everyone. However, your dog cannot verbalize their opinions in English; remember to always "listen" by watching their posture with your eyes.

BOOKMARK

If you think your dog's leash skills may be playing into their reaction, see Chapter 10 to learn more about leash reactivity.

Counterconditioning and desensitizing in the world beyond

As you walk together, remember that your dog's heightened sensitivity likely keeps them on guard. Keep your eyes scanning the environment so that when your dog looks at you, they see that you're the one on guard, ensuring their safety. Avoid staring at and chatting with your dog nonstop; this conveys the opposite message — that you're looking to them to serve as guardian and protector.

Before you begin, review these important directions from Chapter 3 as you create outings to help your dog feel more secure in venturing beyond their familiar home, yard, or neighborhood:

>> "Sit and watch"

>> "Stay"

>> "Find It"

>> "Down"

>> "Under"

Honor your dog's preference; allow them to choose who they want to engage with and who they'd rather avoid.

Structure outings with familiar mats, chews, and toys. If an outing involves sitting, such as in a park, animal hospital, café, or restaurant, arrange your dog's space to encourage them to rest at your side or under your legs. Now, let's get started with counterconditioning and desensitizing your dog to people in the world beyond:

1. **Identify interactions that trigger your dog when out on a walk or exploring the world.** They might show anxiety when someone approaches to engage you or pet them, or simply upon seeing a crowd or gathering. This example uses the trigger of someone approaching to pet them.

2. **Have a helper play the role of passerby.** Invite your helper in, stand with them, and wait until your dog is calmer and can remain on all four paws to play the I Spy or Treat-Retreat game.

3. **After two to three minutes of a game, give the bag of high-value goodies to your helper.** Teach them to toss the treats on the ground and say "find it" each time your dog approaches them.

4. **If your dog is still hesitant, review the Approach-Avoid game in Chapter 3 and stop after a couple of minutes to leave your dog wanting more.** If they approach the person after the game, ask them to toss treats on the ground, playing "find it."

5. **Once your dog is keen on this game, try it with a less familiar person, and then with someone unfamiliar.** Soon, just having the helper reward your dog with five to ten yummy treats, and they'll be your dog's best friend.

This process may take weeks or months, so be patient and consistent. Work your way up slowly by first introducing your dog to acquaintances and eventually to complete strangers. Go at a pace your dog is comfortable with, and never push them past their threshold. With time and dedication, you'll help your dog feel more comfortable and secure around people in the world beyond.

If you're concerned that your dog might bite someone, ensure that they are accustomed to wearing a muzzle before putting anyone at risk.

Navigating the world

Understanding and addressing your dog's social anxiety is a journey that requires patience, empathy, and consistent effort. By recognizing their triggers, incorporating food, fun, and games, and advocating for their needs, you can help your dog navigate the world with confidence and comfort. Remember, you are their strongest ally, and with your guidance, they can overcome their fear, learn to reference you before reacting to stressors in their environment, and remain emotionally centered in their interactions with people. A win-win for sure!

Chapter **12**

Managing Resource Guarding and Other Aggressive Reactions

esource guarding is a protective instinct in dogs and other animals, including humans! Think about how often you demonstrate this behavior, from protecting your counters and trash bins to asserting ownership over your food and possessions. It raises the question: Do we model resource guarding from the moment we bring our dogs home?

If your dog guards their resources, it's likely to upset you. Severe resource guarding may manifest as freezing, staring, growling, or snapping, like someone shouting "back off" at the top of their lungs. Dogs also subtly communicate mild unease, which many people overlook. This chapter explains why your dog guards certain things and how to manage and alleviate their reactivity, whether directed toward you, a child, visitors, or strangers.

WARNING

Aggression is a serious issue. If, at any point when working with your dog, you are afraid for the safety of anyone in your home, call a professional to help you or rehome your dog before the situation worsens. Dogs who bite are more likely to bite again; in many states, dogs who bite are frequently euthanized. While resource guarding can be managed or controlled, be honest with yourself and those around you. Does your lifestyle support having a dog who may use resource guarding, and do you have the capacity to work with them?

Understanding Resource Guarding

Imagine you're enjoying a piece of the pie in your kitchen at the end of the day. If a neighbor were to barge in, grab a fork, and start eating from your plate without hesitation, you might be too shocked to respond. However, the next time, you'd likely cover your plate and eat faster. You might even feel compelled to lock yourself in the bathroom to enjoy your pie in peace. Dogs are no different when enjoying food, toys, spaces, and even people.

The root of their reaction

Dogs guard their resources for various reasons. They may be genetically prone to resource guarding or have learned to protect their resources due to punitive discipline techniques, past traumas, or negative experiences. Understanding your dog's motivations is the first step to addressing and managing resource guarding.

Pain and Sudden Onset Resource Guarding (SORG)

If your dog suddenly exhibits resource guarding, your first step should be to visit your veterinarian to rule out pain as a possible motivator for this reaction. Dogs can suffer from various illnesses and injuries that cause discomfort and long-term pain. Since your dog can't tell you how they feel, they often suffer silently, showing discomfort only through their mood and guarded behavior.

Another instance of SORG can occur when an otherwise trusting dog feels threatened, frightened, or is handled roughly. It can leave lasting trauma, especially if this happens during a young puppy's fear impression period (as detailed in Appendix A). Even well-meaning professionals like veterinarians, groomers, and other pet care providers may inadvertently trigger fear or pain responses that lead to wariness of all strangers. Other scenarios might include being hugged too tightly by a child or being harshly corrected by a utility or homecare worker.

TIP

Sometimes, you can't protect your dog from discomfort, especially when they must go to the veterinarian or groomer. Appendix C contains tips on making these unavoidable interactions more pleasurable. If you're concerned your dog may bite, use a muzzle. Chapter 5 contains tips on positively conditioning your dog's muzzle.

Trauma

Rescue dogs and puppies may have been deprived of various resources in their past lives, from necessities like water and food, to emotional needs such as affection and attention. It's not uncommon for dogs with a history of deprivation to exhibit heightened resource-guarding tendencies, even after being adopted into loving homes. This can manifest in various ways, including guarding food, water, toys, or even affection from their people. Dogs who have experienced scarcity may develop a strong attachment to the resources they have, fearing that they might lose them once again.

Discipline

People can unintentionally frighten dogs and puppies by invading their personal space or wrestling an object or piece of food from their mouths. Professionals who promote domination over communication, e-collars, and other punitive measures to cope with this problem only incite more fear and reactivity.

Mommy issues

Not all dog moms are created equally. Some moms are too ill or neglected to care for their puppies, leading them to miss out on that critical five-week social time where impulse control and emotional regulation are reinforced. Singleton puppies can also be more prone to resource guarding, as they never learn the art of sharing.

Why resource guarding escalates

Resource guarding varies in intensity and can manifest differently depending on the situation. Some dogs may be comfortable with their family members but exhibit protective behavior when approached by strangers or unfamiliar individuals, including caregivers or children. Other dogs may remain reserved and quiet around outsiders but express frustration or aggression toward those closest to them.

A common reaction when dogs grab our belongings or exhibit resource guarding is to admonish them while quickly retrieving the item. Many people chase their dogs and pry their jaws apart. Besides being dangerous, this response conveys what I call *prize envy*. If something they have inspires us to combat them for it, then the object must hold great value. The dog learns that they should either grab objects when people are out of the room or hide and covet these "treasures."

A WORD ABOUT CHILDREN

Dogs often perceive children more like prey animals or puppies rather than people. Impulsive and often unaware of boundaries, children often express affection physically, whether toward a person or a pet. This can lead to unfortunate incidents, as kids love hugging, making them the largest demographic for dog bites.

Parenting can be stressful, and sometimes, this stress affects our dogs. A more effective approach involves counterconditioning: associating the presence of children with positive experiences for the dog. Engage children in activities like feeding and fun games like Alligator Island, Hide and Seek, or Catch Me if You Can! This not only builds confidence and intelligence in both the child and the dog, but also fosters a positive relationship between them.

It's important to note that dogs who exhibit resource guarding are not necessarily happy. Protecting their possessions can be stressful and may lead to aggression. If you're unable to address this issue safely on your own, seek professional help or consider finding a new home for your dog where they can be happier and less anxious. While rehoming a dog can be emotionally challenging, if they consistently exhibit anxiety or aggression around children, they may be better off in a household without them. If you choose to keep a dog that resource guards around children, never leave them alone with a child and share your management strategies with all caregivers.

Territorial behavior, such as barking and rushing at people approaching their home or yard, is common among many adult dogs. However, this ritual can be rooted in fear or frustration. When anxiety motivates behavior, it's generated from insecurity and anxiousness. When pressed, a frightened dog's reaction can be intense. A bite may occur when the person doesn't heed the dog's warnings.

Reference the pyramid shown in Figure 12-1 to gain more insights into the intensity of your dog's reactions and mark your starting point. This behavior intensity pyramid can help you assess the severity of your dog's reactions and serve as a starting point for intervention. Since dogs communicate their emotions through body language and behavior, it's crucial to recognize these signs early and take appropriate action.

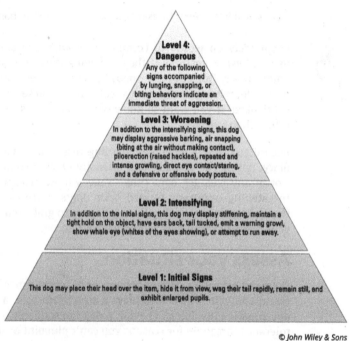

Level 4: Dangerous
Any of the following signs accompanied by lunging, snapping, or biting behaviors indicate an immediate threat of aggression.

Level 3: Worsening
In addition to the intensifying signs, this dog may display aggressive barking, air snapping (biting at the air without making contact), piloerection (raised hackles), repeated and intense growling, direct eye contact/staring, and a defensive or offensive body posture.

Level 2: Intensifying
In addition to the initial signs, this dog may display stiffening, maintain a tight hold on the object, have ears back, tail tucked, emit a warning growl, show whale eye (whites of the eyes showing), or attempt to run away.

Level 1: Initial Signs
This dog may place their head over the item, hide it from view, wag their tail rapidly, remain still, and exhibit enlarged pupils.

© John Wiley & Sons

FIGURE 12-1: This pyramid of warning signs can help you assess the severity of your dog's reactions.

Recognize their back-off signals

When dogs feel crowded while resting, playing, or eating, they exhibit predictable "back-off" gestures. Humans have their own actions for similar situations. Here are some warning cues your dog might use:

- **»** **Body language:** Dogs may crouch or stiffen, pin back their ears, or lick their lips.

- **»** **Eye expressions:** Dogs might stare intensely or show "whale eye," where the whites of their eyes are visible.

- **»** **Avoidance:** Dogs might freeze, run away with an item, or stand guard over it.

- **»** **Blocking access:** Dogs might obstruct others from reaching the resource.

- **»** **Vocal behaviors:** Dogs may snap, snarl, growl, or bark.

REMEMBER

People rely on words to communicate with one another, only using physical gestures if they're having difficulty getting their point across. Dogs are the opposite! They use postures to communicate, relying on dramatic vocalization if these visual cues are overlooked. If you want to know what your dog is saying, watch rather than listen.

Record your dog's resource-guarding reactions in your behavior diary, noting the distance and intensity of their communication. Notice any changes over time? Take a more relaxed and non-threatening approach toward your dog's gestures, reassuring them that you are coming by to give, not to grab. You may notice your dog's reaction gets more relaxed, too.

Assess your situation

Dogs can prioritize different things at different times and in different contexts. Stress also plays a significant role, as it does in any situation involving behavior. A dog can suddenly be over their tolerance threshold for reasons you can't pinpoint or predict.

TIP

Remember the importance of keeping a behavior diary and logging these questions and other details of your dog's reactivity. Record each resource-guarding incidence, ending each entry with a summary of the exchange. Stick to the facts and leave out the emotions. For an example entry as well as a downloadable template, visit SarahHodgson.com.

A PAGE FROM THE DOG TRAINER'S DIARY

I once worked with a dog named Jake, a German Shepherd/Husky mix. He adored playing with his ball. When his dad instructed him to "drop," Jake released the ball and eagerly awaited another throw. However, when his dad came home from work late, Jake became possessive of his toy and sometimes would growl if approached by the children. In the past, his dad had yelled and removed the ball for this behavior, but this only reinforced Jake's perception that the presence of the children meant the loss of the ball, exacerbating the situation. The new goal was to change Jake's associations with the children using the desensitization and counterconditioning steps outlined in this chapter.

In this scenario, Jake's behavior illustrated how his response to the same stimulus could vary based on circumstances and stress levels.

Here is a list of questions to help you determine what's important to your dog and to clarify a pattern to your dog's reactivity.

What does your dog guard?

>> Food dish
>> Bones/treats/toys
>> Bed/other sleeping areas
>> Stolen objects
>> Specific person/people
>> Doors/passageways
>> Home/neighborhood/yard
>> Outside areas

Is there a time of day that your dog shows resource guarding?

>> Morning
>> Mid-day
>> Late afternoon

>> Evening

>> Anytime

List the people who trigger a reaction from your dog:

>> Pet professionals

>> Strangers/visitors

>> Children

>> Pet parents

>> Everyone

Where does your dog resource-guard?

>> Only at home

>> In the yard

>> Away from home

>> Animal hospital/groomer/daycare/kennel

Is there a consistent consequence to their guarding?

>> Removal of the guarded item

>> Verbal reprimand

>> Physical intervention

>> Being ignored

>> Attention is redirected

Understanding where, what, and who your dog guards will help outline your rehabilitation process. If they guard things from strangers or unfamiliar visitors, they may act out of defensiveness, protectiveness, or territorial behavior. The root of their reactivity can stem from fear or frustration. If they only guard resources from pet care professionals, it could indicate distress from feelings of abandonment or fear during your absence. In such cases, your dog may benefit from your presence during examinations or short-term medication to alleviate emotional stress.

Don't take it personally if your dog exhibits resource guarding toward you and other family members. Remember that resource guarding is a normal behavior exhibited by humans *and* dogs.

Recognize their behavior as a plea for respect for their space and boundaries.

If you react aggressively to your dog's fear-based reactivity by claiming or overtaking the resource they're defending, you'll reinforce your dog's fear that you are competitors.

PREVENTION

While a dog who feels the need to resource-guard with people may resort to this behavior when they feel cornered or threatened, you can manage the issue and prevent incidents from occurring. Use this chapter to help your dog reevaluate your relationship and see you and others as non-threatening.

Prevention is your best course of action, especially if you have a busy household filled with family and friends who are young, old, or otherwise unable to read your dog's intentions. Don't take chances, especially the kind that would set you back, such as your dog reacting to a young child. Toddles have less impulse control than dogs! Here are four tips to lower your dog's reactivity:

- **Remove all objects your dog guards, such as bones, toys, balls, and so on.** If your dog guards their food bowl, consider scatter feeding, outlined in Chapter 3, or feed your dog in their crate or behind a gate.

- **If your dog guards resting spots, areas on the couch, other furniture, or even your lap, prevent access using boxes or other objects to block them.** Relocate their bed to another area of the room or in a gated area. Consider tethering your dog to their mat location. If your dog guards their crate, put the crate in a separate, less trafficked location and consider a crate cover.

- **Limit their space by using a pen or gated room to prevent access to areas where resource guarding may occur.**

- **Attach a five-foot drag leash, preferably light nylon, when supervising your dog.** Hold the leash to prevent any potential episodes of resource guarding and teach them to relax by your side calmly, especially when your household is active.

If you have concerns about your dog's behavior, consider conditioning them to wear a muzzle, outlined in Chapter 5.

Managing Resource Guarding

Managing resource guarding isn't straightforward. Dogs guard different things for unique reasons and at different times. Your dog might react to everyone who approaches them when they rest or enjoy a bone, or they might only react with family members. Before you begin the rehabilitation process, read through and gather all necessary information and tools.

Tools that can help

Managing your dog's resource guarding boils down to keeping them happy and reassuring them that you're their caregiver, not their competitor. Gather some useful tools to work through your dog's defensiveness. Since the end goal is to help them feel at ease when you're together, tools that inspire sharing and caring, not fear and domination, are essential.

Determine what you'll need by considering what your dog is guarding, how big they are, their level of reactivity, and who is being targeted.

>> **Clickers:** A clicker is a training tool that marks desired behaviors with a sound, providing clear communication and positive reinforcement. A word marker can work equally well, such as pairing the word "yes" with a treat. Use this practice to reassure your dog that your presence is always a positive thing. (Chapter 3 has more on clickers and other word markers.)

>> **Treat cups:** You can easily create a treat cup by putting treats in a cup and pairing the cup's shaking sound with positive food rewards. This DIY training tool is especially handy in rehabilitating recourse guarding, which will pair your approach with treats and positivity!

>> **Crates:** A crate provides a safe and secure space for your dog, which can be used to manage their behavior and limit access to certain areas of the home.

>> **Gates:** Use gates to block off specific areas of your home and control your dog's access to certain rooms or furniture that trigger their guarding behavior. Gates can also be used to isolate your dog when eating or enjoying a chew. They come in handy in multi-dog households as well, a topic covered in Appendix D.

- >> **Playpens:** Playpens provide a confined space for your dog to play and relax, offering a controlled environment to manage their behavior.
- >> **Cushioned wedges:** These physical blocks can limit access to furniture or even your lap if it prompts guarding behavior.
- >> **Distasteful or odorous sprays:** These can be applied to areas or items your dog may be inclined to guard, deterring engagement and allowing you to redirect them calmly. Many commercial distasteful sprays are available. For some dogs, a mix of vinegar and water or lemon juice can do the trick.
- >> **Dragging leashes:** The best dragging leashes are made of lightweight nylon and are at least five feet long. Tailor your drag leash by cutting off the handle to prevent it from catching on doors and other objects. Let your dog wear the leash when supervised so you can step in and redirect your dog's behavior without overstepping their boundaries.

TIP

When choosing a drag leash, ensure the clip is sized to your dog's head: Big clips can be too heavy for small dogs.

Create a safe space

Your dog needs a safe space, somewhere comfortable, cozy, and far away from the demands of everyday life. Especially if your dog feels threatened, they need a place to enjoy their food, bones, bed, and so on, without the constant fear of confrontation. A lovingly outfitted pen, gated room, or crate is ideal. When your dog goes in, lower the lights and play calming music. At least once a day, let them have something they treasure and leave them in peace. If you do need to go by, walk by without challenging or staring. Carry a treat cup and toss treats into their area as you walk by.

WARNING

If you have children or your dog targets certain family members, locate your dog's safe space away from their foot traffic. If need be, lock the room to prevent mishaps.

FUN FACT

Dogs need way more rest than people. Lack of quality rest can feed into your dog's insecurity and agitation. Think about how you feel when you're exhausted and overstimulated!

The next section teaches you how to reassure your dog when they feel threatened, instilling trust and friendship instead of fear. You also learn a kinder way to teach them the concepts of "leave it" and "drop," allowing you to retrieve things when necessary.

Rehabilitating a Dog Who Guards Their Resources

We don't need to assert dominance over our dogs — they already know we're in charge. We control their environment, provide their meals, and dictate their routines. When dogs guard resources, they experience an emotional reaction and perceive you as a competitor rather than their caregiver. Use the following techniques to reassure them that you're a caregiver, not a competitor. Avoid reacting aggressively, as you only reinforce their fear.

As you work through your dog's guarding habits in the pages ahead, pay attention to and record these three variables:

>> **Distance:** The precise distance you can comfortably approach before your dog signals discomfort.

>> **Red flags:** Body cues your dog uses to signal unease.

>> **Level of aggression:** The intensity of your dog's reaction.

Note these variables and update your notes in your behavior diary as new information arises.

WHAT NOT TO DO WITH RESOURCE GUARDING

The Internet and many trainers still advocate using e-collars, prong collars, and rough handling to address aggressive responses. This falsely portrays aggressive dogs as dominant and seeking to control their household. That would be like saying a two-year-old wanted you to hand over the keys whenever they had a temper tantrum! Nothing could be further from the truth!

Using such collars may produce immediate results, but I think of that as the "robotic cure." While the dog may appear subdued and obedient to the untrained eye, their lowered tail and head, stiff body movements, and lack of engagement with their environment suggest otherwise. These techniques rely on fear and intimidation to suppress natural responses, which are ignored and may resurface unexpectedly, such as resource guarding with children, more lenient family members, or strangers.

Puppies are typically more inhibited and less prone to using aggression to defend their resources until they reach sexual maturity (around 12-18 months) or emotional maturity (2-3 years of age). Occasionally, you may observe level one or two behaviors in an adolescent puppy that suddenly worsen when their "back-off signals" are misinterpreted, disciplined, or ignored.

Build a better bond

Rehabilitating your dog's resource guarding is less about confronting their aggressive reaction and more about establishing better communication skills between you and your dog. By linking rewards and fun to your interactions, your dog will be more optimistic and joyful.

Dogs who feel happy act happy. Simple five-minute lessons can help build new pathways toward mutual respect and understanding. Teach your dog words you can use when they're feeling crowded or stressed.

Red zones and safe zones

Recognize that your dog's behavior isn't random or unpredictable — dogs who consistently resource-guard highly value their personal space. As explained in Chapter 2, you must identify your dog's red zone and safe zone. When your dog is in their red zone, they are reactive, unsettled, and threatened. Their fight, flight, or freeze reaction comes into play as their body floods with stress hormones. In this physiological state, you cannot reason with them. The only proper reaction is to acknowledge and measure this zone. Your goal is to earn your dog's trust over time and shrink this zone.

Once you're outside of your dog's red zone, they grow less reactive. You're now in the safe zone. Your initial steps in soothing their intensity involve reducing your dog's fear of your presence by periodically tossing treats and offering other positive engagement.

Avoid crossing into your dog's red zone and sparking a guarding episode. In the pages ahead, you learn how easy it is to change your dog's perceptions. Don't rush this process. You're ready to begin your work once you understand and acknowledge your dog's signals and can differentiate between their stress and comfort levels.

Build a solid foundation

As you work on your dog's issues, organize the weeks ahead to limit their guarding impulses and reshape their perspective.

>> Limit your dog's access to places, food, and objects that trigger their resource guarding.

>> Block access to other dogs and people who might trigger reactivity.

>> Set aside time to practice the following exercises twice daily for five days only.

REMEMBER

If your dog becomes defensive around children or visitors, use a muzzle. In addition, place your dog on a dragging leash for calm intervention or redirection.

WARNING

If you feel your dog is a bite risk or you're concerned about your safety or others, your dog can likely sense it. Remarkably, dogs can smell the slightest shift in the hormones related to your moods. Devise a few guaranteed focus-shifting activities — quick actions to redirect your dog away from an object or favorite place, such as grabbing a leash, shaking a treat cup, or offering attention to another pet or person.

Let the rehabilitation begin

Your goal is to help your dog feel less threatened by people in their presence, especially when they're resting or guarding food or objects. Remember, your dog is constantly aware of your movements and becomes particularly sensitive if they feel their autonomy is threatened. Throughout this process, do everything you can to ensure your dog welcomes each person's approach with excitement rather than dread. Help them associate joy and relaxation with enjoying food and toys around people.

While curing this condition involves many variables, including the intensity and duration of the problem, there is always room for improvement. Reassuring your dog that you're coming to give, not grab, is a behavior problem that continually improves over time.

While the goal is to increase your dog's comfort level in all situations, begin practicing the counterconditioning steps with the least valuable objects first. The best time to work with your dog is when they're relaxed and calm, after a good meal and a walk or playdate.

>> **Pot of gold:** First, find the treat your dog loves more than anything else. Cut-up chicken or turkey excites most dogs, as does dried liver and hot dog slices. Don't scrimp on this step.

Reserve these high-value treats for these exercises alone. Many dogs like their food and will do tricks for a cheerio, but this resource-guarding routine is serious business.

>> **Train your brain:** Avoid facing your dog head-on, especially if your approach triggers their staring. Remember, people are the only animals that view face-to-face greetings as friendly; dogs see this pose as confrontational.

>> **Don't utter a sound:** Don't yell, even if they growl. Shouting is interpreted as barking and won't help your dog.

>> **Monitor all interactions:** No one can read your dog's social cues as well as you can. Monitor children, less interested adults, and other vulnerable people or pets.

If your dog is a bite risk, confine them in a room, pen, or crate before working through these exercises. The goal is to regain their trust and help them feel safe. If you do not see an improvement in one week, hire a professional to help you and keep them on a muzzle around children or visitors.

Desensitizing and counterconditioning exercises

Dogs who resource–guard are concerned that people might steal their belongings or invade their space. They don't know what we value or that we have no interest in their meals or toys. It's your job to reassure them you're not out to get their stuff. Start with these steps:

1. **Walk by or approach your dog at a slight angle, toss one of your high-value treats in their direction, and then quickly walk away.** This will leave your dog wanting you to come back.

2. **As you practice these walk-bys, vary the number of treats you toss from one to five.** Each approach should leave them guessing and wanting more!

3. **Leave quickly and instruct them to sit or go to a place before giving them attention should they follow.**

Since every situation varies, there is a wide range of approaches:

>> **Change your focus:** Your dog thinks you want what they have, so staring and shouting reinforces their suspicions. But what if, while you are at a safe distance, you change your focus and do something else? Like emptying the dishwasher, organizing the spice cabinet, or even just reading a book? This is called *desensitizing* your dog to your presence.

>> **Avoid prize envy:** Remember, your dog doesn't know you don't eat their food or play with their toys. Play the Find It game within view by yourself or with a friend or family member. Your dog might lose interest in their item and leave their resource to play with you. Let them in on the game.

>> **Practice walk-bys:** Do the same thing when your dog rests or plays with a toy, food dish, or another triggering item or place. Initially, walk by them well outside their red zone so they do not view you as a challenge. Also, be in the vicinity at a safe distance without acknowledging your dog's actions. Your actions and activity contradict their view that you're only there to steal their stuff.

Use a treat cup to alert your dog that you're in their vicinity. While keeping track of their reactions, do not make a big deal if they stiffen up or growl. Reassure them that you come in peace — to share, not steal. Follow these guidelines and use what works.

If your dog seems more interested in you and the treats you share, you're on the right road! Should they get up and come toward you, ask for a "sit and watch" or a trick before tossing the treat. If you can, redirect their focus with attention or an activity.

If your dog reacts to other people in your household, make sure they also understand the process. If you're concerned they cannot identify your dog's cues, use a gate, crate, or pen to separate them. Once you've practiced the counterconditioning game, ask them to be alongside you as you do the steps together.

The best games for addressing resource guarding

Practice working with your dog in relaxed settings, away from the areas or items they would typically guard, such as resting spots, other pets, or feeding areas. Start with simple directions, gradually adding more words as your dog responds consistently. Once your dog reliably follows the cues, incorporate them into everyday interactions.

For instance, if your dog consistently responds to "sit," ask them to sit before giving them things they desire, such as treats, toys, or access to certain areas like the door or the couch.

Keep the training sessions short — about five to ten minutes — and use your dog's attention span as a guide. If you notice signs of distraction, such as itching, shaking, or fidgeting, it may indicate that your dog is losing focus. Consider taking a short potty or exercise break.

BOOKMARK

Refer to Chapter 3 for more in-depth directions on each of the following directions:

>> Find It

>> Sit and Watch

>> Place

>> Down

>> Get It

>> Drop

>> Off

>> Away

>> Leave It

FUN FACT

Dogs learn words from hand signals, not the other way around. When positively redirecting your dog's behavior, use both hand signals and familiar words to shift their focus!

Play training

Dogs only play when they feel safe in their company and surroundings. The ability to let loose and have fun can be atrophied in traumatized or stressed dogs. Here are my top games for helping dogs who guard their resources:

>> Catch Me if You Can

>> Alligator Island

>> Lily Pad

>> I Spy

BOOKMARK See Chapter 3 for more detailed instructions. These games inspire communication over domination, encouraging a relationship based on sharing and fun as your dog learns to look to you for rules of play!

Acclimate them to your touch

Once a dog with resource guarding learns to tolerate your approach, conditioning them to your hands reaching out can be an added step. If your hand signals that you're grabbing something from them, they're likely to react swiftly to protect their space or treasure. Try these steps:

1. **Using your high-value treats, practice hand-focusing games from their safe zone, such as Find It, Feed the Chickens, Treat-Retreat, and Catch, as described in Chapter 3.**

2. **As your dog participates willingly, gradually move closer to your dog, remembering to stand sideways, not straight on.**

3. **Throughout the day, reinforce the idea that hands are for giving, not grabbing, by keeping treat cups around your home or in your pocket.**

4. **If you find your dog chewing or playing with a toy, prompt them to drop the item by offering a treat.** Say the word "drop" when they choose to give up the object.

TIP If your dog has something you'd rather they didn't, approach them with treats and prompt them to "drop." Then, scatter a handful of treats to their side. As they collect the treats, calmly remove the forbidden object.

Redirect them

List all the games and activities your dog loves. If they have favorite toys and bones, include those on the list. Use these items to redirect your dog's attention to fun and games when they feel scared, overstimulated, or defensive. Use whatever excites and makes them happy to shift their defensive behavior, such as games like Catch Me if You Can or Two Toy Toss.

One of my stress-prone dogs loves carrying a stuffed toy around like a pacifier. Whenever he's overstimulated, we direct him to "get your toy!" Do whatever gets your dog's tail wagging to lighten the mood. That's the whole focus of counterconditioning — to shift their focus from fear to fun!

REMEMBER

Redirection offers your dog a graceful way out of any stressful situation. You can suggest a game like fetch, take them for a ride, or practice a trick. Redirecting shouldn't be complicated; it should provide a fun, interactive alternative to a stressful encounter.

Consider medication

BOOKMARK

Don't wait until your dog's resource guarding is out of control, or they've bitten someone to seek professional help. Dogs who use aggression to defend their resources are more likely to act this way again. Make an appointment to speak to a qualified trainer or veterinary behaviorist, who can meet you virtually or in-person to explore pharmaceutical options, dosage, and other supportive products. To read about medicinal options, review Chapter 5.

If your dog's resource-guarding behavior is sudden, make an appointment with your veterinarian to rule out pain or illness.

Dealing with Special Scenarios

Every dog is an individual. Regarding resource guarding, no breed, gender, or personality trait is immune. This section lists the most common things dogs resource-guard and how to apply what you've learned to various situations.

REMEMBER

Remember that dogs who use aggression to defend their resources are not necessarily aggressive. Most are simply insecure or have learned through human retaliation about prize envy.

Food dishes, trash bins, and other areas

It shouldn't come as a shock that some dogs resource-guard their food, as humans similarly guard our food all the time. The worst advice is that people should discipline or assert dominance over their dog in these situations. Instead, consider your long-term goal. This behavior clearly indicates that your dog perceives you as a competitor, not a caregiver. Reacting with aggression or taking food from your dog only reinforces this perception.

Help your dog feel more comfortable with your presence around their dish by using the techniques mentioned in desensitizing and counterconditioning tips. If you have young children, do not expect them to exercise restraint around your dog's feedings. Instead, it's best to place your dog in their crate, behind a gate, or in their pen during meal times.

Toys and bones

Use the same counterconditioning and desensitization techniques to help your dog feel more comfortable with your presence when they guard toys and bones. Respect their space as you reinforce your approach by giving them rewards and reassurance.

TIP

Use these opportunities to teach your dog the "drop" cue. As you approach with a high-value food reward, say "drop" as your dog spits out their object to receive your offering.

Beds/other sleeping areas

If you've allowed your dog up on your couch or bed only to notice they've begun to guard their prized resting spots, it's time to reassess the situation. Being allowed on the furniture should be a privilege, and one that's lost if they become possessive. Instead of shouting when they warn you or other family members off, use tools to prevent their access to these areas while you engage in desensitizing and counterconditioning techniques to ease their concerns.

Use a dragging leash if you need to move your dog into another room. In this case, there is a direct reaction to your dog's resource guarding, namely, they are moved to another location. Remember, no anger. At the same time, treat cups can help your dog reassess your approach as non-threatening. Respect your dog's red zone and don't push it. The goal is always to keep them under their threshold.

Stolen objects

To your dog, any random object they find is a treasure. If you go so far as to chase or threaten your dog to get it back, you're setting a bad example. Too many aggravated assaults over gum wrappers and paper towels can result in a dog who covets what they find. Be mindful of getting too near your dog if they've shown aggression over stolen bits, whether it's a muffin from the counter, a dead frog they picked up outside, or a napkin. This can be unsafe for children too, as your dog will likely hide and covet novel prizes.

Use the same approach as you do with toys and bones — approach only as close as they are comfortable and try to redirect your dog if you need the object. No matter how vital the situation might be to you, getting upset will only reinforce your dog's resistance to giving it up.

Specific people

It's common for mature dogs to be more attached to one person or feel responsible for young children in the home. It's less common for dogs to use aggression to guard people, but it can happen. Initially, the guarding behavior is endearing, and people often unconsciously reinforce their dogs by laughing and giving them attention. It doesn't take long for any aggressive behavior to lose its charm.

If you notice your dog guards you from your partner or friend, try to busy yourself when your dog is around and let your significant other play the good cop, rewarding playing and practicing games like Catch, Find It, or another game or activity they love.

If you have a dog who guards your lap, some surefire fixes include sending your dog to their "place" or instructing them to "down." You can also get up and walk away so they have nothing to guard. Dogs are masters of the action-reaction connection. If an action gets a reaction, the action will be repeated. The reverse is also true; if an action gets no reaction, it will diminish. If they guard you and you walk away, the behavior will end.

Doors/stairways/passageways

Doors, hallways, and stairways are tight passageways for dogs. If you notice yours blocking or throwing their weight around in these areas, take notice. Sometimes, a dog will passively lie down and prevent traffic flow; while stepping over or navigating around them might be tempting, don't. This can lead to dogs actively guard these thoroughfares. Other dogs are more demonstrative in their action — crossing in front or standing ground when you or another family member tries to pass. If this sounds like your dog, take action immediately:

1. **If your dog has not used aggression, use your body to block or scootch through their body as you say a phrase like "excuse me."**

2. **Leave your dog on a drag leash, calmly moving them aside as you direct them "away."**

3. **Practice directions from Chapter 3, including "sit," "stay," and "wait."** Ask your dog to remain on one side of a passageway until you release them.

TIP

I'm also a fan of "away," as it's taught with treats and toys and takes the heat off everyday conversations. If your dog's behavior is more ingrained, get professional help.

Outside areas

Dogs who love the outdoors and have a propensity for resource guarding may show this behavior in unexpected places, such as a doghouse or den-like area or when digging holes or hunting where squirrels gather.

For example, your otherwise totally chill dog suddenly bears their teeth over a decaying carcass or a savory bit of garbage. Often, dogs will resource-guard when someone grabs their collar in the heat of the moment. Do not take this personally; don't be upset with your dog. Imagine someone grabbing you when you were working hard or preparing a meal (what I consider the equivalent of a dog's hunting instinct).

If you have a dog who consistently resource-guards an object outside, use all the techniques mentioned in the desensitization and resource-guarding sections. The same rules apply.

The car

A car is a quintessential fishbowl. Many dogs develop a resource-guarding habit when traveling in the car, throwing a hissy fit anytime a person or dog approaches and often when they see a dog out the window as you're driving around.

Counter-condition them by placing a comfy bed in the backseat or hatch, giving your dog a savory chew, and playing calming music while you drive. If your dog moves about in the car, use a leash or seat belt to secure them in one area.

If that's not working, try this version of the I Spy game:

1. **Park your car far outside your dog's red zone, in a parking lot, or a street away from a triggering area.**

2. **Roll down the car window closest to your dog halfway through and stand outside it with several high-value treats as your dog remains in the car.**

3. **Whenever your dog alerts you to a distraction, say "yes" or mark the moment with a clicker.** When they look back to you, reward them.

4. **You're in their red zone if they don't look back and get reactive.** Drive farther away until your dog can see the triggering activity while still prioritizing your interaction.

Remember — addressing resource guarding doesn't involve asserting dominance or control over your dog. Rather, it's about nurturing trust and communication. By understanding your dog's instincts and motivations, introducing new engagement techniques, and staying alert to their cues, you can positively manage and reduce their reactive behavior.

SOCIAL AND DOG-TO-DOG ANXIETY, FEAR OF VETERINARIANS, AND OTHER PET CARE PROFESSIONALS

A home or yard can take on a fishbowl effect: Envision a dog anxiously defending what is, to them, their personal space. With the advent of round-the-clock deliveries, a dog's anxious alert barking can reach a deafening crescendo every time they see or hear a person off in the distance. This situation falls under both resource guarding and social anxiety. You'll find help for this social anxiety in Chapter 11. Dog-to-dog anxiety, while also rooted in resource guarding, has its own rules. Appendix D walks you through multi-dog household stress and interacting with dogs outside your home. Regarding fear of pet care professionals, you'll find ways to calm and soothe your dog in Appendix C.

5

Calming a Sensory-Sensitive Dog

Chapter **13**
Rehabilitating Storm and Sound Sensitivities

M any dogs (and people) are naturally fearful of loud noises. An unexpected sound piercing an otherwise peaceful day can startle and frighten your dog. Unfamiliar noises, such as construction tools, fireworks, vacuums, and thunder, can signal danger and elicit fear unless your dog has been conditioned to similar sounds at a young age. If this fear is routine and unaddressed, it may lead to chronic anxiety. Fortunately, addressing sound sensitivity is often straightforward. This chapter explores various strategies for managing this issue.

Understanding the Root Causes

When there is an unexpected noise, your dog's survival instincts come into play, much like an unfamiliar noise that startles you. The noises that upset your dog may be easily recognizable, or they could be so routine that you barely notice them. Either way, your dog's first goal is to regain a sense of safety. If your reassurance doesn't calm them, do whatever it takes to help them regain their composure, including leaving the area and returning home.

Many factors affect a dog's sound sensitivities. No two dogs are alike, so avoid comparing your dog to others you've loved or known and let go of expectations. The following sections describe a few factors that can contribute to a dog's fear of certain noises.

Genetic and parental influences

A puppy's mom sets the first example of how to cope with noises and people. Sound sensitivity can manifest across generations, so knowledge of your dog's pedigree is valuable. The mother's coping skills are your puppy's first example and shape their worldview until you adopt them, so when possible, ask to "meet the parents" and note their demeanor. The mother's health and emotional well-being also plays a significant role in determining the potential stress levels of the puppies, as her hormones are transmitted through her milk, and her overall well-being impacts her interaction with the litter.

Lack of socialization

Puppies undergo an intense socialization period, from 5 to 14 weeks, during which they acclimate to the world around them. Since most people adopt puppies around eight weeks old, the first month at home can have a lifelong impact. Early socialization is crucial to familiarize them with the sounds and experiences they will encounter.

One consequence of a dog's lack of early experiences is that everything unfamiliar becomes suspect. When an older puppy or dog is startled by an unfamiliar noise, their autonomic nervous system activates, flooding their body with adrenaline and causing them to react with alarm and suspicion. This can lead to anxiety, especially if the people around them are unaware or unsure of how to respond.

TIP

For more on raising confident puppies and learning about their fear-impression periods, flip to Appendix A.

The startle effect

When a sudden noise startles your dog, they enter a fight, flight, or freeze mode. Dogs experience sounds more intensely than we do, as their hearing is exceptionally acute. Even everyday noises like a truck or a vacuum can be stressful.

If your dog gets startled while walking down the street or on a pathway, they might be more anxious since they're away from home. The farther dogs with anxiety stray from home, the more inhibited and on guard they are likely to be. If your dog gets startled, don't hesitate to take them home.

REMEMBER

A little training goes a long way with dogs with anxiety. Identifying the meaning of a few words lights up their brain. Using these words throughout the day and rewarding their cooperation will give you a vocabulary to use when they're stressed. In addition, direct your dog where to go and what to do so they see you as a positive role model. Refer to Chapter 3 for helpful tips on training and engaging in interactive games.

The age factor

Dogs, young and old, want to feel secure. Old animals experience sensory decline and Cognitive Dysfunction Syndrome (CDS), which is like Alzheimer's. When normal sounds are unrecognized or distorted, generalized anxiety may develop. Appendix B provides more on the effects of aging on your dog's well-being.

At the other end of the age spectrum is a young puppy, who, until approximately eight months, is a defenseless prey animal dependent on their caregivers for protection. Unfamiliar noises signal danger. Young puppies want to return to the den for cover and rely on you to deal with the provocation.

Trauma

Trauma is not uncommon in dogs, even those raised in loving homes. It's easy to overlook that each dog is an individual with a different threshold for stress. What one dog might tolerate, another might panic over. For example, if you've rescued a dog that has experienced trauma, they might cower when you raise your hand or voice. This reaction reflects their past experiences.

Recognizing Natural Attempts to Self-Soothe

When your dog becomes startled, their attempts to self-soothe can lead to impulsive reactions. Picture stress as the buildup of steam inside a tea kettle; it needs release. Similarly, stressed people might chew their nails, scribble, or twirl their hair. Dogs release stress in various ways, from barking and pacing to cowering and biting.

Consider these ways your dog might react when frightened by an unfamiliar noise or weather–related event.

>> **Running away:** A century ago, dogs weren't enclosed, so they'd just run off until they felt better. We never gave a second thought to their emotional distress. Today, some dogs still have an instinct to flee when encountering loud, unpleasant, or unfamiliar noises. These dogs will run until the source dissipates or they find shelter. The distance varies based on each dog's sensitivity and the event's intensity, but running miles away for safety is not uncommon. When they are unable to escape the anxiety-inducing noise, dogs may resort to desperate measures, like clawing through screens or chewing walls to flee.

Ensure your dog's microchips and ID tags are up to date in case they run off during a storm.

>> **Redirecting tension:** When their freedom to flee is inhibited because they're trapped inside or restrained on a leash or fence, dogs with sound sensitivity will exhibit distress in various ways, such as pacing, panting, vocalizing, shaking, hiding, drooling, destructive behavior, and even self-injury. Other dogs may dig or chew to release some of their built-up tension.

>> **Eliminating inside:** Extreme fear can stimulate your dog's digestive tract, potentially triggering the expression of their anal sacs, which leaves an oily stain around their bum and emits a repugnant odor akin to decomposing fish. Even housetrained dogs may experience fear-related accidents or stress diarrhea, as their bodies instinctively divert resources from digestion, leading to lose stools and, in severe cases, colon inflammation. Likewise, chronic stress can exacerbate gut health issues.

These incidents are beyond your dog's control. Disciplining your dog for their reaction may exacerbate their anxieties, leading to more stress-related accidents, not fewer.

TIP

When you anticipate a stressful event, take your dog out for a potty break beforehand. It's a win-win-win — quality time together, serotonin-releasing exercise, and an empty bladder!

>> **Hiding:** To your dog, home is their safe place, or at least it should be. When life gets chaotic, loud, or frightening, your dog may choose to evacuate into what I like to call the "inner sanctum of the den," which might be their crate or a warm closet, especially one padded with familiar smells. Closets can be ideal for blocking noise and static electricity, waiting out a storm, or auditory disruption, although dogs will choose anywhere they think they might be safe (see Figure 13-1). If your dog has a chosen closet, lay a fleece or cozy blanket at the far end and appropriate chews to comfort them. Sitting calmly nearby and breathing steadily can also calm your dog and promote a sense of security.

© Getty Images

FIGURE 13-1: Attempting to hide is a common reaction to fear and anxiety in dogs.

TIP

Crates can also be a comforting refuge for your dog if they prefer this spot. Fearful dogs often seek solace away from windows in a darkened area. Remember this if you need to move their crate during a storm or another anxiety-inducing event.

TIP

>> **Grounding in the bathtub:** Many dogs with anxiety plant themselves in the tub, shower, or by the toilet during a storm. While it might seem perplexing, this has more to do with static electricity than their wanting a bath. Ceramic surfaces block electricity and can be a safe hiding place to sit out a storm. There is more to reassuring them than overcoming noise interruption: Storms can cause them pain!

Rather than forcing your dog out of the tub, consider joining them in the bathroom with your phone, knitting, or a good book. Breathe calmly to set a relaxing example.

Helping Your Dog Overcome Sound Sensitivity

Although dogs can be triggered by a wide range of noises, soothing their sensitivity follows a similar pattern. This section covers techniques, games, and interactions that help resolve noise anxiety. In the pages ahead, I refer you to this section and the more detailed explanations of the techniques found in Chapter 3 as I tackle each category, from thunderstorms and fireworks to household appliances and outdoor commotion.

Desensitizing and counterconditioning

Desensitization involves gradually introducing your dog to a stressful noise at a low volume during everyday interactions. The hope is that your dog will process the noise during normal interactions, enabling you to slowly increase the volume over time until it no longer elicits a fearful reaction.

Counterconditioning involves introducing pleasing activities while the noise event occurs. The goal is that your dog will link the noise to pleasure. Combining these two efforts can help your dog develop a new lease on life!

Here's a play-by-play using this dual approach to help your dog overcome noise phobias:

1. **Record the sound of fireworks, thunderstorms, a siren, or any other sound your dog reacts to.** You can also find these recordings online.

2. **Engage in positive activities that your dog loves, like hide-n-seek, fetch, or tug of war, as you play the recording at a low level.** You can also try massaging them, practicing training lessons with high-value food rewards, or practicing synchronized breathing on a mat. Note the volume that captures their attention without causing distress (indicated by a slight head tilt or ear twitch).

3. **Once you determine the proper volume, play the recording for two to three minutes as you interact positively with your dog.** If at any point your dog seems distressed (won't take treats or engage with you), reduce the volume or turn off the recording.

4. **Gradually increase the volume until your dog is no longer bothered by the trigger.**

WARNING

If the recorded sound is too loud, it can have an adverse effect, potentially exacerbating your dog's fear. Be mindful of your dog's tolerance and ensure the volume is kept at a level that doesn't overwhelm them or damage their hearing.

Each dog has unique sensitivities, so what works for one may not work for another. Some dogs do not associate recordings with the event itself. Sometimes, there is more than the sense that's disrupting them, as with static electricity during a thunderstorm, odors with vacuums and fireworks, and machinery vibrations.

Games and positive redirection

I Spy is a great game designed to help your dog manage their triggers by transforming stressful stimuli into a playful activity. By playing this game, your dog will learn to shift their focus from the trigger to you. I Spy also helps dogs become more mindful of changes in their environment, reducing anxiety and improving their ability to cope with challenging situations.

Operation Cooperation is a great tool for improving communication between you and your dog. The game encourages your dog to signal their comfort or distress through behavior, promoting a deeper understanding of their emotional state. It's a fun and therapeutic way to turn potential stressors into positive experiences.

BOOKMARK

For tutorials on I Spy and Operation Cooperation, refer to Chapter 3.

Relaxation techniques

Anything that can help your dog release tension is helpful. Some dogs respond to touch or interaction moments after a startling noise event; others may flinch, show more distress, or even growl if you interfere with them. For these dogs, relaxation techniques are most effective once they retreat from the scene or after the storm or episode has passed. Honor your dog's timetable. Relaxation techniques like synchronized breathing, massage, and aromatherapy can help your dog release tension and regain a sense of calm. Techniques such as TTouch, music therapy, DAP, and anxiety wraps are effective ways to soothe and relax your dog.

Flip to Chapter 3 for more on massage, synchronized breathing, and other relaxation techniques.

BOOKMARK

Medication, supplements, and products

Sometimes, a little medicinal relief can go a long way in helping your dog handle their sound sensitivities. A veterinarian, behaviorist, or certified trainer can guide you through the many alternative approaches. A veterinarian or board-certified behaviorist may recommend prescription medications to ease your dog's stress as you help soothe your dog's reactivity to given sounds.

Chapter 5 provides more information on medication, holistic alternatives, and helpful products. Always consult your veterinarian before giving your dog supplements or making any changes to their diet.

BOOKMARK

Considering and Curing Common Sound Sensitivities

For dogs who suffer from phobias, panic, and post-traumatic stress due to specific sound events, daily life can be fraught with sudden and terrifying disruptions. This section explores considerations for specific instances – from thunderstorms and fireworks to at-home and outdoor noises.

SENSITIZATION

Sensitization results from repeated exposure to a feared event, leading a dog to become more sensitive to the trigger. Dogs can also become sensitized to unrelated objects or stimuli associated with the initial trigger. For example, your dog might become anxious simply by seeing you open the closet where the vacuum is stored, even if you're not using the vacuum.

Thunderstorm phobias

Studies have shown that thunder is only a fraction of the reasons dogs experience anxiety during storms. If your dog suffers from storm phobia, the sensation of static electricity tingling their fur can contribute to their distress. In a domino effect, some dogs correlate rain to thunder; others may associate wind and the sound of rustling leaves with the feared event. The good news is these dogs can be helped. Dogs prefer feeling confident over fearful and respond eagerly to the games outlined in this section. See Chapter 3 for more games you can try.

As you work through your dog's fears, note both the timing and intensity of your dog's reaction. Consider the environmental factors and whether your dog is triggered by pre-storm events or by the feared occurrence.

As the storm approaches

If your dog becomes fearful in the moments leading up to a storm, try to identify the specific sound or effect that triggers their anxiety. If your dog reacts to a particular sound, consider recording it or finding a similar recording online and practicing the desensitization exercise described previously.

When the storm is upon you

To help your dog during a storm, you can try several of the previously explained approaches. Test these methods calmly, allowing your dog's reactions to guide you. For example, while a gentle massage might calm some dogs, touch may stress others. Focus on what works for your dog and cross off strategies that don't.

WHAT TO DO WHEN YOU CAN'T BE THERE

Sometimes, you can't be with your dog during stormy weather, fireworks, or other intense noise events. It's critical to have a plan in place, and there are several steps you can take to prepare.

Containment

Ensure your dog's safe space is accessible. Keep their favorite closet open and equipped with comforting materials like blankets, toys, or clothes with your scent. If your dog seeks solace in their crate, place it away from windows and use music or a sound machine to drown out noise.

Dog Sitter

Arrange for a trusted dog sitter to stay with your dog during these events. Provide them with details about your dog's anxiety triggers, preferred comforts, and any potential hazards to watch out for (running away or destructive behaviors). Consider giving them a copy of relevant reference materials, such as this book and your anxiety log, with notes.

Prescription Medications, Supplements, and Other Remedies

Consult a veterinary behaviorist about medication or natural supplements for your dog's anxiety. Monitor your dog closely when starting any new medication or supplement, especially before leaving them alone.

Some people find relief for their dogs by using specifically designed security wraps, available online or through pet stores or veterinarians.

As you experiment with different strategies, manage your own stress levels. Remain rational and composed, even if you must fake it. Dogs are sensitive to our emotional cues, even when our actions are well-intentioned.

Fireworks

To your dog, fireworks and similar noises are anything but normal. Typically occurring after dark, when dogs sleep, fireworks disrupt their natural biorhythm. Imagine someone unpredictably making deafening noises while you are sleeping. Moreover, bombs and gunfire closely resemble this sound and often emanate from our TVs and phones.

A lack of early socialization or previous trauma related to these sounds can also lead to phobic reactions if they're inadvertently reinforced during an episode.

Should your dog suffer a fireworks phobia, consider if other similar sounds set them off. If they are unreactive to similar everyday noises, their firework reaction is considered *episodic* and your efforts should be straightforward:

1. **Ensure your dog's microchips and ID tags are up to date in case they run off during a storm.**

2. **Take your dog for a long walk before the festivities begin to promote restful behavior and ensure they have an empty bladder.**

3. **Play sound-canceling music or leave a TV show on that your dog finds soothing to help drown out the storm's noise.**

4. **Create a safe and comfortable space for your dog to retreat during the storm, such as a cozy den or a quiet room with familiar bedding and toys.**

5. **Consider investing in an anxiety wrap, exploring calming supplements, or consulting a veterinarian for short-term medication.** Utilize these options in the hours leading up to the storm, but avoid using them once your dog's fear has taken hold.

6. **Provide fidget chews and mentally stimulating toys before and during the storm to help distract and comfort your dog.**

7. **Keep your dog indoors during the night to minimize exposure to fireworks and other loud noises.**

8. **Stay with your dog during the event or ask/hire a familiar person to be with it.** Experiment with various calming techniques. Share these soothing handling tips with your dog sitter but instruct them to discontinue anything that increases your dog's stress level.

9. **Practice synchronized breathing.** Relax your body, releasing all tension as you inhale for three seconds, hold for three seconds, and exhale gently for a count of four. This will help your dog mirror your sense of calm.

10. **Don't be upset if your dog snubs directions, invitations to play, and even food when triggered.** Fear, food, and fun don't mix!

If your dog triggers similar noises and shows anxiety throughout the day, a combined effort of desensitization and countercondi-tioning can mute their association or redirect the noises to more positive associations.

While these mental activities can distract your dog from an impeding celebration, they should be practiced *before* the fire-works begin, lest the interaction be associated with fear. I out-lined these methods; here, you learn how to relate them to these specific sounds.

» List noises that stress your dog and events or objects associated with the noises that may trigger your dog's anxiety, such as turning on the television.

» Discover how far your dog must be from these stimulations to feel safe.

» Working at this distance, pair positive interactions, brain games, and sensory activities, like I Spy and Operation Cooperation, to instill confidence, focus, and resiliency throughout the day.

Vacuums, appliances, and other household noises

Vacuums and other audibly alarming appliances and machines can be particularly distressing to dogs, especially because they occur inside their "den" where constancy should reign. Keep in mind that your dog's auditory perception is sharper and more refined than yours (see Figure 13-2).

FUN FACT

Did you know that dogs can hear noises at higher frequencies than us? This heightened auditory sensitivity can make encounters with machinery and household appliances even more unpleasant. Other sounds your dog may hear that we can't include electronic devices, high-pitched winds, and distant animal calls.

© Getty Images

FIGURE 13-2: Although you might find utility in your vacuum, you dog might just find it to be a menace.

Regardless of the noise triggering your dog, there is a lot you can do to help them return to a calm state. Try out the different strategies described in this chapter, like synchronized breathing, massage, or a pleasurable game. Test one activity at a time to better assess their effectiveness in soothing your dog's reactivity.

TIP

As you have more control over these sounds than the weather event or fireworks, ask a helper to activate the specific sounds in a distant room when practicing desensitization and counterconditioning techniques.

Sounds outside your home

Dogs are intelligent, and when startled by a sound, they instinctively know how to react: distancing, defending, or freezing until the stimulation passes. The problem is that humans get in the way. Some may grip the leash too tightly, pull them toward the trigger when they want to retreat, or fail to observe their cues. But you can change that.

If your dog is unexpectedly triggered, observe the situation and their reaction to it closely. If they want to hunker down and lean into you, remain still, breathe calmly, and offer comfort. If they prefer to flee from the noise, move swiftly, waiting to comfort them until they feel safe. If they want to go home, listen to them and head back.

At first, you may not always know what triggers your dog — and that's okay. The most important thing is to get your dog to a safe place, whether redirecting them home, putting them in a car, or moving away from what's upsetting until they calm down. Review the information on your dog's red zone, safe zone, and turning point in Chapter 2.

Follow these steps the moment your dog becomes startled in the world beyond:

1. **Try to identify what is causing your dog's upset and record it in your behavior diary.** This could be a loud truck, a construction vehicle, people shouting, a vacuum or coffee grinder, a siren, a train, and so on.

2. **Observe your dog's posture and movements.** Keep the leash loose as you quickly respond to their cues. If circumstances prevent you from following your dog, such as in busy or hazardous environments, backtrack the way you came.

3. **If your dog seeks comfort from you, assess whether providing reassurance is enough to calm them.** Persistent pawing or climbing on you is generally considered a fearful or phobic response; it's better to distance from the source of their distress until they're calm.

4. **If your dog wants to return home, allow them to do so.** Once inside, offer a chew or engage them in a stimulation activity to help them relax (e.g., chews, licky mats, puzzle toys, or frozen treats).

5. **Once your dog has recovered and is receptive to interaction and treats, continue your walk in a different direction or engage in other enjoyable activities.**

For information on leash reactivity, refer to Chapter 10.

Using a Mindful Approach

There isn't a one-size-fits-all formula for soothing anxiety in dogs: Some may find comfort in petting, while others prefer personal space. Certain dogs can be redirected with treats, while others may be too overwhelmed to respond. Your dog might shake off a scuffle with a neighbor's dog, while another may feel reluctant to leave the safety of the front porch. Restoring a dog's confidence varies greatly, depending on each dog.

When working on your dog's sound anxiety, experiment with various solutions to find what is most comforting. You might discover that a combination of approaches suits their needs or that one method works initially, but another is better suited as your dog becomes more confident.

By taking the time to understand your dog's natural self-soothing behaviors and employing a range of techniques outlined in this chapter, you can help your dog regain a sense of calm. Remember, patience, dedication, and empathy go a long way in supporting your dog through their fears.

IN THIS CHAPTER

» Identifying the cause of noise anxieties

» Recognizing your dog's scent and taste anxieties

» Addressing your dog's touch anxieties

» Learning to soothe your dog in the moment

» Making positive associations with triggers

Chapter **14**

Alleviating Other Sensory Sensitivities

oise aside, our modern world can be confusing to dogs. Offensive candles, home renovations, other animals on TV, and unpleasant car rides — dogs can be easily unnerved by any shift in their sensory world. Depending on your dog's sensitivity, something as simple as rearranging the furniture can be upsetting. Another dog may fear storm drains after getting their foot caught in one.

This chapter explores how interruptions in your dog's sensory world may contribute to their anxiety and what you can do when fear takes hold.

Sensing Something's Out of Whack

Your dog's life is devoted to sensory interpretation. Routine exposure to something unfamiliar or previously linked to a danger can leave your dog in a state of generalized or episodic anxiety. Consider the following everyday experiences from your dog's perspective and embrace empathy over anger.

Sight reactivity

While dogs' sight isn't as sharp as humans, they can see at night and detect even the slightest motion. Changes in their familiar environments, however, may appear unrecognizable. For dogs prone to anxiety, these visual interruptions can trigger a startling and unsettling reaction.

Unfamiliar objects

A sudden appearance of something new and unfamiliar in your home, yard, or neighborhood can alert danger for a dog prone to anxiety. Common reactions include lowering and swinging their head, pinning their ears back, cautiously approaching, suddenly darting away, and growling.

Once your dog's autonomic nervous system engages, nothing save distancing will realign their focus — even favorite treats might fail to get their attention. Still, you can desensitize them to the object once they have calmed down.

I recall an instance with my nervous Shepherd mix when we encountered a deflated bouncy castle in the field near our house. He became extremely agitated until I led him back about 20 yards. We then played the I Spy game and watched my other dog, Wahoo, approach and parade all over it. While Skippy never engaged to that degree, he overcame his initial distress.

Even seemingly insignificant changes, such as a new lawn ornament in your neighbor's yard, can catch your dog off guard. If you're unsure about what's upsetting your dog, pay attention to where they exhibit signs of discomfort. Kneel down and view the surroundings from their perspective.

Reflections

It can be endearing for a puppy to notice their reflection for the first time. However, having a dog that routinely startles or barks incessantly at a mirror or their reflection on the glass can upset everyone involved, especially the dog. Their body language — such as lowered posture, a throaty growl, and attempts to attack or escape the reflection — clearly convey distrust and fear. If your dog experiences reflection anxiety, you've probably realized that avoiding the situation entirely is nearly impossible.

Television

Modern television has made a significant impact on the dog world. High-resolution images and improved audio systems make them more alert and stimulated than ever. This heightened awareness isn't entertaining and often leaves dogs anxious and aroused throughout the day. What may seem like an engaging response, such as barking at the TV while watching images, is an automatic reaction to an uninvited stimulus. These stimuli can cause more distress than enjoyment. Reassuring, shouting, or restraining your dog furthers the startle factor, increasing their anxiety!

REMEMBER

Are you stuck in the arousal loop? Many think high-arousal activities like extended walks, fetching, and tug-of-war lead to a calm companion. This is not true. Routine arousal leads to a dog who needs similar stimulation day after day. For brain games and other activities that engage your dog's brain, see Chapter 3.

Nighttime worries

Nighttime can add another layer to your dog's anxiety, especially if you live near wildlife or the commotions of a busy metropolis. Your dog may hear predators or sirens off in the distance and be too afraid to venture out on their own. This holds particularly true for young puppies, small breeds, and older dogs who depend on group security for safety. Sudden apprehension about going out after dark can also be a sign of an underlying ailment or illness.

TECHNICAL STUFF

As dogs age, they may start experiencing Cognitive Dysfunction Syndrome (CDS), as explained in Appendix B. The confusion and disorientation associated with CDS can heighten anxiety, particularly at night. Declining senses of sight or hearing can also make dogs more on edge at night, as noise phobias may intensify when visibility becomes limited.

Distorted human forms

While dogs have relatively good eyesight, it's not as sharp as ours. Their vision tends to be more near-sighted. It's important to understand how their eyesight influences their behavior and emotions. If your dog becomes anxious upon seeing a person in uniform, with a physical disability, or someone carrying a box or equipment, you're not alone. They may not even recognize you if you're in a costume or wearing bulky clothing, such as a hoodie, hat, or heavy coat. In such situations, verbal reassurance or a sniff will provide comfort. However, when the source of their anxiety is someone like a plumber or yard crew, it's time to act.

Identifying triggers can be harder in situations closer to home, such as interactions with children. Dogs who experience anxiety around children may have been hugged or squeezed frequently while resting, eating, or otherwise occupied. Even well-meaning people who insist on carrying their dogs or constantly interacting with them through chatting, hugging, and doting on them can inadvertently contribute to generalized anxiety.

Trauma

If you've adopted a dog with a history of trauma, you might notice that it's easy to keep their anxiety at bay most of the time. However, certain sounds, like boots on a wood floor or the jangle of metal, or sights like a baseball cap, can transport them back to a place or time when they were powerless. When a haunting memory resurfaces through a particular shape, smell, or sound, it can transform your sweet, loving dog into a puddle of despair. They may exhibit lowered posture, sinking their head and tail and defensively barking or slinking away.

CROSSOVER TRIGGERS

Dogs have a mirage of senses that intersect and influence each other. The smell of a chipmunk may prompt them to explore, while the sound of another dog might lead to a visual scan. However, with anxiety, various stimuli can become sensitized, even if they have no direct relationship to the source of the fear or anxiety. Here are a few examples of seemingly innocuous occurrences that can trigger anxiety; the potential triggers are limitless.

- **Rain: Thunder.** A dog might associate the sound of rain with the accompanying thunder, even if the two don't happen simultaneously. This can make the dog anxious during thunderstorms *and* when it rains.

- **Leash: Neighbor's dog.** If the neighbor's barking dog triggers fear and an impulse to retreat inside, the dog may eventually associate the sound of the bark with being leashed, even if the two events don't co-occur.

- **Opening closet: Vacuum.** Many dogs have a fear of vacuums. Some dogs note the sequence of the closet door opening and may develop anxiety each time the closet door is opened, regardless of what happens next.

- **Beep of any electrical device: Electronic collar.** Electronic collars often have a warning beep that signals an impending shock. While I don't endorse their use, I frequently encounter dogs with a phobia of beeps, from phones to household appliances, due to their association with electronic collars.

Attending to Scent and Taste Aversions

Dogs rely on their sense of smell to navigate and understand their environment, much like how we use our eyes to see. Some scents create an emotional memory that can be recalled days, weeks, or years later. Just as different sights can evoke various emotions in us (seeing someone we adore versus someone who annoys us), the same holds for dogs.

If you notice that a particular scent triggers your dog's anxiety, it's likely not just your imagination. Dogs can associate scents with people, weather conditions, and past events. Taste can also play a role in triggering anxiety, although it's rare and typically occurs because of a sensitizing event. For example, a dog may associate the smell or taste of peanut butter with anxiety-inducing fireworks if peanut butter was offered to them during the event.

Smells associated with people and animals

Scents of other dogs, people, or animals can trigger fear, especially if your dog associates fear or trauma with those odors. For example, does your dog react anxiously when brought to the veterinarian, becoming distressed by the familiar antiseptic smell? This scenario is not uncommon.

If your dog has experienced a negative encounter with another dog or been startled by loud barking, similar situations may provoke an anxious reaction. Anxiety can also stem from interactions with other animals, such as cats, horses, and wildlife.

Scent marking

Dogs and other animals mark territory for various reasons, including communication. Studies show that quickly sniffing another dog's urine can reveal their sex, diet, stress level, age, and social status. This underscores the importance of allowing your dog to dictate the pace when walking — they need time to "read" all the "pee-mail" left by other dogs!

If your dog becomes anxious during a walk or shows reluctance to go in a certain direction after sniffing an area, it's important to respect their instincts. A dog prone to anxiety will be mindful of whose scenting and which areas are best to avoid.

Anal gland expression

Every dog has two anal gland scents located on the side of their bottom. Most dogs express these glands when they poop to intensify their scent mark. However, when a dog is hyper-aroused or anxious, their muscles can contract involuntarily, emptying these glands and releasing a repugnant, fish-like odor.

Understanding Touch Anxieties

Your dog's sense of touch is integral to their association with you and the world. Touch can either soothe anxiety or contribute to it. A gentle touch — whether a loving pat or a deep pressure massage — can be incredibly reassuring and help a dog transition from a heightened state of arousal or stress to a state of calmness. You learn more about the therapeutic use of healing touch later in this chapter. This section focuses on how unfamiliar or negative tactile experiences can evoke various levels of distress, ranging from simple anxiety to strong fear responses.

FUN FACT

Touch is significant for both dogs and humans. Psychiatric service dogs are trained to apply deep pressure to individuals experiencing severe mental distress, eliciting a calming response — just like what you can do for your dog!

Surfaces

As most of your dog's sensory neurons are in their feet, they are particularly sensitive to changes in footing. Many free-range dogs that have never set foot indoors can be wary of wood and tile flooring. The lack of grip on these surfaces can make it feel like walking on ice. Surfaces like cement, sand, and snow can initially cause stress for dogs who didn't experience these stimuli as puppies.

FUN FACT

When laboratory beagles are finally released from their sterilized cages, they often hesitate to explore unfamiliar surfaces. However, a few minutes under the warming sun with no restrictions can ignite their hearts, and soon, most of them leave their anxiety behind and burst with joy.

Human touch

Touch can inspire deep reassurance in dogs, triggering the release of oxytocin, a calming hormone. It's the sense they're born with, connecting them to life and their mother. In ideal circumstances, touch links their earliest experiences with future ones, fostering the bond between dogs and humans across generations.

However, touch can also lead to reactivity or discomfort. Certain dogs have specific "no-touch" zones that can trigger feelings of distrust. Here are a few examples:

>> **Waist:** Your dog's kidneys are located just behind their ribs near the surface of their waist. Hugs or handling in this zone can cause pain, distress, or a defensive reaction.

>> **Neck:** Some dogs may feel uncomfortable or defensive when touched around the neck, especially if they've had negative experiences in the past.

>> **Top of the head:** While many dogs enjoy being petted on the head, some may find it unsettling or uncomfortable, particularly if they're approached too quickly or forcefully.

>> **Belly:** Although belly rubs are often portrayed as enjoyable for dogs, some dogs may feel vulnerable or anxious when touched on their belly, especially if they're approached in a way that feels invasive or threatening.

REMEMBER

A puppy's early socialization window is the clearest predictor of their future comfort with human affection as adults. Missing out on early handling can lead to constant apprehension in the presence of people. For more about puppies, check out Appendix A.

In the worst-case scenario, human touch can evoke anxiety, especially if a dog has experienced abuse or rough handling during their formative stages. When abuse occurs after a dog has already developed trust in a human, the impact of the traumatic experience can be severe and long-lasting.

If you've adopted a dog for whom touch is associated with negative experiences or triggers stress or aggression in specific areas of their body, the situation is not hopeless. Solutions are explored in the following pages.

Understanding Car Anxieties

Car anxiety involves a medley of sensory disruptions. Streets speed by through the window. People, animals, objects, and other cars remain just out of reach. The sounds and smells of our chaotic world fluctuate. Many dogs experience motion sickness, while others feel trapped or triggered by past traumas. Pair this with unsettling destinations like the vet, groomer, or daycare, and it's no wonder some dogs are so averse to being trapped in a moving machine.

Rehabilitating car anxieties depends on the specific nature of your dog's concern. While there are general measures you can take to address motion sickness, tackling more complex car phobias typically requires desensitization and counterconditioning techniques.

Motion sickness

Puppies are typically more prone to car sickness than adult dogs, and many dogs grow out of this as they mature. However, for those who continue to experience discomfort, there are steps you can take to alleviate their symptoms:

>> Maintain a cool temperature inside the car.

>> Allow fresh air by cracking the windows.

>> Limit your dog's food and water intake a few hours before the trip.

>> Consider using dog pheromones — available as collars, diffusers, and sprays — to mimic the scent of a nursing mother dog.

If motion sickness persists, consult with your veterinarian regarding motion sickness or anti-anxiety medication.

Car phobias

Rehabilitating a dog's fear of cars requires desensitization and counterconditioning. Try these steps:

1. **To begin, identify where your dog feels comfortable and relaxed, whether in the back seat or about 15 feet away from the car.**

2. **As you gradually approach the car, reward your dog with something enjoyable, such as a special toy, tasty treats, or a meal.** Engaging in games or trick training sessions can also be beneficial. The objective is to help your dog associate the car with positive experiences.

3. **Advance to the next stage only when your dog is completely at ease with the current stage.** If your dog stops eating or playing, you may be progressing too quickly. In such cases, take a step backward until your dog relaxes, then continue. Remember, the duration of the training process may vary, so patience is key, and progress should be tailored to your dog's pace.

4. **Once your dog is comfortable being near the car, gradually introduce other elements associated with driving, such as sitting in the driver's seat, closing the doors, or activating the remote locks.**

5. **Pair each step with something enjoyable for your dog, like tossing treats in the back seat or playing tug-of-war together.**

6. **Ensure your dog's safety by securing associated non-related objects and stimulation like leashes or voices to the experience (known as sensitization) with the noises and subtle movements.** Allow your dog to associate the engine's sound with positive experiences like food, fun, and games without driving anywhere.

7. **Once your dog is comfortable with all the sensations in a car ride, begin traveling short distances.** Gradually increase the duration of the trips in small increments.

Taking Action to Alleviate Sensitivities

If your dog seems frightened by anything, respond right away. Whether you recognize the source of their fear matters less than your immediate validation. Early signs of sensory-induced anxiety may include freezing and reluctance to move forward, dropping of ears, tail, posture, and other body indicators detailed in Chapter 2.

WARNING

Some people overlook these cues, unintentionally keeping their dog in trigger situations, exacerbating fears instead of providing comfort. Actions like tightening the leash, insisting on a sit-stay or focus cue, or forcibly dragging your dog toward a trigger can heighten their anxiety. With repeated occurrences, a dog may develop a phobia of the initial event and associated objects and stimuli like leashes or voices.

As with other sensory triggers, the two most reliable ways to soothe fear and anxiety are to:

>> Distance yourself from the trigger

>> Give your dog time to calm down

As you've learned, when a dog experiences anxious emotions, the body releases stress hormones that take time to regulate.

Relaxation exercises

If you enjoy watching TV and want your dog to relax with you, it's important to help them process and detach from the images on the screen. Consider the emotions your dog experiences, which are likely a blend of fear and frustration as they react to foreign sights and sounds in their home.

You aim to shift your dog's attention away from these intense, emotionally charged reactions and involve them in cognitive games that ignite curiosity and playfulness. This way, they can comprehend that what they see on the screen does not affect their behavior or interactions.

1. **Find the distance from the TV where your dog is less engaged in the screen; initially, you may need to mute the sound.** While it's okay for your dog to notice the TV, the

goal is to have them far enough away that playing and engaging with you outweighs the screen distraction.

2. **If you haven't already discovered the games, puzzle toys, and treats your dog finds most engaging, see Chapter 3 and use the brain games that engage your dog's thinking and mental processing.**

3. **Review the I Spy game and make the screen the focus of choice.** Each time they look at the screen (and remain quiet), mark the moment and reward their turning away from the screen. The longer they keep their focus on you, the longer you reward them as you gradually shrink the distance from the screen.

4. **As with any interaction involving food rewards, your goal is to eventually phase off treat dependency.** Introduce other rewards gradually, such as special pats, scratches, or your dog's favorite chew toy.

Change anxieties to positive associations

You need a well-thought-out approach to help your dog overcome their chronic fear, arousal, and anxiety. Mindlessly exposing your dog to triggering situations, day in and day out, will intensify their fears and could create anxiety about non-related objects or stimulations as well.

Supporting your dog properly is never too late. Here's how to get started:

1. **List all the things that startle your dog and cause them anxiety or fear.**

2. **Arrange this list in order of least upsetting to most.** Start with the lesser triggers to build your dog's confidence.

3. **It's easiest to orchestrate exposure with another's help. So, ask someone to channel Animal Planet, lean a ladder against a tree, wear a hat, or hold a stethoscope to simulate a veterinarian.**

4. **Approach the situation being mindful of your dog's reaction. When your dog is startled, pause and walk back a foot or more until they're only mildly alert to the distraction.** At this point, stop and engage them in a game of I Spy or treat cup sequence training.

5. **Gauge how far from the triggering event you are and gradually move closer.** You are switching their fear of objects and events with treats and games.

I Spy is a fun game. You start inside with a familiar object. Reward your dog for looking at an object you hold or one moving like the TV or a person. Gradually practice this game outside and eventually with triggering objects or sensory triggers.

Reintroduce scary sensory disruptions

Another way to desensitize your dog from triggering objects or events is to stage gradual exposures. Bring the events inside and begin rehabilitating your dog where they feel most safe. Use short, coordinated sessions and expose your dog to a trigger as you use food and fun to engage them simultaneously. Repeat exposures in various locations and times, paired with pleasure activities and attention, will nullify their reactivity over time.

Dogs with anxiety feel most safe at home, surrounded by people who comfort and help them contain their intense emotions. To your dog, the home is their den, the yard is their territory, and everything else is the great beyond.

Here are some ways to reintroduce triggers safely:

>> For a dog who triggers when passing a schoolyard, it's helpful to play recordings of children interacting at a low volume during fun and feeding times. Or, go to the periphery of a playground, where your dog might engage in busy activities or play-training exercises.

>> Many dogs find visiting their veterinarian terrifying, associating medical prodding with offensive smells and unforgiving footing. Desensitizing your dog to this necessary experience can start at home. Pair antiseptic smells with positive interactions and expose your dog to routine checks more than once a year. This can make the actual veterinary visit less stressful and startling.

Avoid over-exposing your dog to triggering events or objects. The pros call this *flooding*, and it can backfire, causing phobic association and trauma.

When your dog is startled, there is a lot you can do to help them regain their confidence:

1. **First, meet them where they're at emotionally.** If your dog needs to leave a particular place, you can use the Hurry, Hurry game described in Chapter 3, simply by saying "hurry, hurry" as you leave the area.

2. **Next, guide them to their safe place and surround them with comforting blankets and familiar toys.** Once they are settled, sit by their side and practice synchronized breathing.

3. **Since your dog's body will have just experienced distress, give them time to relax and invite them to choose one of their chews or busy toys.** This can help them return to a state of calm.

REMEMBER

Whether you're trying to help your dog with visual disturbances, unfamiliar scents, or touch anxieties, empathy is the first step in rehabilitating any sensory sensitivity. By approaching these challenges with patience and consistency, you can help your dog overcome their fears and integrate better into our crazy, modern world.

The Part of Tens

Chapter **15**

Ten Plus Confidence Building Exercises

Busy Toys

Busy toys can be bought or made at home. A quick search online will show DIY tutorials and ready-made products, offering a plethora of activities to keep your dog entertained. Unlike high-energy games, which can leave your dog supercharged, these mental activities stimulate your dog's brain and promote calmness. Busy toys bolster your dog's confidence as they reap rewards for solving the puzzles. More examples can be found in Chapter 3.

Scent Games

Dogs love to search for things, especially their favorite toys, chews, and treats. Encourage your dog to stay in one room while you hide their toys, balls, or food goodies around the house or yard. Encourage your dog to use their sensory stealth to locate them. This is another confidence-boosting game! You can also try *scatter feeding*, where you portion out your dog's food to let them forage for it. For more detailed instructions, visit Chapter 3.

Parlor Tricks

Teaching your dog silly parlor tricks is a great way to bond with your dog. After all, fun serves as the ultimate remedy for worries. Select tricks that align with your dog's natural abilities and won't strain their physique; for instance, dance might be perfect for a Toy Poodle but not as suitable for a Great Dane! Assigning words to tricks such as "paw," "belly up," and "dance" adds an enjoyable way to bond with friends, family, and admirers!

Passion Pursuits

Passion pursuits include activities that tap into a dog's instincts and interests, such as chasing, tracking, or herding. Engaging in activities that align with a dog's passions can enhance their fulfillment and confidence. For example, participating in scent-focused activities allows dogs to use their keen sense of smell to search for hidden objects, boosting their confidence as they successfully locate targets. Whether you have a purebred dog or a mixed breed, watch them to determine what they love. Do you have a water fanatic? Time to fill up a doggie pool or find a place for them to swim!

Target Training

Targeting is a training technique where a dog learns to touch a specific object, such as a target stick or a hand, with their nose or paw. Targeting can be used to teach your dog a variety of behaviors, from tricks to walking politely to going to a place. Check out Chapter 3 for more training instructions.

REMEMBER

Target training can help dogs overcome social and sensory anxieties. It focuses your dog on a rewarding task when they might otherwise be preoccupied with a triggering distraction.

Socialization

If your dog loves interacting with other dogs or new people, set up playdates or arrange group adventures. Although a confident, friendly dog won't erase all their fears, having a good friend to meet and play with will give your dog something to look forward to and a successful social interaction. Assign a quick phrase, like "Chloe's coming over!" to highlight the guest meet-up. Some dogs love their dog walker or pet sitter, and a visit from them can be exciting! Friendship and fun will give your dog a happy reprieve from their troubles.

WARNING

Dog parks can be too chaotic for dogs with anxiety. The entrance can be a stressful transition, and unknown dogs frequently squabble over a ball or a favorite person. If you find a well-run park, be mindful of your dog's stress level when playing with other unknown dogs.

Sniff and Strolls

One of the best ways to bond with your dog is to take them on adventure outings. By giving them the freedom to sniff and explore new terrains, you'll enrich their day and break up the monotony of everyday life. Explore a few new areas a month and return to the places your dog likes best. My dogs and I love the forest trail behind my house and get even more excited when meeting friends there.

Obstacle Courses

Set up a simple obstacle course using cones, tunnels, and low hurdles in your backyard or living room. Guide your dog through the course with a treat, toy, or target wand, gradually increasing the number of obstacles before rewarding them.

If you have a yard, consider getting a home-spun obstacle course with tunnels, weave poles, jumps, and a platform table. I have six obstacles in my backyard and my dogs love trying to guess the order I'll call them out.

Play Doctor

Throughout their life, your dog will need to be handled. Occasionally, playing doctor or groomer with your dog is a great way to get them accustomed to body handling. Don't insert a thermometer in your dog's behind, but expose them to latex gloves, stethoscopes, scissors, hairdryers, and so on. Gently examine their ears and mouth to get them used to these new sensations. Playing the Operation Cooperation game detailed in Chapter 3 use rewards and fun to expose your dog to handling they'll need to endure throughout their lifetime.

Daycare and Group Training

Bringing your dog to a daycare if they love free play with other dogs or enrolling them in a dog class together are great ways to boost their morale. If your dog gets anxious during car rides to the veterinarian or groomer, they might resist initially, but keep the mood light and reward them.

WARNING

Choose your daycare or group classes wisely. Some facilities may use punitive measures to correct behavior and to prevent dogs from getting into confrontations.

TIP

As car seats are slanted, they can be discomforting; the leather-type material is difficult for a dog to grip. Make your car more comforting by providing a big, oversized blanket or fleece, or purchase a cozy car seat specially built for dogs!

Pet Therapy

If being around people soothes your dog, and they're as comfortable cozying up to just about anyone, they might be the perfect candidate for pet therapy! Pet therapy is a team activity where you visit nursing homes, libraries, and other facilities to bring love and joy only dogs can provide. Visit AKC.org to learn more about getting started with pet therapy.

Canine Sports

If your dog is an activity junky and spends too much time keeping track of all your comings and goings, consider joining a dog sport activity group in your area. Canine sports are all the rage and have expanded from agility and flyball to dock diving, and even dancing competitions.

Chapter **16**

Ten Plus Ways to Address Separation Anxiety

Stay Calm

Remaining composed during departures and arrivals helps reassure your dog that leaving is routine and nothing to worry about. Dogs pick up on their people's emotions, so it is best to maintain a neutral and confident attitude.

Create a Safe Space

Designate a comfortable area in your home, such as a crate or a specific room, where your dog can feel secure when you're away. Decorate the area with cozy beds or blankets, familiar calming chews and toys, and clothing that has your scent. Your scent can be very comforting to your dog when you're gone.

Use Calming Music or White Noise

Turn on soothing music or white noise in the background to create a calming environment for your dog. Dogs don't like silence. In your absence, your dog will tune into noise outside your home. Certain types of music or sounds can help reduce stress and anxiety.

Turn Off Lights

The goal is for your dog to rest when you're gone, not pace about anxiously or destroy things to vent their angst. To encourage calm, turn off the lights and pull the blinds. Dogs are more alert in bright light.

Turn Off the TV

TV is full of drama these days, especially with commercials! Your dog may notice other animals and become alert to dog sounds. But the TV isn't a substitute for your company. Your dog's arousal means increased stress hormones, which can lead to reactivity or anxiety, especially when you're not home to balance them. If your dog seems triggered by the TV, turn it off when you leave and opt for music or white noise instead.

Use Comforting Scents

Aromatherapy has been shown to have a calming effect on dogs. Find a scent like lavender, vanilla, or ginger, and use a diffuser throughout the day and when you leave. Pheromones that emit an odor similar to a nursing mother can also be effective; discover if this odor works to relax your dog.

Reinforce Self-Soothing Activities

Be less accessible even when you're home. Encourage your dog to engage in self-soothing behaviors, like chewing on or engaging with a busy toy (which you provide) or settling in their bed. These activities help your dog relax and cope with anxiety constructively.

Make Departures Gradual

Acclimate your dog to your departures gradually, starting with short absences while you are home. When leaving for a moment, say, "Be right back," then go for less than a minute or two. If your dog is anxious when you return, stay calm and practice synchronized breathing, described in Chapter 3. Once your dog is calm, reconnect with them for five seconds, then behave nonemotionally. After a few days of progress, try a casual departure, using the same phrase as you leave. Should your dog's separation anxiety worsen or continue indefinitely, see Chapters 6 and 7 for more detailed tips on leaving your dog home alone. You might also want to consider a professional consultation.

Encourage Impulse Control

Teach your dog impulse control exercises to help them regulate their emotions and behaviors. Games like those outlined in Chapter 2 teach your dog to control their excitement and sudden arousal, which can empower your dog to manage separation anxiety and stay calm in your absence.

Use Doggy Daycare or a Pet Sitter

If your dog still suffers when you leave, consider enrolling them in doggy daycare a few times a week or hiring a pet sitter to provide companionship and stimulation when you're away.

WARNING

Choose your daycare or group classes wisely. Some may use aversive measures to correct behavior and to keep dogs from fighting.

Play Mind and Body Games

Avoid playing high-intensity games like fetching or tug of war right before you leave, which can amp your dog up when it's important for them to calm down. Instead, opt for mental enrichment activities before you leave. Take an ambling walk or hike, try a sniff and stroll, as described in Chapter 10, provide busy toys, or set up indoor treasure hunts for a more calming engagement before departure.

Run Through Lessons

Dogs love training sessions — even just five or ten minutes a day. Going over familiar directions or teaching them new ones can be rewarding. They're just as happy learning a new trick as practicing the basics, so mix it up to keep it fresh. You are engaging your dog's brain power by using treats or favorite toys as they figure out how to earn them!

Consider Supplements and Medication

In severe cases, your vet may recommend supplements, products like Thunder Shirts, or medication to help manage your dog's symptoms. Chapter 5 goes into detail on the various options. Prescription medication should be used under vet guidance alongside behavior modification to address anxiety causes.

Practice Patience and Understanding

Above all, be patient and understanding with your dog as you work through their separation anxiety. It may take time and consistent effort, but with the right approach, many dogs can learn to manage their anxiety and feel more comfortable alone.

IN THIS CHAPTER

» Addressing your puppy's
vulnerabilities and fears

» Recognizing your puppy's key
development stages

» Making learning fun for your puppy

» Creating a supportive and structured
environment for your puppy

Appendix **A**
Anxiety in Puppies

Every puppy should have a safe, trusting, and joyful environment in which to grow up, one that promotes learning and encourages curiosity and exploration. Unfortunately, this is not always the case. When a puppy feels too confined or misunderstood, anxiety can set in.

A puppy can experience stress for a variety of reasons, from their own mother's poor health or neglect to miscommunication or trauma once they've been brought home. Even their temperament can play a factor in their insecurity.

People often distress their puppies despite their best intentions. While loving a puppy like a child feels natural, puppies are not children and may not always understand our reasoning and values. Many puppies can be overwhelmed by discipline and human demands. This appendix explains the complexities of puppyhood and how to start things off on the right paw.

Appreciating a Puppy's Vulnerability

Like all young animals, puppies are prey animals. Unable to defend themselves, your puppy will bond with you as their guardian — like a child to their parent — and your home as their den. They'll instinctively want to stay close to the den and to you for protection. Due to their vulnerability, a young puppy is uniquely attuned to unfamiliar sights and sounds that could indicate danger. Fear and anxiety can manifest during this stage if their emotions are ignored or unrecognized.

A puppy knows what they need. Do not force your puppy if they are avoidant or refuse to move in a certain direction.

Recognize where the fear begins

Nothing is more exciting than bringing home a new puppy! They're cute, curious, and sometimes mischievous but nonetheless charming. All too often, though, our natural impulses can unsettle them. For example, when we pick up a baby, we hold their head to the ceiling and gaze into their eyes lovingly. A puppy, however, needs to be held spine to ceiling, belly to floor, and direct eye contact may seem threatening to them. Our expressions of joy, excitement, and love can appear scary, bizarre, and downright predatory. Start by avoiding these types of interactions:

>> **Any fast, head-on motion:** This may be seen as an attack, causing an impulsive freeze or flee response when approached by family, caregivers, or strangers. Remember, mature dogs approach their young nonchalantly. Approach a puppy calmly and at an angle.

>> **Hands descending above your puppy (the classic head pat):** This can be interpreted as predatory. Urge everyone interacting with your puppy to kneel or bend sideways and keep their hands where your puppy can see them. Remember this phrase: Hands are for giving, not grabbing.

>> **Rough play and physical corrections:** Puppies nip to play, especially with their original littermates. When people engage roughly or physically correct them, they act more like puppies than parents. It's best to redirect and disengage when puppies become impulsively playful.

>> **Pulling or grabbing at your puppy:** Puppies have a life-sustaining freedom reflex, an instinct humans possess as well. Puppies will instinctively pull away from force or pressure. Think of a puppy caught in a predator's mouth — being dragged on a leash is a similar sensation.

>> **Forced leash walks or collar dragging:** These can create a negative association with both, often resulting in excessive

fear and frustration. Improper leash handling can develop into leash reactivity.

REMEMBER

The leash is for a dog walk, and a bike helmet is for a bike ride. Your relationship guides your puppy. Chapter 10 includes instructions for leash training the right way.

>> **Forced interactions:** Puppies are completely defenseless. If they are forced to meet dogs and people too often, they can develop deep-seated insecurities that raise cortisol and adrenaline levels.

>> **Behaving erratically and inconsistently:** Puppies are self-centered — their only goal is survival. Bonding starts early, but teamwork develops during their emotional maturity, around one to two years. Dogs cooperate best after puppyhood is filled with calm, trusting parenting and consistent routines.

All puppies start out loving unconditionally, but there's no guarantee that an adult dog will feel the same way. It's your job to honor the relationship you've been gifted.

Understand imprinting and socialization

Between 5–14 weeks of age, your puppy goes through an important socialization period when life experiences, even jarring ones, are normalized. If a puppy is sheltered during this time, they will have a harder time acclimating to new experiences. This can lead to them being more fearful and anxious about new situations. As this short socialization window sets the stage for the rest of a dog's life, taking advantage of this time is critical.

THE IMPORTANCE OF SLEEP

If I could give puppy parents only one tip, it would be to honor their puppy's sleep schedule. An overtired puppy is like an overtired toddler — with sharp teeth! Puppies need a safe, uninterrupted place to rest with sound-canceling, soothing noise to block out the sounds of everyday life. If you aim to share your life with a well-adjusted dog, track your puppy's sleep needs at different stages. Like children, puppies need sleep to grow and develop.

The focus of a puppy's first month at home should be exposing them to the many sights, sounds, and sensations they will experience in their lifetime.

Your veterinarian may advise against socializing before certain key vaccinations as their immune system is still developing. However, there are several workarounds for when a puppy's vaccine schedule limits their socialization:

>> **Nylon playpens:** Safely erected and positioned at a comfortable distance, these playpens can help puppies experience the world while being safe. Treats and toys can also distract the puppy while they are sensitized to the world around them.

>> **Strollers or enclosed wagons:** Puppies can experience the world around them while you observe and influence their reactions with treats, reassurance, and attention.

>> **Slings:** For puppies light enough to be carried, slings can provide a safe way to expose them to the environment. See Figure A-1.

>> **Car engagement:** If your puppy has already developed insecurities or these other options don't work, you can take them in the car. Park in a targeted area, crack the back window, and stand outside between the puppy and the environment. Reward and engage them as they socialize.

© Getty Images

FIGURE A-1: A puppy sling can make a puppy feel secure while out experiencing the world.

If your puppy appears fearful, overstimulated, or vocalizes during a meet-and-greet with another dog or person, calmly move away. Once they can disconnect from the experience, kneel or sit next to them, talk lovingly, and soothe them with loving strokes and calm rhythmic breathing. If the situation involves respectful adults or children, or if a calm dog remains present, stay; otherwise, withdraw from the situation. Be your puppy's role model for how to act in all situations, maintaining a parental sense of assurance. Never leave your puppy unattended outside the home.

Understanding the Fear Impression Period

All puppies go through the same developmental stages, regardless of breed. One of the most critical periods in your puppy's life is between 8 and 16 weeks of age, known as the *fear impression period*. During this time, puppies categorize the world around them as either safe or dangerous. Some experiences are brushed off as normal, while others can leave a lasting imprint of fear or caution.

During the fear impression period, your puppy may be startled by things, people, or other dogs that previously didn't cause a reaction. Sudden changes in their sensory environment, whether shifts in sights or sounds, can cause alarm where there was none before. Even more perplexing is that your puppy might be fine with something like a puddle or loud noise one day but afraid of it the next.

Handling this phase correctly is crucial for your puppy's emotional stability. Events during this time can be traumatizing. Potentially frightening encounters include interactions with children or other dogs, sudden dislikes of strangers or unfamiliar dogs, shocks from invisible fences or e-collars during routine activities, unexpected weather events, loud celebrations, and grooming mishaps. Avoid pulling or forcing your puppy to approach what they fear or in a direction they'd rather avoid. Instead, calmly explore the area or object to show them there's nothing to fear. If they follow your lead, reward them; otherwise, ignore their reaction.

WARNING

Be mindful of your puppy's sensitivities during their fear impression period and avoid bringing them too close to triggering situations. Check out the Approach-Avoid game in Chapter 3 for tips in helping your puppy overcome their fears.

Interpreting Puppy Behavior

Puppies display cute, engaging gestures that can be both adorable and annoying. Many of these behaviors disappear by young adulthood, which is around 12 to 36 months, depending on the breed.

>> **Licking the chin:** A puppy will lick someone's face for several reasons. Primarily, it's a sign of respect! Your face likely tastes good, too — and as some mom dogs regurgitate food for their pups, perhaps they're hoping you will, too!

>> **Front groveling:** This one is known as an appeasement gesture. When a puppy grovels in front of a person or dog, they may have been disciplined and groveling to avoid further reprimand or confrontation.

>> **Play bows:** Puppies have endless energy and love to play. If your puppy goes down on their front legs with their rump in the air, they're eager to play with you! As play is the opposite of anxiety, take every opportunity to create fun memories.

>> **Frenetic random action patterns:** Two to three times a day, puppies get a burst of energy and look like cartoon versions of themselves, running in rapid circles or bouncing off your furniture like a gymnasium. Some people call these the *zoomies*.

>> **Need for persistent interaction:** Puppies do not feel safe on their own, especially outside, where they are vulnerable to predators. Forced isolation becomes traumatizing for many puppies, who often end up with anxiety and heightened arousal to everyday noises.

>> **Nipping:** Puppies nip and mouth things from birth until about six months of age. They have two types of nipping behavior:

   • *Soft nips* are localized in the front of their mouth, with less pressure or intent to harm.

   • *Hard molar nips* rolled back into their mouth. These nips often indicate a need or overstimulation. If necessary, bring your puppy to a quiet area to calm them down.

>> **Chewing:** Puppies, like babies, love to pick stuff up! Babies use their hands, while puppies use their teeth. Keep various chews and toys in designated areas around the house, like a toy basket. If your puppy chooses one of your things, direct them to their stash and swap it out.

Making Learning Fun

It is never too early to engage your puppy as you teach them words and impulse control. Chapter 3 devotes an entire section to various games, lessons, and fun activities. Here are a few ways to sharpen their skills, establish positive habits, and encourage good behavior from the start:

>> **Word association:** Pair words with everyday routines, such as inside, outside, car, and crate. Puppies love feeling included and learning the meaning of words. The more words they know, the more they can participate! Assign words to all your routines — your puppy will be too busy keeping up to sit around waiting for the other shoe to drop!

>> **Play training:** Engaging a puppy in playful activities is a great way to enhance their learning experience. Incorporating games into their routine can sharpen their skills while fostering positive behaviors. From interactive toys to structured play sessions, play training provides a productive outlet for your puppy's energy and curiosity. With patience and consistency, you can turn every playtime into a valuable learning opportunity. Chapter 3 contains lots of play training exercises to try.

>> **Frustration tolerance:** There is such a thing as healthy doses of fear and frustration. These short, guided intervals build resiliency and help your puppy develop emotional regulation. Frustration exercises include holding a treat or toy over your puppy's head or lining treats on the countertop and waiting until your puppy sits calmly to reward them. An example of healthy fear might be teaching your puppy to navigate the stairs or taking them to an unfamiliar location, putting them down or in an enclosed playpen as you wait, and reinforcing their resiliency.

>> **Touch desensitization:** Socializing a puppy to touch is an important part of their development, laying the foundation for trust and comfort in various situations. Gentle handling and positive reinforcement help a puppy associate touch with safety and security, reducing anxiety and fearfulness. Use food and fun to make happy associations to foot handling and faux examinations of their ears, eyes, and belly. Desensitization and reward-based interactions go a long way to conditioning a puppy to accept physical interactions! This can come in quite handy during trips to the vet.

>> **Crate training:** Puppies need plenty of sleep for proper growth and development. Just like children, overly tired puppies may become more fearful and reactive. Crates function as their safe space, and like cribs, can help establish sleep routines for nighttime and nap periods (see Figure A-2). This structured sleep schedule also aids in housetraining. If your puppy isn't crate trained, surround the crate with an open pen and fill it with familiar items, such as old sweatshirts with your scent, toys, chews, and food. Covering the crate creates a cozy den-like environment. For a free sleep and housetraining schedule, visit SarahHodgson.com.

© *Shutterstock*

FIGURE A-2: Crate training helps a puppy feel secure while sleeping.

FIRST DAYS HOME

Your puppy's first transition will be leaving their mom and littermates and coming to live with you. The first two weeks in a home should feel safe and routine. Surrounded by positive experiences, a puppy will develop confidence in the world around them. Use treats and toys to teach them impulse control and reward good choices, like sitting for attention and learning new words!

On the first night home, you may notice your puppy whining — they're likely calling out for their littermates. Reassure them by sleeping nearby, even by simply placing your fingers in their crate and making calming noises (like shh, shh, shh) until they feel safer in their new home. Socialization, good sleep habits, and calming interactions are the best things you can do to offset anxiety.

>> **Housetraining:** Puppies have predictable potty routines. They need to potty after they wake up, eat and drink, play and chew, or come out of confinement. A potty schedule should coordinate with a puppy's sleep schedule. Routinely take your puppy to their potty area, saying "time to potty" as you follow a consistent route to their potty spot. When your puppy goes potty, say another cue phrase like "get busy." Praise them calmly when they potty.

Handling Special Circumstances

A lot goes into a puppy's life experience before you bring them home. From day one, they begin learning about life beyond the womb through interactions with their littermates, their mom, and their first associations with people.

This section discusses a few situations that can cause puppies stress before being adopted into a loving home. Unfortunately, early stress can impact an adult dog's ability to cope with generalized anxiety and regulate their fear responses.

Irresponsible breeders

Poor breeding practices can significantly affect the well-being of puppies. It's important to recognize that not all individuals who claim to be breeders uphold ethical standards. Breeders prioritizing quantity over quality may struggle to provide attention and socialization to each puppy, compromising their development. While dogs from various backgrounds, such as those from puppy mills or hoarding situations, deserve love and care, they need homes with the resources and dedication to address the specific challenges stemming from their early experiences.

Rescues

Rescuing puppies from shelters presents unique challenges. Suppose a puppy is transported without their mother and possibly separated from their littermates, particularly during or after their fear impression period. In that case, their anxiety levels regarding certain events, such as car rides and meeting new people, may be severe. These puppies often begin their lives with a predisposition toward fear and may develop generalized anxiety as a result. Successfully helping them overcome these challenges demands commitment and patience. Are you prepared for this responsibility?

Puppies from pet stores or hoarding situations are often stressed from the beginning. Like rescue dogs, many of these puppies start with generalized anxiety and specific fears.

Orphans

Some puppies are abandoned or separated from their dog mom before eight weeks. Sometimes, they may even be isolated from their littermates and raised alone. A puppy's dog mother imparts key lessons on impulse control, fairness, and emotional regulation that are challenging for humans to replicate. As these puppies mature, they often exhibit limited frustration tolerance and may grow difficult when their desires are unmet. Considering these factors when dealing with a puppy in these circumstances is important.

Above all else, puppies need a supportive, structured environment. They require a role model who'll stay calm, especially when they get overwhelmed. Empathy and patience are the cornerstones of raising a self-confident puppy who learns early on where to turn when life gets unpredictable.

Appendix **B**
Anxiety in Senior Dogs

ogs, much like humans, age predictably. They experience sensory decline, physical changes, and cognitive deficiencies that influence their routines and interactions with the world around them. However, unlike humans, they can't articulate their discomfort or confusion. Consequently, many aging dogs develop anxiety, which manifests through a host of notable behaviors. These symptoms are typically attributed to the effects of aging and are diagnosed as Cognitive Dysfunction Syndrome (CDS). Here is a checklist of common symptoms:

- ❏ Nervous behaviors

- ❏ Anxiety/increased irritability

- ❏ Depressed and sluggish behavior instead of usual activities

- ❏ Sudden confusion

- ❏ Getting lost, stuck, or unable to navigate familiar locations.

- ❏ Pacing or wandering

- ❏ Gazing or fixating on objects

- ❏ Obsessive activities such as licking, self-mutilation, or persistent itching

- ❏ Vocalizing, particularly repetitive barking and howling

- [ ] Withdrawal from social interactions with new and familiar dogs and people
- [ ] Aggression when approached or handled by groomers, veterinarians, or even familiar individuals
- [ ] Clinginess
- [ ] Increased or repetitive activity levels
- [ ] Changes in appetite
- [ ] Anxiety about being separated from family members
- [ ] Sudden onset of generalized anxiety
- [ ] Restless sleep and waking up frequently during the night
- [ ] Loss of bladder or bowel control (incontinence)
- [ ] Elimination indoors in random locations in front of you or family members
- [ ] Decreased interest in activities they previously enjoyed
- [ ] Reduced responsiveness to directions or cues
- [ ] Increased sensitivity to noise or touch
- [ ] Change in grooming habits, such as neglecting personal hygiene
- [ ] Restlessness or aimless wandering
- [ ] Decreased ability to recognize familiar people or objects
- [ ] Reduced problem-solving abilities
- [ ] Episodes of staring into space or appearing disconnected from surroundings
- [ ] Increased startle response to sudden movements or noises

Although many of the behaviors can be frustrating for you, they're even more distressing for your dog. Your first step is to schedule a veterinarian visit, as many behaviors are symptomatic of underlying conditions. If nothing else, they will confirm whether your dog has CDS and help you craft a long-term plan, which may include meeting with a trainer or behavioral consultant to address these issues.

Understanding Generalized Anxiety in Aging Dogs

As dogs mature, their behavior will adapt to accommodate their strength and sensory awareness changes. They grow feeble and dependent and become more nervous about being left alone. General anxiety can develop and persist regardless of whether a feared event is occurring. I refer to this internal state as the *cortisol drip*: a continuous stream of the stress hormone that keeps the dog hyper-alert to potential danger and prevents relaxation in normal situations. Over time, this chronic stress can increase their susceptibility to diseases such as cancer, Cushing's disease, and other health issues.

FUN FACT

Dogs age differently depending on their size and breed. Small dogs can be considered senior at 11 or 12 years old. Medium sized dogs become seniors at ten years old, large dogs at eight years old, and giant breeds at seven years old.

Fortunately, dogs desire inclusion and affection and long for safety and love. Here are steps you can take to make the transition to old age more bearable:

>> **Maintain a consistent schedule.** Like people and young puppies, older dogs find comfort in familiarity and are unsettled by change. Consistency is key to alleviating anxiety in older dogs. Predictability in their daily lives helps them feel secure — including regular wake times, walks, meals, playtimes, and bedtimes.

>> **Modify beloved games like Fetch, Tug, or Hide-and-Seek to accommodate their physical or sensory decline.** Teach new games that rely on their sense of smell, such as Find It and Scavenger Hunt.

>> **Interact with your dog.** Dogs love company — even more so as they age and feel more vulnerable. Of course, you know they're safe, but your dog doesn't see their world through your eyes. As they return to the dependency of puppyhood, their need for unity increases.

>> **Minimize alterations to their environment.** For example, keep their food consistent, maintain the location of toys, and avoid frequent furniture rearrangements.

Despite life's unpredictability, every effort to maintain stability for your older dog contributes significantly to their well-being.

Dealing with Separation Anxiety

When life becomes blurry around the edges, it gets harder to be left alone, especially for dogs grappling with CDS. Separation anxiety ranks high in aging dogs and can lead to distress even before you depart. Signs may include trembling, panting, pacing, or excessive licking. When they are left alone, dogs with separation anxiety may bark incessantly, engage in destructive behavior, or have indoor accidents.

REMEMBER

The book's motto especially rings true here: Choose empathy over anger. Resist becoming frustrated with your dog. They need you now more than ever, and fortunately, many things can help ease your dog's worries.

Keep these tips in mind to combat separation anxiety:

>> **Ask family and friends if they can offer some time to doggie sit.** Company is key! While you may have other pets, they don't provide the same comfort as having a familiar person close. Most people can operate portable electronics anywhere now. Being home is preferable to being dropped off in an unfamiliar location.

>> **If you must leave your dog home alone, leaving music or the TV on can create the impression that you're still around.** However, pay attention to your dog's reaction and see if this increases their anxiety instead of helping to soothe them. An indoor pet camera can come in handy.

>> **Limit your dog to a comforting room or area to soothe them.** Many dogs prefer curling up by the door you've left from. Leave clothing with your scent to comfort your dog.

>> **Establish a calming environment during the day and ensure your dog is comfortable at night.** Evenings can be challenging for dogs with CDS, leading to episodes of waking up and vocalizing in distress. Keep them close by and offer reassurance if they call out.

MAINTAIN A POSITIVE ENVIRONMENT

Remember that your dog mirrors your emotions; maintaining calm can help alleviate their anxiety. Resist punitive reactions to behavioral issues and instead focus on providing love and acceptance. Engage in activities that bring you joy, nurturing a bond that has lasted a lifetime.

>> **Desensitize your dog to your absence by starting with short, non-emotional departures and arrivals.** Practice synchronized breathing before you leave and when you come back. Gradually increasing the duration can help them learn that you will return.

For much more on separation anxiety, check out Part 2 of this book.

Don't introduce a crate if your dog isn't already comfortable in one. The combination of confinement, separation anxiety, and aging can stress them out even more.

WARNING

Attending to Stranger Anxiety

Even previously sociable dogs may develop stranger anxiety as they age, displaying signs such as skittishness, tail-tucking, urination, or aggression when approached by unfamiliar individuals. As dogs age, they become more vulnerable and bound to home, routine, and familiar people. They may show little interest in meeting new dogs or people and become uptight or aggressive when unfamiliar individuals invade their personal space. This is all normal.

People are the only animals that perceive face-to-face, teeth-baring, body-enveloping greetings as normal. All other animals, especially dogs, see this interaction as confrontational and threatening. Don't allow anyone to approach your dog in this way. Rather, have them keep their hands where your dog can see them and approach them from the side instead of head-on.

REMEMBER

To support your dog's social anxieties, follow these tips:

>> **Respect your dog's boundaries and don't force them to interact with anyone they're uncomfortable with.** Don't hesitate to fend off polite admirers; your dog's need for safety should always come first.

>> **When interacting with kids, encourage gentle interactions by placing a treat or toy in the adolescent's hand and allowing your dog to approach at their own pace.** Avoid interactions with toddlers, as their movements and interactions are unpredictable.

>> **Modify walks and adventures as needed.** Dogs with social anxiety can still enjoy tailored adventures. If they enjoy car rides, take them to familiar places, crack the window, and allow them to explore new scents while you stand outside the window, offering comfort and rewards. If they're comfortable exploring outside, let them lead the way.

>> **Be an advocate for your dog.** Remember you're their family; they need you to advocate for them if someone misjudges their abilities. Remove them from stressful situations when necessary.

>> **Prioritize your dog's well-being over calorie counting.** If something makes them feel better, whether it's a new toy, a comfy bed, or an adventure like a trip to the beach, indulge them!

For much more on stranger anxiety, check out Chapter 11.

Addressing Medical Issues Common in Elder Dogs

Aches and pain besiege the elderly, and your dog is no exception. Aging is tough, causing acute pain, physical discomfort, and mood disorders. Signs of pain in dogs can include limping, difficulty rising or lying down, reluctance to climb stairs or jump, decreased activity, and changes in appetite or sleep patterns. Many aches and pains can result in behavioral changes that may not indicate illness or injury.

Consult Table B-1 for common illnesses and behavioral symptoms in older dogs. Chapter 5 contains more information about medical issues that dogs of all ages can experience.

TABLE B-1 Elder Dog Behaviors and Related Illnesses

Behaviors	Symptoms	Condition
"My dog no longer responds to familiar cues like 'come' or their name. They startle easily, often vocalize, and constantly bump into objects."	Cloudy eyes, dilated pupils, bumping into objects, lack of response to auditory cues	Vision and hearing loss
"My dog is reluctant to move, has trouble rising and lying down, and has a decreased activity level."	Limping, favoring certain limbs, swelling or warmth around joints, audible joint cracking	Arthritis
"My dog is reluctant to eat and often paws at their mouth."	Red or swollen gums, tartar buildup, loose or missing teeth, oral infections	Dental disease
"My dog is lethargic, exhibiting a loss of appetite and weight, and seems to have less energy overall."	Visible lumps or bumps, abnormal swelling, non-healing sores, difficulty breathing or urinating (depending on tumor location)	Cancer
"My dog is constantly thirsty and experiencing weight loss despite an increased appetite. They seem lethargic and urinate more often."	Sweet-smelling breath, cataracts, weakness in hind legs (in severe cases), urinary tract infections	Diabetes
"My dog is constantly hungry. They also seem confused and lethargic and is experiencing vomiting and diarrhea."	Jaundice (yellowing of the skin and whites of the eyes), abdominal swelling (ascites), increased drinking and urination	Liver disease
"My dog is always thirsty, urinating more frequently, experiencing a loss of appetite, and generally lethargic."	Weight loss, dehydration, vomiting, pale gums, bad breath	Kidney disease
"My dog appears weak and fatigued. They cough frequently and show a low tolerance for exercise."	Irregular heartbeat, difficulty breathing, fainting episodes, fluid accumulation (edema) in the abdomen or legs	Heart disease
"My dog keeps urinating in the house and constantly licks their genitals."	Wet fur around the genital area, urine odor, redness or irritation of the skin	Bladder disease (e.g., incontinence)

REMEMBER

Contact your veterinarian or veterinary behaviorist before reacting to any change in your dog's behavior. It's important to rule out and treat medical issues first.

Dealing with Anxiety from Failing Senses

One of the more notable signs of aging and CDS is a decline in senses, with sight and hearing being the most common. Many older dogs develop a noise phobia toward loud, unpredictable sounds like thunder or fireworks. This decline often brings about anxiety, leading to a fear of being caught off guard when familiar environments are disrupted. Hearing loss may lead to misunderstandings with loving family members, who may mistake their delay for disrespectful behavior.

It's important to remember that your dog is more vulnerable in their older age, and they may revert to a puppy-like state, feeling more vulnerable and in need of protection. Consider these tips:

>> **Use your dog's remaining senses to help shape their environment.** Create a comforting atmosphere using pheromones and aromatherapy while eliminating unpleasant odors to dogs. Common options include lavender, chamomile, and cedar wood. Use repugnant odors like citrus and oregano to warn of danger zones like pools and ledges.

>> **When dealing with sudden noise aversion, ensure that someone stays with your dog during celebrations and weather events.** Confine them to their favorite room with comforting blankets and familiar clothing items with your scent, and be surrounded by pillows for tactile comfort. Join them in the room and use synchronized breathing to model calmness. If you can't be there, arrange for a familiar person to stay with them so they don't have to face it alone.

>> **Encourage everyone who loves your dog to approach calmly and accommodate their reduced senses.** Navigating the world with diminished senses is like walking on thin ice. For a blind dog, announce your arrival verbally or with a gentle touch. Wave your arms for those with hearing

loss, and consider using distinct visual signals or vibrations to get their attention. Maintain a consistent routine and environment to provide stability and predictability.

>> **If possible, consider sleeping with your dog to provide tactile comfort and reassurance.** Sleeping patterns may be disrupted in older dogs, leading to insomnia at night and increased exhaustion and irritability during the day. This disruption can also lead to separation anxiety, as sleep can feel like a form of abandonment. Try keeping a light on and using a sound machine to drown out nighttime disturbances. Always offer gentle and loving touches to your dog when they're feeling stressed to help soothe them.

>> **To enhance your dog's quality of life, engage them in mentally stimulating activities tailored to their abilities.** Consider puzzle toys, interactive games, or scent-based challenges to keep their mind active and engaged. These activities provide mental stimulation, help maintain cognitive function, and prevent boredom, which can alleviate stress and anxiety in older dogs.

SUPPLEMENTS, MEDICATION, AND OTHER HELPFUL PRODUCTS

Consider supplements like Omega-3 fatty acids and cognitive support formulas for dogs with CDS or other age-related anxieties. Pheromones and aromatherapy can help reduce anxiety, while medications may be necessary for severe symptoms of separation anxiety or noise phobia. Consult your vet for tailored recommendations and guidance on managing your dog's specific needs. Various products can help dogs with conditions like incontinence and anxiety. Diapers can assist with managing incontinence, while calming wraps, also known as anxiety wraps or pressure vests, can help alleviate anxiety and sensory sensitivities.

Addressing Anxiety from Loss of Bladder/ Bowel Control

As dogs age, their muscles, like ours, lose tone and contractibility, leading to overall weakness. This weakening extends to their bladder muscles, affecting their ability to control urination and often affecting their housetraining. Symptoms of CDS may also contribute to their disorientation and incontinence.

To minimize accidents, consider increasing outdoor bathroom breaks, adjusting your schedule, or seeking assistance from neighbors or a dog sitter. Doggy diapers can help manage frequent and unpredictable eliminations. Remember to respond to accidents calmly and avoid punishment, as your senior dog is doing their best. Be sure to consult with your veterinarian for guidance on managing any underlying medical conditions contributing to their incontinence.

IN THIS CHAPTER

» Learning to understand your dog's fears

» Helping your dog tolerate the vet

» Normalizing visits to the groomer

» Helping to make daycare fun

» Calming your dog with trainers and other pet professionals

Appendix C

Addressing Fear of the Veterinarian and Other Pet Care Professionals

nteractions with pet care professionals can be challenging for even the calmest or most outgoing dogs. After all, it's easy to get unnerved when someone is blasting an industrial-sized dryer in your face or jamming a thermometer into your nether regions. While some dogs may enjoy their time with a dog walker, at daycare, or with an overnight pet sitter, others may feel anxious and utterly abandoned.

When these destinations are unavoidable, a dog with these anxieties may take days to recover, can develop new triggers like containment or separation anxiety, or might even cultivate a state of generalized anxiety that consumes their day. This appendix is dedicated to all the dogs with anxiety who resist anyone handling them outside their family.

Understanding Your Dog's Fears

Dogs with anxiety are typically not comfortable with anyone handling them but their family. From vets to groomers, to daycare facilities and dog sitters, many dogs with anxiety become withdrawn and depressed, refusing to eat or, on the flip side, reactive and snippy with even the most well-intentioned caregiver. Further, sensitive dogs and those with separation anxiety quickly become sensitized to secondary activities like car rides, triggering a phobic reaction even when that destination is not intended.

REMEMBER

When my son was young and afraid of needles, a doctor insisted on pinning him down hastily, claiming we were wasting his time. I left and never returned to that doctor. Regardless of what your dog chooses to do, their behavior is neither good nor bad. It's simply communication — their way of dealing with the energy and stress they're experiencing at a given moment.

WARNING

When a dog shows aggression, people assume the dog is inherently mean and is attempting to assert dominance. This is rarely the case: Aggression is often a bodyguard of fear. As violent reactions require great energy, dogs, like people, only resort to aggression when other signs of distress have been ignored.

To help your dog overcome their fear of pet care professions, you must make new, more positive associations with the journey, experience, and people. Eliminate dated techniques like pulling or dragging a dog against their will or hoisting them off their feet like lifeless stuffed toys. Dismiss professionals who dismiss your dog's emotional sensitives or who rely on rough handling as a means of control. Find open-minded professionals who embrace food, fun, and gentle-handling techniques to soothe your dog's insecurities, helping them feel safe even when the interactions are unpleasant. By allowing your dog to acclimate at their own pace, you'll develop strategies to foster positive relationships between them and those who help you care for them.

Helping Your Dog Tolerate the Vet

The veterinarian's office can be overwhelming for dogs. It offers unfamiliar surroundings, strange odors, and separation from their humans. This is especially daunting for dogs who fear strangers or react negatively to other dogs, as a routine checkup can mean facing both. Moreover, the shock of experiencing discomfort and unfamiliar handling further a dog's stress, and it can reach a tipping point.

While many dogs can be comforted with a treat and a friendly pat on the head, a dog with anxiety can swiftly transition into their emotional fight, flight, or freeze brain and can cling to a memory that triggers fear the moment you turn into the parking lot. Consider whether your dog's anxiety is triggered by any of the following:

>> Leaving home

>> Riding in the car

>> Being separated from you

>> Anxiety during medical procedures (including handling by veterinary technicians, full-body examinations, rectal temperature checks, and receiving shots)

>> Strangers

>> Nervousness around other dogs, possibly triggered by the scent of another dog

>> The tile flooring

>> The scale

>> Being placed on the table

FUN FACT

Dogs are highly attuned to our emotions. If your anxiety mirrors theirs, it can reinforce their perception that something bad is happening. If your dog fears a situation like visiting the veterinarian, model confidence. A calm attitude goes a long way in helping your dog feel safe. Take deep breaths, gently pet them if it calms your dog, and envision a positive experience.

Even the most confident dogs can lose their mojo at veterinarians. Without our guidance, visiting the veterinarian or — in more serious cases, staying overnight — can induce panic and distress. Gradual exposure, counterconditioning, and desensitization can help make these visits tolerable, a bit more interesting, and perhaps even a little fun.

Play veterinarian

You can get your stethoscope or children's doctor kits and some empty droppers from the drug store to "play veterinarian" at home. Before starting the game, hold each item out for your dog to sniff. Give them treats when they do so they're not tempted to treat them like toys.

In addition to your examination tools, have licky mats, favorite chews, and treats ready. Move at your dog's pace: Pair faux examination touches as your dog focuses on a helper giving them treats or a licky mat. Initially, one touch, one treat; try a few momentary touches while your dog enjoys a their chew toy or licky mat. Should they turn to you, stop touching them and freeze in place. By giving them agency over the tempo of the examination and pairing touch with positive reinforcers, your dog will look forward to experiencing examination equipment.

WARNING

Scales can stress dogs out before they even enter the exam office. Since they are often positioned in corners, dogs can feel trapped and resistant to getting on them. Place your dog mat on the scale, ask them to zero out the scale, then use treats and toys to lure them on. Do not drag and force; this will trigger your dog's anxiety.

In addition to playing veterinarian with equipment, rehearse gentle-handling techniques to simulate an examination. This can include touching your dog's paws, ears, and mouth and gently restraining them. Again, reward your dog for calm behavior during these sessions.

If your dog is uncomfortable with handling, tricks can help.

>> Teach "paws up!" Have your dog balance their front paws on your forearm or other object. Use this during weigh-ins and to help with examinations.

>> "Chin rest" is another helpful behavior, where your dog rests their chin on your hand, aiding in low-stress handling during exams.

>> Other tricks like "spin," "roll over," or "high five" can make exams cheery. These tricks and more are covered in Chapter 3.

Choose a vet your dog likes

Choose a veterinary hospital your dog feels comfortable with that responds kindly to your dog's special needs. Pre-determine if you can accompany your dog to exams; if not, consider a veterinary hospital that offers that option.

In addition to the veterinarian, their front staff and technicians may also influence your decision. You're paying for their service, so spend time choosing where you and your dog feel comfortable. Bring your mat, treats, and toys, and use the other tips in this section to make the trip more pleasant. Explain your efforts with the staff and the specialized techniques you use to ease your dog's anxiety.

Visit for fun

Use food, fun, and plenty of positive encouragement each time you set off for a veterinary visit. Begin play and engaging walks before you leave to boost your dog's serotonin, the happy hormone, and release energy. Keep the treats coming as you bring your dog into the building and during the exam! Offer others a treat cup, ask them to shake it, and reward your dog a few times before routine check-ups and vaccinations. Use familiar mats, chews, and favorite toys to distract and comfort them during examinations or procedures.

Use the Fear Free approach

Fear Free is an initiative dedicated to preventing and easing fear, anxiety, and stress in pets. Founded by Dr. Marty Becker, "America's Veterinarian," in 2016, with the collaboration of hundreds of experts in behavior, medicine, and handling, Fear Free offers education to veterinary professionals, pet professionals, animal welfare communities, and pet parents. Fear Free-affiliated practices are well-prepared to provide care to dogs. This approach is especially comforting to sensitive dogs. I'm honored to be part of the Fear Free board.

Try calming supplements or medication

You can use anything to ease your dog's stress during a veterinary visit, including products, supplements, and short-term medication. Chapter 5 lists calming options; speak to your veterinarian or veterinary behaviorist about the various options.

Take regular car rides

Once a dog associates car rides with vet visits and other negative destinations, the car may provoke anxiety. If this situation sounds familiar, link being in the car to more positive outcomes, such as attention, food, favorite chews, or busy toys. Once your dog is more comfortable entering the car, go on rides that end somewhere fun, such as a park, playdate, trail, or town. You know what your dog enjoys most!

Normalizing Groomer Visits

Regardless of how wonderful your groomer may be, many dogs don't develop a strong attachment to them. A single negative experience at the groomer can lead to a phobic reaction, affecting car rides, home brush-outs, and future visits altogether. For dogs with containment anxiety (covered in Chapters 8-10), being confined to a crate on top of these stressors can worsen their already frightening condition. If your dog experiences severe separation anxiety, it's best to avoid leaving them anywhere, especially during the rehabilitation process.

Normalizing visits to the groomer involves similar principles to those used for vet visits, focusing on desensitization, positive reinforcement, and gradual exposure. Here are some steps you can take to help your dog become more comfortable with grooming appointments:

>> **Desensitize at home:** Gradually introduce grooming tools such as brushes, combs, and nail clippers to your dog. Allow them to sniff and investigate these tools while rewarding calm behavior with treats and praise. This helps your dog familiarize with the grooming process in a relaxed environment.

>> **Play Operation Cooperation:** This is a great game for desensitization, used throughout the book. It gives your dog more agency over uncomfortable situations and allows them to communicate their comfort level. Best of all, it's fun, easy to learn, and strengthens your bond. For an in-depth explanation, see Chapter 3.

>> **Try short, positive visits:** Ask your groomer if you can occasionally bring your dog into the store to pair the route with food and fun. Pop in for short, positive visits that result in treats, favorite busy toys, and affection. Gradually increase the duration and complexity of the visits as your dog becomes more comfortable.

>> **Choose a groomer your dog likes:** Just like with vets, it's beneficial to choose a groomer that your dog feels comfortable with. Look for groomers who have experience working with dogs with anxiety and who prioritize gentle-handling techniques.

>> **Incorporate regular brushing:** Incorporate frequent brushouts, depending on your dog's coat. Ask your groomer which tools are best for your dog's coat. This will reduce the cost and stress at the groomer and reduce the need for a full body shave down, which is only done when the coat is matted. A bonus of routine maintenance is your dog's increased comfort level at the groomer.

Helping Your Dog Love Their Sitter or Walker

For dogs experiencing anxiety, the presence of a pet sitter or dog walker might trigger feelings of abandonment or confusion. If you notice your dog's tail drooping or they resist interacting with the helper, and you cannot avoid using their service, try using rewards and engaging games to help your dog feel more comfortable with the current helper, or alternatively, seek out someone better suited for dealing with your dog's temperament. Here are a few tips for helping your dog love their sitter or walker:

>> **Start by introducing the new person to your dog in a neutral environment, such as at a park or outside your home.** Allow your dog to approach the person at their own pace and sniff them to become familiar with their scent.

>> **Tell the dog sitter what treats, toys, and touches help to calm your dog down.** For example, hot dogs, toys, music, and loving touches like ear massages and bottom scratches.

>> **Outline familiar interactions, games, and directions.**
Teach your helper what movements to avoid, such as fast motions, head pats, or other moves that upset your dog.

>> **Ask your helper to stick to your dog's routines and walking routes while you're away.**

Pet sitters and dog walkers play an important role, especially with dogs with anxiety, as they provide much-needed company during solitude. By gradually increasing your dog's time with them, you can help them build a comforting bond.

Making Daycare Fun

Dogs with anxiety don't thrive in chaotic situations. While a romp in a big room with various unfamiliar dogs and no potty rules might sound fun to you, dogs who have anxiety disorders prefer the security of home.

TIP

Pay close attention to your dog's body language when you bring them to daycare. If you notice their tail, ears, or body drooping, or if they resist going into the facility, it's worth reconsidering this option. As anxious children may not thrive in loud, chaotic situations, your dog may also prefer the familiarity and security of home.

If this option is unavoidable due to work commitments and time constraints, find a facility that:

>> Groups dogs according to temperaments.

>> Offers downtime when necessary and throughout the day.

>> Listens to your concerns and special requests, such as using provided bedding and toys during rest time.

>> Clearly likes and enjoys your dog.

Alone time can be more difficult for dogs with anxiety. Having a trusted group that will prioritize their individual needs and sensitive temperament can be incredibly valuable when you must be away.

Normalizing Trainers and Board-n-Train Facilities

If you've hired a trainer who instills fear in your dog, seek a new trainer. Prioritize someone with experience in working with anxiety and explore virtual training options. Based on my experience with virtual training, I've observed that it shifts the focus away from the dog's response to the trainer and strengthens the bond between the dog and their family.

A negative experience with a trainer or kennel can lead to fear or avoidant behaviors toward similar handling situations, training lessons in general, or specific individuals. This often occurs with underground electric fence trainers who tend to rush and handle dogs within a routine rather than individuals. In such cases, dogs may be dragged across shock zones and subjected to trainers yelling at flags to "warn" them from approaching. The problem? The dog undergoing such "training" does not understand what's happening or where their person went. It's common to see a spike in social anxiety, separation anxiety, and nervous reluctance any time someone else takes the leash. One traumatic experience can ruin a dog's trust indefinitely.

WARNING

An overnight training facility may not be the best option for dogs with anxiety. Many facilities now use battery-operated collars to deliver shocks or various stimulation to modify a dog's behavior. If being away from home isn't stressful enough, being handled and shocked by strangers can shut down a dog with anxiety, making it hard for them to trust new people and novel experiences.

Take the time to find professionals who will be patient and sensitive toward your dog's anxiety. With the right support, you can help your dog navigate these situations confidently and easily.

conflicts arise

» **Creating routines to prevent conflict**

» **Communicating effectively with multiple dogs**

» **Managing tiffs**

Appendix **D**

Managing Multi-dog Households

L iving in a multi-dog household where all the dogs get along, respect each other's things, and listen to your direction is rewarding and enjoyable. Unfortunately, not all multi-dog households are this harmonious. Chronic stress and insecurity can cast a shadow over your household, leaving everyone on edge and nervous.

This appendix explores the nuances of living with multiple dogs and provides insights into understanding and addressing dog-to-dog aggression. Managing space, preventing conflicts, and fostering friendships can be surprisingly easy once you establish clear rules, routines, and boundaries. As the mediator, it's important that you keep your cool. If you're not confident in managing this situation, don't hesitate to seek professional help.

Understanding Dog-to-Dog Relationships

Dogs love role models. If you want your dogs to get along, establish yourself as their parental figure: Dogs love a leader with grit and good ideas. Are you worried you might be too late for the game? Fortunately, it's never too late to assume this role. If you have a dog or dogs who spar over resources and accessibility to good stuff, it's time to establish some ground rules!

TIP

How often does your dog look to you throughout the day? Five times? Ten times? Every five minutes? Each glance carries a message: "I'm bored; What should I do?" "Let's play!" Maybe even, "I need a potty break." If your dog constantly prompts you for engagement, it shows they have difficulty self-soothing or settling down.

All dogs, like people, have unique personalities and special gifts. When you live with multiple dogs, you must act as their social director or parent. Sometimes, they'll spar over a toy, a resting spot, or your attention. Knowing how to manage their interactions at their best and worst is critical if you want harmony in your household. Here are my top tips:

>> **Teach each dog their name so you can call to them individually:** Each dog needs to react to their own name in order for any multi-dog training to be effective.

>> **Be the one to watch:** Establish routines, directions, games, and quiet time. Assign words to routines, objects, and people to give your dog insights about their day.

>> **Be calm, cool, and collected:** Dogs are perceptive and can pick up on emotions. When you remain calm and composed, especially during conflicts or stressful situations, your dogs are more likely to mirror that behavior.

>> **Avoid sustained glaring and direct eye contact:** Humans are the only mammals that see conversational eye contact with smiling as polite. Other mammals interpret direct eye contact with visible teeth as confrontational or an invitation to play rough. While some dogs seek eye contact when relaxed, remember: When teaching your dog, say and show, don't say and stare.

>> **Enforce the rules:** Several rules are necessary for multi-dog households, such as using the four-paw rule, sitting calmly for attention, using food toys, and place training. A bonus is teaching your dogs to wait until their name is called before entering a door or gate. No dog should proceed out a gate, car, or fenced area until their name is called. Finally, it's not theirs if you didn't give it to them!

WOULD ANOTHER DOG HELP?

Some people think that having two dogs will alleviate separation anxiety. A recent study at Tufts University showed that the opposite is true! Separation anxiety tends to increase with another dog in the house. This is likely because emotionally reactive dogs control the mood when you're gone. Having multiple dogs is like having a group of children; no single dog can replace the role of a parent.

> **>> Don't play favorites:** Nurture and appreciate each dog's personality and gifts. Make an effort to spend individual quality time with each dog, engaging in activities they enjoy.

WARNING

Dogs only fight to defend a need or resource, such as a bone, toy, space, or even you. Dogs with anxiety more often cling to their people. When the neediest dog is reinforced with constant affection, this can create tension in multi-dog households.

Logging the Conflicts

Many people interpret dog aggression as mean, vindictive, or dominant. In most cases, aggression is simply the bodyguard of fear and is used as a last resort when other warning cues are ignored. Resource guarding is a tipping point when a dog's anxiety and defensiveness ignite, which happens more frequently in a multi-dog household.

What is there to fight about?

Dogs treasure their possessions as much as we do. They may unravel and begin bickering over simple things like food, toys, resting spaces, and your attention when they lack routine and structure. While some dogs share more easily than others, many are insecure and guard what little control they have. Confident dogs rarely engage in fights over possessions, as they understand what's theirs.

If your dogs bicker, grab your behavior diary and jot down your observations dog by dog. Cover topics such as who is most coveting of food, toys, doorways, company, and your attention. Does one dog have a favorite resting spot? Note how each dog conveys their aggravation. Do they growl, snap, lunge, hover, or outright attack? Does one dog give warnings while another snaps without warning? Confident dogs typically give warnings, while insecure dogs may escalate quickly. Consider this list of resources your dogs may fight over:

>> Leash, couch, bed, and so on

>> Food (treats and meals)

>> Personal space

>> Tight passageways, hallways, or doorways

>> Bones and toys

>> Attention from their favorite person or visitors

>> Territory or leash circumference

>> Countertops

Next, record your response. Do you yell, physically separate them, or attempt to intervene with props like a chair mimicking a lion tamer? Finally, create a section labeled "What You Should Do" and fill it in after reading this chapter.

Where do most fights occur?

As you work to understand, direct, and calm your dogs' aggressive responses, remember that all dogs prefer peaceful interaction and getting along. Conflicts stem from fear: fear of there not being enough resources, lacking an authority figure to organize and structure daily routines, and possible stress-related illnesses from walking on eggshells. Rest may be interrupted, too, as heightened arousal levels can interrupt much-needed sleep patterns.

Take note of where fights often happen, whether by a window with a view of outside activity, at the door where they greet visitors and family members, or where they eat during feeding time.

When do most fights occur?

Conflicts between dogs can erupt during various routine activities and interactions:

>> Mealtimes often become a battleground as dogs compete for food.

>> Chewing on a bone may also lead to disputes, with possessive behavior over the prized object.

>> Playtime can turn sour when one dog reacts over a personal space violation or a favorite toy or object.

>> Seeking attention from you can often spark jealousy. Whether with family members or familiar visitors, greetings can trigger territorial instincts or provoke insecurity. Even simple gestures like petting can escalate tensions if one dog feels slighted or left out.

>> Certain locations within the home, such as doorways, stairs, hallways, or the kitchen, may serve as hotspots for conflicts, as dogs feel the need to defend their territory.

The bottom line: Fights can start during any routine activity or interaction, driven by underlying instincts, territoriality, or emotional responses.

Other factors that contribute to conflicts

Bickering over resources, vying for attention, and jostling for positions are common sibling rivalry moves. At the root of all these conflicts is resource guarding. If your dogs had a more free-ranging lifestyle, they'd figure it out; dogs rarely invest energy in bickering when given enough space. However, when dogs are confined in small houses, often lacking stimulation and feeling bored, tensions can escalate, leading to quarrels. These conflicts may be triggered by the excitement of greeting or observing others behind a fence or window. With limited outlets for their energy, dogs may fixate on possessions and status, leading to competitiveness or redirecting their frustration onto one another.

Confinement with other dogs

We often see dog-to-dog reactivity as a dog problem when it's really a consequence of their place in our modern society. In a multi-dog household, dogs are often confined indoors or behind fences, under constant supervision, and forced to share resources and space. We've created a fishbowl effect, which can leave dogs anxious and frustrated. Constant frustration can escalate their reactivity, leading them to lash out at each other.

An abundance of pets

While I'm all for growing families, but bringing home a new dog or puppy is more exciting for you than for your pets.

Nobody lives with somebody without conflicts now and then, and dogs are no different. When people clash, we use words and sometimes raised voices; dogs often growl and show teeth when they quibble. Dogs rarely draw blood unless we spawn a greater divide with our interference.

Perpetual anxiety

Stress motivates conflict, no matter the species. When tensions rise, dogs switch to their reactive, emotional brains. Cortisol and adrenaline increase as they react quickly with little emotional regulation. Triggers can include passersby, other dogs, visitors, resources (like sleeping areas, food, water, treats, toys, and people), and disputes between people.

Some dogs, like people, are born with a greater need for reassurance. With little self-confidence, they may imagine the worst possible outcomes, straining relationships and increasing conflict. Recognizing the role anxiety plays in your dogs' conflicts is critical. Understanding each dog's unique needs and using specific strategies for managing anxiety is essential for creating a harmonious and stress-free environment for everyone. Stay calm and confident and take action to guide them effectively.

WARNING

Avoid shouting or scolding your dogs for squabbling. Reacting in the heat of the moment only reinforces their reactivity. Instead, model a good attitude and a calm demeanor. Use the rest of the chapter to devise a plan ahead of time. Implement the methods that work and eliminate those that don't. Be the model of calmness for your dogs.

Rough play and tug-of-war

While some dogs love rough play and tugging, these games lead to hyperarousal and dysregulation. When two dogs get aroused, it's not uncommon for their roughhousing to become confrontational or for one to turn on the other.

Adverse or negatively reinforced training

Avoid training methods that frighten your dog or heighten their stress, such as punitive measures or e-collars. When a dog feels powerless, they can become susceptible to another dog's stress, especially if they're also experiencing a disciplinary environment.

Territorial reactivity

All dogs bond to their home as their den and a yard or neighborhood as their territory. When multiple dogs sound off at the fence line or window, tensions rise, and without a proper outlet, dogs often turn on each other.

Age differences

Age-related changes, such as introducing a puppy, can trigger stress and conflicts, as resident dogs may feel threatened or irritated by the persistence of the new addition. Similarly, adopting a mature dog can pose challenges, as the resident dog may react to being sidelined and frustrated with the presence of another adult dog.

Pain

Illness, pain, or discomfort can trigger aggressive responses in dogs, either as a defensive reaction to protect themselves or increased irritability due to physical discomfort. Healthy dogs may also jockey for authority and, in some cases, bully an impaired dog.

Homecoming after grooming, vet visits, or errands

When one dog leaves for a medical or grooming appointment, they might return home stressed, disoriented, or smelling unfamiliar, not to mention those who come back with the dreaded cone of shame or with injuries. Resident dogs may react by turning on their usually affectionate sibling as if an alien presence has invaded their home.

Boredom

Boredom or lack of mental stimulation can lead to reactivity, as dogs may seek stimulation through confrontational interactions with other dogs.

Gender issues

With same-sex pairings, female dogs are proven to engage in more intense and prolonged altercations compared to males, and same-sex pairs are more prone to aggression.

Loud noises and weather events

Many dogs have an innate fear of fireworks and weather events. Their fear reaction can have an adverse effect on puppies or younger dogs in the home, especially those experiencing these events for the first time (because they mirror what's modeled). Older dogs may also get dysregulated by stress pacing, clinging, and acting out in unfamiliar ways.

Breed differences

Certain breeds, especially those originally bred for fighting or protection, may be genetically predisposed to dog-on-dog aggression. While variations exist, breed tendencies toward aggression can influence a dog's behavior.

Trigger stacking

While a dog might be able to endure one stress, add two or three or four, and they might reach their breaking point. When you live in a multi-dog household, if one dog gets frantically upset, the other dogs will respond in what can quickly become a bruhaha. If you want to live with multiple dogs successfully, learning to identify triggers and soothe each dog as an individual is mandatory.

Creating Routines with Multiple Dogs

The goal of having more than one dog is for them to have more company when you're out and enjoy being with them at home. It's a good goal! But sometimes, living with multiple dogs takes effort, energy, and eyes-in-the-back impulses, at least initially.

Dogs love predictable routines — predictable sleep, play, and eating schedules. Dogs who are fed predictably, potty predictably, too. No matter how much the Internet touts the need for constant stimulation, restful dogs have been shown to have lower stress hormones and live more peacefully with one another.

Living with multiple dogs doubles the responsibility and the need to structure interactions throughout the day. Without order, interactions can sow seeds of confrontation. Don't let that happen! Assign words to each need, as explained in Chapter 3.

The following sections cover five ways to organize your day so that each interaction brings more cooperation than conflict.

Predictable mealtimes

Assign each dog an area or mat and instruct them to sit calmly before presenting their meal.

With proper planning and execution, mealtimes can become opportunities to reinforce good manners and self-control in your dogs, establish yourself as the parental figure, and address resource-guarding behavior. The goal is for each dog to wait calmly (ideally sitting) in their usual spot while you prepare and serve their food, eat without guarding it, and leave the area without attempting to eat others' meals. Consistency and structure are key to success here.

WARNING

If your dogs are contentious around mealtimes, divide them with a crate, pen, or gates. Enact structure and reinforce mealtime rules to calm these interactions. Also, enforce that each dog looks to you and stays in one area when eating.

Orderly drinking turns

When one dog is drinking, teach the other to wait. If you see one poaching or crowding in, instruct that dog to "wait" for their turn. If they ignore you, have the pushy dog dragging a leash so you can supervise them and enable calm interference.

Coordinated sleeping areas

Limit sleepy time resource guarding by assigning each dog a sleeping area. If the dogs are contentious, assign areas in separate crates or rooms divided by a gate or pen.

Orchestrated potty times

When dogs potty together, one can interrupt the other mid-stream or clutch. Teach each dog their individual name so you can call to either should they interrupt each other.

Manageable playtimes

The bottom line is that you need to teach each dog impulse control. No matter how reeved-up playtime gets, periodically stop the play and insist the dogs sit or lay down and pause for a varying amount of time (3-20 seconds).

Nothing levitates moods or relationships more than fun and games. Before addressing friction, do anything you can to counter tension. Here are four games that can unite a multi-dog household:

>> **10 O'Clock, 2 O'Clock:** When two dogs face you for treats, toys, or attention, imagine the area in front of you like a clock. With you at 12 o'clock, remind both dogs to "stay," then toss one treat to your left at 10:00 and the other to your right at 2:00, as shown in Figure D-1.

>> **Treat-Retreat:** Toss the treats close to your feet (treat) and back behind your dog (the retreat) in the 10 o'clock, 2 o'clock formation. If this causes tension, divide the dogs via a gate. This game is exciting and keeps the attention focused on you.

>> **Catch Me If You Can:** With a treat cup in hand, shake the snacks and run in the opposite direction as you call your dogs. Initially, keep it short. After five to ten turns, hold your hand like a traffic guard, saying, "stop!" Reward your dogs in the 10 o'clock to 2 o'clock formation. Keep this going for three to five minutes.

>> **The Nickname Game:** Dogs can quickly learn to respond to their names once they join your household. To establish this connection, associate their name with a favorite toy, a treat, or the sound of a shaking treat cup.

TIP

Here's a fun twist: Teach them their individual names and the collective name you use when addressing them together. For example, if you have dogs named Gus and Chloe, they can learn to respond to "Guys!" when called together.

FIGURE D-1: The 10 o'clock, 2 o'clock formation.

ENRICHING ACTIVITIES FOR MULTIPLE DOGS

When weather or time constraints derail plans, many enrichment toys can keep your clan satisfied and happy. Here are some of the treats and toys I rely on; check out Chapter 3 for more games, toys, and activities.

- **Pupsicles:** Frozen treats, such as bananas, strawberries, yogurt, and peanut butter, provide a refreshing and enjoyable way for dogs to cool down on hot days, while also offering a tasty snack.

- **Treat dispensers:** Interactive toys that dispense treats as your dog plays, providing mental stimulation and rewarding activity.

(continued)

(continued)

- **Licky mats:** Silicone mats designed to hold treats or peanut butter, providing a long-lasting, engaging licking activity that helps calm and entertain dogs.
- **Fresh chews:** Natural, long-lasting chews, such as bully sticks or antlers, satisfy your dog's instinct to chew while promoting dental health and keeping them busy!

Building a Vocabulary with Your Dogs

Lessons help dogs associate your presence with structure and assign meaning to various words. Incorporating freedom, food, and fun during lessons fosters a sense of teamwork. If lesson time becomes overly stressful, it can elevate adrenaline and cortisol levels, especially in your presence, leading to heightened tension. Once you've taught each dog to recognize a specific word, use it when your dogs are together, rewarding them only when they respond.

In a multi-dog household, dogs will look to you for direction. If you stop each time they do and focus all your affection on that one dog, the others may seek their share, leading to sibling rivalry. Instead, try a new approach. When your dog looks to you, give them a direction, even if it's just a simple "sit" or "get your ball." Reward them for initiating the interaction with you.

With more than one dog, you need to teach and train them separately before you direct them together. This section describes the top five words my family and I use daily with our dogs. I've included other words you may find helpful. Choose your go-to words or phrases.

Sit and watch

Sitting is the equivalent of saying "please." Use it before all positives, including treats, food, toys, going out the door, your attention, and more. If following "sit," they don't look to you, remind them to "watch" before rewarding them.

Teach your dog to wait until their name is called to receive a treat or be released. Don't play favorites. For a tutorial, hop over to my Instagram account (@SarahSaysPets).

Pair "sit" and "watch" often to create wordless habits — routines so ingrained your dog does them automatically.

Place

This teaches your dogs that all good things happen when they are on their beds, mats, or in their area. Initially, assign your dogs an area in each room you share with them. Place them at least three to six feet apart and near a doorway or heavy piece of furniture should you tether either or both.

Tethering involves attaching a three- to four-foot leash to an immovable object or closing the end of the leash in an adjacent doorway. Use coated wire or chain leashes if your dogs might chew the leash.

If you're experiencing tension between your dogs, another place each dog should know by heart is "in your room," which will signify a crate or private area. Should tension arise, a calmly instructed timeout can help reset the mood. To clarify, there are no hard feelings. Give each dog a chew or busy toy and block direct eye contact with a blanket or piece of furniture, if necessary.

Wait

This direction says, "stop, look, and listen." It has many functions, including teaching your dog to pause before entering or exiting a room, the car, crate, or doorway as needed, on walks to urge them not to race ahead and to check in. It helps you manage them during life's many unpredictable events. The other day, I broke a glass jar on our walkway, bringing my four dogs running. I calmly told them all to "wait," which saved the day (and their paws)!

Get your x

You can fill in the blank here: ball, bone, toy, sock, and so on. Labeling the objects your dog chooses rather than yelling at them will make your dog more likely to share it and, within days, fetch the thing you identify! Each time your dog picks something up in their mouth, identify it and tell them either to "go to place," bring it to you, or let them keep it with loving praise from you.

Hand target and come

The hand target is an easy and fun way to get your dog's attention. Work with each dog separately before using it together in the 10 o'clock 2 o'clock formation described previously.

Hold your hand three to four inches directly in front of your dog's face and reward them when they bop it with their nose. Add touch when you're certain they've caught on. Once your dog learns this cue, reinforce directions like "come" and well-mannered greetings. First, teach "come" as a direction for being together, pairing "touch-come" until both directions can be used interchangeably. Then, extend the distance you call your dog from, rewarding them with praise and enthusiasm.

REMEMBER

We teach our dogs the meaning of words to keep them safe and help them navigate our world. While you can take basic lessons to the next level, it's your choice. Whether your dog retrieves balls, herds sheep, chases squirrels, hunts vermin, or digs up grubs, it doesn't matter. What gives your dog's life meaning is feeling like they are part of a family and experiencing unconditional love from you.

Managing Tension

If only dogs shouted like kids when frustrated, tracking their tension would be a lot easier. While growling is a clear warning, most dogs posture and bluff for many minutes before exploding.

Dogs also behave differently depending on who's home. Make a mental note of everyone interacting with your dogs when you're around. Do they have the same authority or interest in interacting with and managing the dogs? My kids love our dogs, but I do not expect the same level of attention from them that my husband and I share. It's not realistic. Kids will be kids, and dogs will be dogs. Do not leave this to happenstance!

REMEMBER

No matter what's happening, you're the parent. You control mealtime, walks, and play and have access to the best treats. The more cheerful and positive you are, the more your dogs will mirror your attitude. Do you feel out of control, stressed, or sick? Your dogs will sense that, too, and their relationships will suffer.

Use tools

Whether your dogs are outright fighting, occasionally tense, or at different stages of development, these tools will help you manage your household when needed:

» **Crates:** Bedtime can be challenging when a puppy is restless, or when your dogs aren't in the mood to settle down. Crates can be used like cribs: Have one for each dog and separate them to prevent overdependency. If you have a puppy, maintain a strict schedule that you can download from my site and ensure they have designated rest times, allowing the other dog or dogs to long for their company rather than becoming annoyed. Appendix A covers lots more about puppies.

» **Gates:** Gates are incredibly valuable for managing house-training, feeding, and providing each dog with space to enjoy chewing and mastering puzzle toys without interruption. They are also indispensable for diffusing arising frustrations or disagreements between dogs.

» **Playpens:** Playpens can be beneficial for isolating a young puppy and separating a dog that may be causing frustration or pestering other dogs for food, bones, or toys.

» **Muzzles:** Muzzles are essential when fights have escalated to the point of physical harm. Refer to Chapter 5 for more information on conditioning your dog to wear a muzzle.

» **Treat cups:** Treat cups are a fantastic way to redirect a dog's attention with the sound of shaking treats.

» **Tethering leads:** Tethering leashes are excellent for teaching your dogs a group stay and providing you with a means to separate them for training or a timeout. Tethering can also provide a necessary break if one dog bothers the others or steals their food or toys. Designate separate locations in your various rooms, ensure that the item used to secure the dogs are strong enough to hold them, and place a mat down in each area to designate their timeout spot.

» **Drag leashes:** Avoid grabbing your dogs if you need to separate them. Grabbing dogs can trigger an emotional response, escalating fear or frustration. Instead, allow them to drag a four- to five-foot leash when you can supervise them. This will enable you to separate them calmly.

Predict altercations

In most cases, your dogs will exchange a series of gestures to attempt to head off an argument before a fight breaks out. Like calling someone's bluff, the goal is to deter interactions that could result in injury.

Calming signals

Some dogs offer a calming signal, such as ducking their head, turning around, and walking away. Chapter 2 has a full list of calming signals. When another dog or (more often) a puppy persists, the more patient dog may snap.

Should this happen, do not discipline the dog who tried to head off the situation; calmly isolate the bothersome dog or puppy for a time out. Better yet, isolate the persistent dog or puppy before your usually patient dog loses their cool.

WARNING

If you start shouting when your dogs give warning signals, it's like pouring fuel on the fire. You're more likely to escalate a fight. Handle the situation mindfully and stay calm.

If you notice your dog making the gestures in Figure D-2, intervene and redirect their attention calmly. Things can quickly escalate!

>> **Subtle gestures:** Certain gestures, like bumping into or standing on each other's backs, are intentional and meant to convey power and authority. Often, they signal immaturity and insecurity, like bullying. Dogs with authority do not need to display it, whereas insecure dogs may be overcompensating. In certain contexts, they may escalate into aggression if not interrupted or addressed appropriately.

>> **Lip-licking:** Dogs may lick their lips as a sign of stress or to appease the other dog, indicating they're trying to diffuse the situation.

>> **Lowering the head (defensive response) or lifting posture and tail while leaning forward (offensive reaction):** These are two contrasting body language signals. Lowering the head indicates submission or fear, while the lifting posture with a raised tail and leaning forward suggests aggression or dominance (see Figure D-2).

>> **Hyper-fixation on an object, dog, or human:** When a dog fixates intensely on something, it may indicate heightened

arousal or potential aggression toward that target. When two dogs focus on each other, it can invite confrontation or rough and confrontational play. Other body cues will clarify whether they're vying to quarrel or play.

>> **Stiffening of the body:** Dogs may become rigid, with their muscles tensing up, indicating readiness for a potential confrontation.

>> **Ears pointed backward:** When a dog's ears are flattened or shifted backward, it can indicate tension, anxiety, or readiness to defend themselves.

>> **Growling:** Audible growling is a warning sign that a dog feels threatened or uncomfortable and may escalate the situation if ignored.

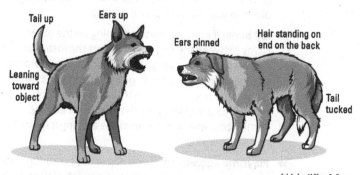

(c) John Wiley & Sons

FIGURE D-2: Offensive reaction (left) and defensive response (right).

Of course, you want to do your best and manage your dog's occasional disagreements calmly and gracefully. Keep reading for effective methods.

Redirect to something pleasant or neutral

When tensions spike between your dogs, you have two options: to completely freak out, which while understandable (no one wants to witness a dog fight) often encourages more stress when you're around. The other option is calm redirection to a more pleasant activity or to a neutral space, where they can regroup side by side or separated with a gate, crate, or pen. Redirection is the art of quickly shifting your dog's mental focus from tension to relaxation or fun. It's easier than you might think.

Most dogs have a tipping point: a level of arousal and excitement that can get out of control. As a good parent, be aware of each dog's triggers and arousal level so you can head off a spat.

To help you get your head around how this works, here are a few examples:

>> **The lap guarder:** This is a common one. One dog is sitting or lying with their head in your lap. Another dog approaches. Do not pick sides or worry about who started it. Stand up and walk away. There is nothing to fight over if there is no lap. After five to ten minutes, redirect them with a game or go outside for a walk. If you go back and sit down, put a big pillow in your lap and ignore the dogs.

>> **My bone!** If one dog starts poaching on the other dog, step calmy between the dogs and instruct the instigator to their mat (tethering or crating them if necessary). If two dogs are sparing over a toy or bone, pick it up and put it away. Bickering is not cool. Take a three- to five-minute pause, then redirect your dog to a new thinking brain activity. Remember, anything that involves earning a reward requires thinking.

>> **Playtime aggression:** If one dog starts posturing during highly charged group activities, like rough play or territorial barking, shift their focus fast! Get the dogs in a 10 o'clock 2 o'clock formation for a game of Treat-Retreat, or call them to the freezer for a frozen toy. If you're too busy to referee, put them in their crates or gate them in separate rooms with a chew or busy toy, deescalating the interaction and giving all your dogs a chance to calm down.

Use counterconditioning

This technique can transform your dogs' perception of being together from tense to enjoyable. It also works well when integrating a new dog or puppy into the household. The key is encouraging them to reference each other for positive interactions rather than react negatively.

Your first goal is for them to establish positive vibes on sight. Each time your dogs are together, engage them with familiar directions and games, making every effort to keep them under their threshold. Here are two-person games to try; each person should stand with one dog:

>> **Two Person I Spy:** Here, each person has one dog. Stand at least 30 feet apart in an open area. Reward each dog every time they look at each other. Use gates, pens, or different rooms to separate them indoors. Keep your dogs on different leashes when outside.

>> **In House I Spy:** In a setup with two dogs, it's best to have them gated, ideally with a neutral zone, like a hallway, in between. One person stands in this neutral zone. When the dogs look at each other without tension or confrontation, reward them with praise, treats, or attention. If their proximity seems to spark confrontation, separate them, or gate the one showing more tension. Stay flexible and adapt to create a scenario that relaxes both dogs. Consistently reinforce them to look at each other comfortably.

While it's easier to practice these with a helper, if you're doing this alone, you can separate the dogs with gates and play the Treat-Retreat game. If one dog becomes reactive, turn away from them and ignore their behavior.

TIP

Dogs respond best to quick, decisive, and calmly delivered reactions. If dogs look at one another and you mark the moment with praise and rewards, then looking at each other becomes something worth repeating. If barking at each other receives a sharp shout like "quiet!" the dogs learn to bark at one another just as easily.

TIP

Once your dogs are comfortable in each other's presence and around you, it's time to reestablish some basic ground rules. Avoid reinforcing behaviors that trigger their excited, reactive state, such as overly arousing greetings, barking, or jumping up for attention. Instead, encourage activities that engage their thinking brain, such as calmly sitting on their mat, waiting patiently to enter or exit doors, and going to their mat for attention.

When Fights Happen

This appendix has addressed various triggers for conflicts, ways to decrease your dog's arousal threshold, and methods to foster friendships among them. However, it's important to acknowledge that fights can still occur. Remember, it's not the end of the world — it's an opportunity to learn and improve the dynamics in your household.

After your dogs have disagreed, separate them. Take a moment to assess what triggered the altercation. Was it frustration over a particular resource? Maybe even your attention? Pause and reflect to see if you can figure it out.

Create an emergency toolkit

If you sense tension in your household, do not wait for a dog fight to break out. Get the right tools on hand. You can never be too careful!

- >> **Buckets of water:** Buckets of water can be used to intervene in a dog fight quickly. Dousing the dogs with water creates a distraction, allowing you to step in to separate them.

- >> **Blankets:** Blankets can be used to safely cover and separate fighting dogs, reducing visual stimuli and helping to calm them down during a conflict.

- >> **Spray deterrents:** Spray deterrents deliver an unpleasant scent or taste when activated; this is a great way to stop dogs from fighting.

- >> **Break sticks:** A break stick is used to break up a dog fight safely and quickly. You insert it between the jaws of fighting dogs to pry them apart.

- >> **Noise blasters:** A noise blaster emits a loud sound that can startle dogs and interrupt a fight when other verbal cues are ineffective.

REMEMBER

Nothing beats a professional opinion. If you feel you're in over your head and you'd like some help, reach out before things get worse.

Now what?

Once you've separated the dogs, isolate them quickly. They'll need to cool down. When dogs fight, their adrenaline and cortisol go through the roof. Once they're separated, check for wounds and visit your veterinarian or an animal hospital if necessary. No matter what unfolds, stay calm. All dogs respond to our postures and respiration, sensing our anxiety with a glance.

WARNING

Perhaps you're mad; that's okay. But do not take it out on your dogs. Remember, they are just dogs. In these situations, expressing your anger would be toxic and will create more stress, leading to more fighting.

It can take hours for your dogs to unwind from a sharp dispute; surround them with comforts that raise their serotonin levels, such as gentle music, chews, or busy toys. You'll also need to process the interaction to see it clearly. Consider consulting a professional with experience in multi-dog houses.

TIP

Take out your behavior diary and record exactly what happened during the fight. Leave your emotions out of it. Assess where each dog was, what triggered the altercation, and your and other family members' responses. Note any extenuating circumstances that may weigh in, like illness, pain, age, recent changes, or other factors.

Now consider the aftermath of the fight: What happened right after? Was one dog amped up while the other was terrified? Consider each dog's mental well-being. One may act like nothing happened, and the other may be more anxious or hyper-alert. Keep the dogs separate and remain neutral. You have work to do.

Before bringing the dogs back together, consider which tools might be helpful. Muzzles are a must if you're worried the dogs might fight. Having each dog wearing a dragline is also wise. If one dog is on edge, a body wrap may be helpful to settle their nerves. If you're working with a veterinary behaviorist, discuss medicines or sedatives that could be helpful.

TIP

I strongly recommend contacting a professional to review the situation and develop a plan to reintegrate the dogs. A good trainer or behaviorist may come with a cost, but it's a fraction of what an emergency room visit could cost if these fights continue.

Desensitization and reintroduction

It may take a few days to regroup and even longer to get an appointment with a professional. Keep your dogs separated until you've developed a desensitization plan. Change is possible, and dogs can learn to coexist peacefully after a disagreement, but it won't happen overnight.

As you start to reintroduce your dogs, ensure that both receive equal attention and care throughout the process. Consider these approaches for reintroduction:

>> **Give each dog separate lessons daily:** Work on increasing their focus and attention to your voice. Brush up on your dog's verbal skills. Positive reinforcement ensures a cheerful attitude. Begin working separately with each dog for five to ten minutes once or twice a day. Reinforce words that you'll use to focus them when they're together, such as "watch," "place," and "stay."

>> **Reintroduce play training:** Focus on games that encourage emotional regulation and impulse control, such as Catch Me If You Can, I Spy, and Treat-Retreat. As you gradually bring the dogs together, use the I Spy game to reinforce positive interactions, reminding each dog to "sit" and "watch" before all rewards.

>> **As your dogs grow more comfortable in each other's presence, ask a helper to handle one dog while you walk them side by side:** Begin with a distance of 10-20 feet apart, using treats and toys to maintain their focus and reinforce calm behavior. With patience and consistency, progressively decrease the gap until they can walk comfortably without tension or confrontation.

REMEMBER

The most difficult animal to control in these interactions is yourself. Stay calm. Your dogs will sense your tension, which, if it only rises when they're together, will make them more tense.

Helping your dogs feel comfortable and safe in each other's presence takes time. If either dog becomes emotionally aroused in the other's presence again, calmly separate them using gates, pens, and crates. If you feel ill-equipped to handle the situation, don't hesitate to consult a professional before another fight erupts.

Rehoming

Dogs act happy when they feel happy. Hostility is bad and has long-term psychological effects. If you're struggling to keep the peace in your home, and your anxiety is skyrocketing, the question begs, "Is this the best home for these dogs?"

If you've come to the conclusion that you can't stressfully manage two or more dogs, rehoming might be the better option. It's a tough decision, but it's important to put your dogs' needs for a safe, calm, stress-free life above all else.

Remember that navigating a multi-dog household is a journey of understanding, patience, and love. While tensions may arise, they are not impossible obstacles, but rather opportunities for growth and harmony.

By embracing the unique personalities and needs of each dog and by creating a calm and structured environment, you can lay the foundation for a peaceful coexistence. Seek guidance when needed, but trust your ability to lead with compassion and clarity.

Index

F

fast, head-on motion, for puppies, 270

favorites, avoiding in multi-dog househol3s, 300

fear
about, 10, 179
as an emotion, 21
containment anxiety and, 141
of people (*See* social anxiety)
of pet care professionals, 289–297
in puppies, 270–273
understanding, 290
of veterinarians, 289–297

Fear Free approach, 293

fear impression period, 273–274

fear tactics, 43

fearful leash personality, 161

Feed the Chickens game, 56

fence anxiety, 138

Fetch, 281

fetching, repetitive, 70

fight, fight, or freeze state, 21–22, 215

fighting, in multi-dog households, 301–303, 318–321

Find It game, 55, 169

fireworks, 238–240

flight risks, as a response to separation anxiety, 106

flooding, 256

focus
changing, 218
externalizing dog's, 155–157

Follow, 48–50, 169

food, for trauma, 153

food dishes, 222

forced interactions, for puppies, 271

forced leash walks, for puppies, 270–271

form, good, for leash-reactive dogs, 165–166

foundation, building a solid, 216

freedom, for trauma, 153

frenetic random action patterns, by puppies, 274

front groveling, by puppies, 274

frustrated leash personality, 161

frustration
as an emotion, 21
containment anxiety and, 141
tolerance of, for puppies, 275

fun, for trauma, 153

Fun Fact icon, 2

"fur baby" paradox, 13–14

G

games
for resource guarding, 219
for senior dogs, 281
for social anxiety, 190
for sound/storm sensitivity, 235

gates
for managing tension in multi-dog households, 313
for meeting visitors, 195–196
for resource guarding, 212

gender issues, in multi-dog households, 306

generalized anxiety
about, 10
in senior dogs, 281–282

genetic factors
about, 108–109
as a cause of anxiety, 73–74
storm/sound sensitivities and, 230

Get your ____, 311

goodie bags, as toys, 58

grabbing, for puppies, 270

gradual departure, 144–145, 267

Grandin, Temple (author), 54
Animals Make Us Human, 14

green light, 62

K

M

R

About the Author

Sarah Hodgson is a dog trainer, pet behavior expert, and the author of over a dozen best-selling books, including *Puppies for Dummies, 4th Edition*. With over 40 years of professional experience, her friendly, force-free training techniques have empowered pets and their people worldwide. Her philosophy is simple: Dogs want to feel safe. Sarah helps her clients and readers understand the motivation behind their dog's behavior, developing lessons and strategies that leave both the dogs and their people feeling understood and empowered.

Through worldwide virtual training, local training in New York and Connecticut, appearances on TV and radio, and her growing social media community, Sarah spreads the word far and wide that we don't have to treat our dogs wrong to get them to behave right. Sarah serves on the board of Fear Free and is an active member of International Association of Animal Behavior Consultants (IAABC), Association of Professional Dog Trainers (APDT), and Dog Writers Association of America (DWAA). Follow Sarah on Instagram and TikTok (@SarahSaysPets) for training tutorials, and connect with her at www.SarahHodgson.com for virtual training, online classes, e-books, recommended products, free downloads, and more.

Dedication

For Nicolas Maucieri, one of the most exquisite human beings it's my blessing to know. Many clients mistake you for my son, and I couldn't be prouder of the person you have matured into — loyal, conscientious, and kind beyond measure. It's been ages since you first began working with me, a determined teenager putting himself through college. Facing every task along the way with professionalism and grace, I had no idea of your innate editorial prowess when I asked for your help to structure this book. I dedicate it to you.

Author's Acknowledgments

I'm overflowing with gratitude for all the people and pets in my life. From my friends and family, both two-legged and four-legged, whose reassurance and unconditional love keep me sane, to all the clients and dogs I've had the pleasure of helping over the years — thank you. I could not have pulled this project off without you. Your spirits have been my guide, my inspiration, and my source of joy. What a life it's been! I'm deeply grateful for the opportunity to know you and be your teacher.

A special thanks to my agent of 34 years, Deborah Schneider. We have walked through this world together. I feel your confidence each time my pen hits the paper. A huge shout out to my technical editor, Marsha Penner, for your meticulous attention to detail and invaluable feedback. And to Kezia — what luck to have you at the helm. Your insightful tweaks and comments raise the quality and comprehension of this book to a height I could never reach alone.

Finally, to Jennifer Yee for your unwavering support and for conceiving this project in the first place. Your vision and encouragement have been instrumental.

I owe all of you immense gratitude!

Publisher's Acknowledgments

Senior Acquisitions Editor:
Jennifer Yee

Project Editor: Kezia Endsley

Technical Editor:
Marsha Penner, PhD, FFCP,
KPA-CTP, CPDT-KA

Production Editor:
Saikarthick Kumarasamy

Cover Image: © Lopolo/Shutterstock